FAITH IS LIKE DANCING

- Moved by faith to grow as a Christian.

Training Guide for Developing Religious Competencies.

DEUS EX MACHINA - Part III.

FAITH
IS LIKE DANCING

- Moved by faith to grow as a Christian.

Training Guide for Developing Religious Competencies.

(DEUS EX MACHINA - Part III).

In the theological book series DEUS EX MACHINA have been published:

- DEUS EX MACHINA - Or: On questioning life (Part I). ISBN 978-3-7583-4022-2.
- Homecoming from the Pope - A Quintessence of Charity (Part II). ISBN 978-3-7693-5795-0.
- Faith Is Like Dancing (Part III). ISBN 978-3-8192-4821-4.
- I will be a female bishop! – The Basics of Sermons on Happiness and other religious policy field analyses (Part IV). ISBN 978-3-8192-2914-5.

Imprint

Circe, Eureka: **Faith Is Like Dancing - *Moved by faith to grow as a Christian. Training Guide for Developing Religious Competencies*.**
Deus Ex Machina - Part III.
Hamburg, 2025.
ISBN 978-3-8192-4821-4

© 2025 Eureca Circe as curator and editor in documentation with AI.
Publisher: BoD · Books on Demand GmbH, Überseering 33, 22297 Hamburg.
Printed by: Libri Plureos GmbH, Friedensallee 273, 22763 Hamburg.
This release has been translated by AI.
Bibliographical references from the German National Library at: https://portal.dnb.de

Eureka Circe is the editor and curator of the book series "DEUS EX MACHINA" and the present volume "Faith Is Like Dancing - Moved by faith to grow as a Christian. Training Guide for Developing Religious Competencies. Deus Ex Machina - Part III."

Also published are: "DEUS EX MACHINA - Or: On questioning life" (Part I), "Homecoming from the Pope - A Quintessence of Charity" (Part II), "I will be a female bishop! – The Basics of Sermons on Happiness and other religious policy field analyses" (Part IV).

With the work "DEUS EX MACHINA", the curator is committed to documenting and, if necessary, discussing the texts of artificial intelligence in a religious and theological context. Her thesis: "Artificial intelligence (AI) represents a profound turning point because it fundamentally changes the relationship between humans, knowledge and access to the world - not only technically, but also culturally, epistemologically and socially. It opens up new access to knowledge and leads to its multiplication and democratization: AI systems make information available at a low threshold - often without traditional reading or in-depth prior knowledge. This fundamentally changes how we think, learn and understand, and at the same time promotes a new form of individualization of thought - which can also be exemplified by spiritual belief. What's more, machines are now generating meaning - texts, images, arguments - where previously only human expertise was required. This has long-term consequences for education, science, politics and religion."

Seen a lot of this before and it ain't over
'Til the day we disappear out of nowhere (out of nowhere)
When you're blinded by the dark, it's an illusion
There's a light inside your heart that keeps you moving,

yeah, yeah
It goes on and on and on and on
On and on and on

And if tomorrow's hopeless
At least we had this magic learning
A memory forever frozen
Because tonight goes on and on and on

freely quoted from respective based on:
Glockenbach

Contents

Exercise 6:

Exercise 7:

Exercise 8:

Exercise 9:

Exercise 10:

Exercise 11:

Exercise 12:

Introduction:
Faith Is Like Dancing

Faith Is Like Dancing - this seemingly poetic comparison is far more than just a beautiful image: it is an invitation, an attitude and a program. Dancing means moving, listening to a rhythm, engaging with others and finding your own steps. It is a movement that opens the heart, a rhythm that carries you away, and a relationship that is characterized by balance, mindfulness and the ability to fully engage.

Faith is also such a movement: not rigid or closed, but alive, personal and always changeable. It is rooted deep within and yet strives to enter the heart of life.

As with dance, there are also many paths and styles in faith: standard or Latin - or rather variations such as line dance, jazz, freestyle, West Swing Coast or disco fox?

Some prefer fixed step sequences, others love free improvisation or new creative combinations. It's about learning a standard sequence of steps or getting involved in new situational steps as a leader or guide, or even creating new steps, directions, combinations and dancing in an existing space yourself.

Tango Argentino, for example, impressively demonstrates how delicate communication and sensitive interaction can create aesthetic, lively movement in a shared space. Like any movement with music, dance is a "coordination work" that can be learned and practiced.

Those who understand faith as a dance also learn to find their own steps, to be sensitive and attentive in harmony and dialog with others - or to stay to themselves and creatively try out new movements, conversations and ideas in the space provided or their own with music and its rhythms.

This book aims to help you remain flexible in your faith and become more flexible: not just to follow the faith of others, but to courageously find your own path of faith, to practice it in a coordinated and sustainable way with others and effectively for yourself, and to consciously shape it - with your head, heart and hand!

The aim of contemporary faith formation is to live faith and charity authentically in everyday life. This requires treating oneself and others with respect, empathy and a willingness to engage in dialog. Religious competence means, in particular, personal development, ethical reflection, spiritual expression and social responsibility.

What makes it special: This book does not follow a dogmatic canon, but a competence-oriented, dialogical approach. It is based on the conviction that all religious education - and religious education in particular - should enable people to believe in a mature, empathetic, discerning and responsible way.

Central personal and social key competencies are presented in twelve exercise sections - be it the ability to engage in dialog, empathy, gender sensitivity or reflective sexual ethics and critical thinking and others.

This is not about abstract knowledge, but about concrete life issues and the skills required:

- *Who am I and what gives my life orientation and meaning?*
- *How do I deal with diversity, conflicts and ethical decisions? And: How do I remain empathetic, authentic and capable of acting?*
- *How do I talk about my faith - with myself, with others, with God? How do I deal with otherness? How can I look honestly at my image of God, my doubts, my longing?*
- *How do I make relationships, sexuality, justice or charity and pastoral care as well as liturgical language inclusive, true to life and lively?*

Each chapter delves deeper into a core area of religious competence development, for example:

- **Develop the ability to engage in dialog and empathy:** enter into dialog with others openly and without prejudice, see differences as enrichment;

- **Gender sensitivity and dealing with sexuality:** promoting a conscious understanding of gender roles and talking responsibly about sexuality;

- **Talk openly about challenging topics:** raise controversial or difficult issues (e.g. suffering, doubt, death) without fear;

- **Strengthening critical thinking and judgment:** reflecting on one's own points of view, substantiating them and reaching independent decisions;

- **Self-acceptance and resilience:** building inner strength, dealing with setbacks and accepting yourself with all your strengths and weaknesses;

- **Ethical action and social responsibility:** not only recognizing values, but also acting courageously in everyday life and taking responsibility for others;

- **Creative spiritual forms of expression:** creatively developing your own ideas of God and images of faith and finding expression for your spiritual experience;

- **Willingness to change:** seeing change as an opportunity, critically and constructively questioning traditions and helping to shape the new.

"Faith Is Like Dancing" is the third book in the *DEUS EX MACHINA* series and is intended as a training book for religious skills.

It is aimed at people who want to consciously reflect on their faith, deepen it and bring it to life - whether in religious education at school, in theological training courses, in church contexts or in personal self-study.

Religious education today is more than just imparting knowledge: it combines faith with personal development and life practice.

The learning is structured like a teacher would teach us a dance with exercises: there are clear learning objectives, practical exercises, reflection questions, suggestions and impulses for teaching, community work and spiritual practice.

The focus is particularly on all believers who want to develop further, as well as young people, people who think and live in a queer way, spiritual seekers - all those who do not (or no longer) fit into old molds and therefore want to spell out the Gospel in a new way.

Those who learn faith like dancing develop an inner attitude of openness, respect and joie de vivre that radiates far beyond classrooms, church services and church halls.

Because faith and religion touch on the fundamental questions of life that affect us all, a pedagogical approach to religious education should focus on such skills: By linking subject content with personal experiences, religious learning becomes a path of self-reflection and personal development.

Religious education in particular can be a unique place to support young people in discovering their own values, practicing important life skills, respecting diversity and finding orientation in a pluralistic world. A credible religious life requires an open willingness to engage in dialog, sensitivity to diversity, the courage to change and responsible action.

This holistic education, which appeals to head, heart and hand in equal measure, should be the pedagogical core of the efforts.

However, it is not only pupils who benefit from this content. Prospective teachers, clergy and theology students will also find valuable inspiration in the methods and exercises presented: this book also supports teachers, pastoral care workers and pastoral workers as multipliers in expanding their personal, social and spiritual skills, reflecting on their own attitudes and discovering new paths in religious education work.

At the same time, the book shows how important support from educational institutions is in order to promote these skills. Schools and universities can make a concrete contribution to the success of holistic religious learning - be it through adapted curricula, participatory teaching methods or targeted further training for teachers. Each section includes clearly formulated learning objectives, inspiring examples of good practice and suggestions for implementation.

And something else is special: this book is part of the theological project DEUS EX MACHINA. All texts were generated using artificial intelligence. The starting point was the second volume in the series, *"Heimkehr vom Papst - Eine Quintessenz der Nächstenliebe"*, whose essential themes were translated by AI - the deus ex machina - into concrete and necessary skills that are required and need to be reinforced in order to really live these messages and the Gospel in everyday life.

This book therefore aims to encourage people to see religious learning as a path to personal development: not just to hear or read more about faith, but to strengthen personal growth, ethical thinking, spiritual expression and social responsibility.

So let's set off together with the Deus in this volume: let's learn faith like we learn to dance - with joy, depth and the willingness to keep developing ourselves. In this way, religious education can become a lively development of skills that transforms us all a little and makes our world a little brighter and more human.

Eureka Circe, in April 2025.

And now to the individual sections and exercises on skills development written by Artificial Intelligence.

Exercise 1:
Learning to think women in leadership: Understanding gender equality and learning to change power structures

The exercise deals with learning to promote gender justice and the critical reflection of power structures in a theological context. Target groups are believers, learners in schools and child and youth welfare institutions, as well as theology, religious education teachers and prospective clergy who want to question traditional gender roles and develop gender-equitable attitudes in life, teaching and the church. Essential skills include the perception of gender-related injustices, the ability to analyze systemically, empathic perception, self-reflection and the ability to act for gender-sensitive practice.

These important competencies include the following additional skills: systemic thinking, gender-sensitive understanding of power, focused attention to subtle gender inequalities and empathic perception ("tender perception"). Reflection and deconstruction skills make it possible to critically question and break down stereotypical gender roles. Personal learning paths promote sustainable skills development through biographical reflection, dialog, practical experiences and changes of perspective, mindfulness exercises as well as continuous reflection and feedback processes.

The didactic methods also include practice-oriented knowledge transfer, case studies, role plays, biography work, empathic exercises, intersectional approaches as well as language and material analysis. These methods promote holistic and sustainable skills development through personal involvement, emotional contact and critical reflection.

Believers, students and teachers can be trained through appropriate learning processes: They develop a heightened awareness of gender equality, greater empathy, confident handling of power structures and enhanced capacity to act. As multipliers, they can initiate sustainable change towards a just and power-sensitive culture.

- **Learning and development objective:** *The most important personal competence is the ability to reflect and deconstruct, as it enables learners to consciously question stereotypical gender roles and act in a transformative way. The learning objective is to critically reflect on one's own and institutional power and gender structures and to change them constructively.*
- **Good practice example:** *Biographical writing exercise in which participants reflect on personal experiences of gender-specific imprints and injustices in writing and then share them in a protected setting. This method promotes self-reflection and empathy.*
- **Church support through:** *Believers and clergy can act as role models and mentors by actively modeling gender-equitable practices in their congregation, encouraging discussion and signaling openness to structural change.*
- **Local budget utilization:** *Financial resources from the municipality could be specifically invested in further training, workshops and seminars on gender equality. Specific expenditure includes fees for external speakers, materials for gender education and grants for projects to implement gender-sensitive measures.*
- **Adaptation of the school curriculum:** *The curriculum in religious education should be expanded to include modules to promote gender competence. Content includes sensitization to gender inequality, questioning analysis of traditional role models and promotion of empathic and power-sensitive communication. This enables pupils to reflect on and constructively shape power relations and gender equality in schools, churches and society.*

A speaker in a workshop on gender equality in education. Such learning opportunities help prospective teachers and theologians to develop an awareness of gender and power structures.

Figure1: Workshop on gender equality.

A committed woman leads a workshop on the topic of gender equality. In the background is a whiteboard with the words 'gender equality' and the symbol for gender equality. The workshop leader speaks to a small group of participants and conveys content on gender equality, equal opportunities and gender sensitization in a professional, open learning environment.

Developing a fair and inclusive attitude towards gender and power is a path of personal and professional maturation. Those interested in theology, students of theology, religious education teachers and prospective clergy are often faced with the challenge of questioning traditional role models and promoting more gender justice in their congregations and classrooms. To do this, they not only need knowledge, but above all certain *skills:* they must learn to see through gender injustice *analytically* and respond to it *in a transformative way* - in their own actions as well as in the structures of their environment. This learning is possible in a practical way and can be designed in an inspiring way so that it leads to a real change in perspectives. The following section describes specific teaching objectives, necessary skills and suitable methods for developing precisely this ability to perceive in a gender-equitable and power-sensitive way. The focus here is on practical pedagogical approaches - without focusing on theological or biblical derivations.

Concrete teaching objectives

The first step is to clarify *which learning objectives* are being pursued. These are clear, tangible goals that learners should achieve. Possible teaching objectives for a seminar or training course on *gender equality and power* could be:

- **Perception of inequalities:** Participants can recognize and objectively name gender-related injustices and power imbalances in their own environment (e.g. unequal participation of women and men in discussions, stereotypical role assignments in the community or school).
- **Analytical skills:** You are able to *analyze* these observed phenomena using suitable concepts - in other words, to understand the underlying causes and connections. This includes, for example, seeing personal experiences in connection with social structures or knowing the historical and cultural background of gender roles.
- **Self-reflection:** A central goal is for learners to critically question *their own* attitudes, imprints and prejudices in relation to gender and power. They should recognize how their own biography and socialization influence their behaviour - and become willing to change ingrained thought patterns.
- **Action competence:** Participants develop concrete *strategies* to act in a gender-sensitive manner in their professional or voluntary context. They learn how to shape their own behavior and also structures in schools, universities, communities or

churches in such a way that more equal opportunities are created.

- **Communication and relationship skills:** The aim is also to achieve empathetic and respectful interaction. Learners practise a communication style that is free of derogatory stereotypes and promote a culture of *appreciation* in which all genders feel heard and taken seriously.

These teaching objectives make it clear that it is not just about theoretical knowledge, but about an attitude and skills that shape action. The end result should be that future teachers or clergy *have gender competence* - i.e. are able and motivated to critically reflect on gender roles and use their knowledge in a practical way for more justice.

With these goals in mind, the necessary competencies can now be determined.

Important skills in gender issues and power analysis

In order to achieve the aforementioned learning objectives, various *skills* need to be developed. Some of the most important - as indicated in advance - are:

- **Systemic thinking in gender issues:** Learners should not view gender as an isolated characteristic, but rather understand it in *a systemic* context. This means that they recognize that personal experiences are always embedded in larger social structures. For example, role models in the church or in school textbooks are linked to social power relations and historically evolved traditions. Systemic thinking means recognizing patterns: For example, how institutions, language or education influence gender roles. If you have this competence, you can *see* the *"big picture"* beyond individual cases - for example, you can understand how ways of thinking, patterns of action and power relations interact.

- **Gender-sensitive understanding of power:** This is about a subtle understanding of *how power and gender are connected.* Future religious education teachers and theologians should be able to perceive where power imbalances exist between the genders - be it in the leadership of a group, in discussion dynamics or in institutional rules. Gender-sensitive means that the person recognizes gender-specific *power dynamics* and questions them critically.

This includes, for example, noticing (and, if necessary, speaking out) when a certain group (such as men) always has the decision-making power, or when women organize a lot but receive little recognition. This competence also includes reflecting *on one's own position of power:* A prospective pastor learns to be aware of the authority of the office and not to unconsciously play it out in a patriarchal or power-oriented way.

- **Focused attention on injustices:** This refers to the ability to *be mindful and attentive* to gender-related details in everyday life. Injustices often manifest themselves in seemingly small things - such as who is interrupted most often in a lesson or seminar, which pronoun is used in images of God, or how tasks are distributed in a group. Focused attention means not overlooking such signals. This skill is closely related to *mindfulness*: The senses are trained to notice what otherwise passes for "normal". A teacher with focused attention notices, for example, when girls and boys are treated differently in class, or when certain perspectives (e.g. of women, LGBTQIA+ people) are missing from teaching material.

- **"Tender" perception (empathic perception):** This somewhat poetic term refers to a *sensitive, empathic way of perceiving*. It refers to viewing reality with an inner *attitude of tenderness* - in other words, with warmth, respect and openness. Why is this important? Because many experiences can be painful, especially when it comes to issues of gender and power. Those who perceive with tenderness and empathy listen attentively and with compassion to the experiences of those affected by discrimination, for example, instead of making hasty judgments. This competence could also be described as *gender-empathic perception*.

It enables us to see the *human stories* behind the statistics and analyses. This is essential for prospective pastors, for example: only with a gentle, appreciative perception can they gain the trust of people who may have experienced marginalization.

- **Reflection and deconstruction skills:** In addition to empathetic observation, the ability to critically *reflect on and categorize* what is seen is required. This includes *deconstructing gender roles* - in other words, consciously taking apart supposedly "natural" ideas of masculinity and femininity. In this context, Andrea Lehner-Hartmann speaks of *"gender-empathetic perception combined with gender-deconstructive work"* as a short formula for gender-conscious teaching.

The formula "gender-empathetic perception combined with gender-deconstructive work" describes a central pedagogical approach for gender-conscious teaching. It means that teachers are sensitive and empathetic to how gender is experienced, represented or evaluated in specific situations - for example, when certain students have less say in class or when role models are presented in a one-sided way in materials. This "gender-empathetic perception" requires a mindful, compassionate attitude that takes the effect of gender on the learners' experience seriously.

At the same time, it is not only about empathy, but also about active, reflective action: "gender-deconstructive work" means the ability to critically question and break down stereotypical or standardizing ideas of gender and to point out alternative ways of thinking and acting. Teachers should not stop at mere observation, but should specifically design materials, language and teaching situations in such a way that diversity becomes visible and discrimination is reduced.

Together, these two elements - perception and deconstruction - form an attitude that enables schools and education to be consciously designed in a gender-equitable and inclusive way.

In practical terms, this means that, on the one hand, you sensitively perceive the inequality that exists and, on the other hand, actively work on breaking down the underlying role models and power patterns. This competence is demonstrated, for example, when students have learned not to think of themselves and others in hasty "pigeonholes" (such as *typically* male/typically *female*), but to *set categories in motion* and look for alternative ways of acting. This loosens rigid boundaries and expands the behavioral repertoire of everyone involved - an important step towards transforming power structures.

All of these skills are interrelated and mutually supportive. Professional knowledge of gender theories and research is the foundation (because it is difficult to analyze without knowledge). Equally important are social and personal skills such as empathy, communication skills and self-reflection. In didactics, we speak of *gender competence* with various dimensions - professional competence, methodological competence, social competence and self-competence - which are basically all addressed here. Those who develop these skills can not only understand gender equality, but also promote it in their own sphere of influence.

But how can such skills be *learned in a meaningful and personal way*? The next section deals with possible learning paths from the perspective of the learners themselves - i.e. how to acquire these skills.

Personal learning paths: developing skills in a meaningful way

Theory alone is not enough to really internalize the skills mentioned. A *personal learning process that* engages the mind, heart *and* hands is crucial. The following approaches help learners (whether students, teachers in training or prospective pastors) to develop the skills in a meaningful and individual way:

1 Reflect on your own biography and influences: One of the first and most important exercises is *self-reflection*. By looking at your own life story from the perspective of gender/power, you will gain new insights and become more aware. Specifically, you can ask yourself questions such as: *What biographical backgrounds have shaped me in my gender role? Where have I experienced advantages or disadvantages because of my gender? How do I deal with this, when I realize that I have misjudged others due to bias?*

Such reflective questions often bring unconscious assumptions to light. For example, a female theology student may remember how she was encouraged or discouraged to speak up as a girl - this experience may still influence how she presents herself in discussions today. Or a prospective religious education teacher realizes that certain feelings (crying, showing vulnerability) were *trained out of* him as a boy, which now influences his ability to empathize. By consciously reflecting on such imprints, you get to know yourself better. You develop the *self-competence* to recognize your own thought patterns and correct them if necessary.

This process is often personally touching - it requires courage to be honest with yourself, but leads to real growth.

"Unconscious bias" describes automatic, unconscious thought patterns that influence our actions, thoughts and judgments without us being aware of them. These prejudices arise from social conditioning, cultural experiences, media and upbringing and are particularly effective in situations in which we make quick decisions or assess people.

Such unconscious biases can relate to characteristics such as gender, age, ethnic origin, religion, sexual orientation or disability. For example, an "unconscious bias" could be that a male applicant is automatically considered more competent than a female applicant, without there being any objective reasons for this. This form of bias can lead to unfair, discriminatory and disadvantageous actions - often unintentionally and inadvertently.

To counteract such biases, it is important to first become aware of them *("raising awareness")* and then take targeted countermeasures *("deconstructing")*. Awareness-raising and training help to recognize such automatic thought patterns and replace them with reflected, fairer decisions. This helps to reduce social discrimination and promote a fairer, more inclusive society.

An e-learning module on the topic of *"unconscious bias"* for universities, theology faculties and church institutions could be structured as follows:

It begins with an introduction that explains the term *"unconscious bias"* and emphasizes its relevance for ecclesial, theological and academic contexts. Typical forms of unconscious bias are then presented, particularly with regard to gender, age, cultural origin, sexual orientation and disability. The module then shows concrete situations and practical examples from everyday life in organizations: e.. personnel selection, student evaluation, dealing with colleagues and pastoral conversations. This is followed by interactive exercises in which participants learn to recognize, reflect on and critically question their own unconscious biases. Finally, the module provides concrete strategies and recommendations on how employees, teachers and pastoral care workers can act consciously and without discrimination. The aim is to sustainably promote an attitude of sensitivity and openness in dealing with one another and to reduce discrimination.

2. exchange and dialog: Learning does not have to take place in solitude - especially when it comes to topics such as gender equality, *dialog with others* is key. By talking to fellow students *or* colleagues, experiences can be shared and perspectives broadened. For example, a male theology student may only learn about the subtle disadvantages they experience in everyday university life (such as not being taken seriously or constantly being asked about their appearance) when talking to a female fellow student. Such conversations promote empathy and shake up your own world view. *Peer learning* in mixed groups is therefore very valuable: different points of view are put on the table and people practise listening to each other. It is important to create a protected space of trust in which everyone can speak openly. Learners can compare and deepen their findings from self-reflection here. The dialogue also trains communication skills - you learn to speak respectfully about controversial topics, recognize your own privileges and look for solutions together.

3. practical experience and change of perspective: Nothing is as formative as *practical experience*. Learners should therefore be given opportunities to apply or at least try out what they have learned in real life. One approach is a *change of perspective*: consciously putting yourself in the shoes of people of the opposite sex. This can mean, for example, swapping roles in a common situation for a day - for example, a male student takes on a typically "female-dominated" task in the church (such as childcare or kitchen duty), while a female student tests out an otherwise male-dominated role (such as leading a church service). Such role reversals or *simulations* sharpen the eye for unseen challenges. Prospective teachers could also do an internship or short work shadowing at an institution that is considered *good practice* for gender equality - such as a youth center that specifically promotes girls or a parish where women and men lead on an equal footing. By *observing* and working on site, you gain experience that brings theory to life. Small projects in your own environment also belong here: for example, a group of students could initiate a project to implement gender-equitable language at their university, or religion students could hold workshops with their classes at school on the topic of gender equality. Such projects combine practical action with reflection and consolidate skills enormously.

4. mindfulness and perception exercises: The previously mentioned focused attention and "tender" perception can be specifically trained through *mindfulness exercises*. This may sound unusual in a theological context, but it has a lot to do with spirituality and presence (without requiring theological content). One exercise could be to record in your *daily diary* when and where you notice differences in the way you deal with gender. Every evening, for example, make a note: *What did I notice today on the subject of gender? Were there situations in which someone was treated differently because of their gender? How did I myself react in such moments?* This focused observation trains your senses. Another exercise: in a meeting or a TV program, consciously pay attention to *who* gets *how much speaking time* and count it internally. Or in everyday school life: observe closely for a day whether you praise or reprimand boys and girls equally often. Such mindfulness exercises often make you aware of *where* gender dynamics are at work that you didn't even notice before. It is important to maintain a *non-judgmental, gentle attitude* - i.e. observing, not immediately judging. This corresponds to "tender" perception: You notice facts and feelings without reproaching yourself or others. Over time, this attentive awareness becomes a habit and flows naturally into behavior.

5 Continuous reflection and feedback: Personal learning does not stop after a workshop or semester. Therefore, learners should learn to *continuously* seek and reflect on *feedback*. For example, you can ask a trusted colleague to observe you in class or in group leadership and give feedback on whether you are including all genders fairly. Or you can introduce an open feedback ritual: At the end of a seminar or community meeting, everyone can give anonymous feedback on whether they felt heard and respected. In this way, you find out where you stand and can continue to work on yourself in a targeted manner. Self-evaluation is also part of this: Always pause and ask yourself, *where am I on my path to a gender-equitable attitude? Where do I have blind spots? What am I already doing better than before?* This ongoing reflection keeps up motivation and constantly deepens learning progress.

These *personal learning paths* turn abstract concepts into lived experiences. The skills grow organically: you *experience* the importance of gender equality and gradually internalize the new ways of thinking and behaving. Everyone finds their own approach - one person perhaps more through theoretical reading and writing, the other through conversation and action. The decisive factor here is that learning always goes hand in hand with personal involvement. In this way, the change in attitudes and perceptions becomes sustainable.

Methods and approaches for teaching

From an educational perspective, the question arises: *What is the* best way to *teach* these contents and skills? Which *methods, approaches and content* are particularly suitable for achieving these goals? For teachers (e.g. lecturers in theological training or trainers in the community), there is a wealth of possibilities for designing lessons in a practical and skills-oriented way. Here are some tried and tested approaches:

- **Knowledge transfer with practical relevance:** The first step is often to impart *basic knowledge* - for example about gender theories, studies on gender roles or the legal foundations of equality. However, this should be done *in a practical way*. Instead of just lecturing abstract theory, short inputs can be given and immediately linked to examples that affect the everyday lives of the learners. For example, *a lecturer* could briefly explain the concept of *doing gender* and then ask: *"Where* do you observe gender being 'done' in everyday (school) life?" The students could give examples in plenary (for example: "At our school, almost only girls choose religion, the boys choose ethics" or "At our school, the pastor always holds women's circles, not the female pastor"). This makes it clear that theory directly helps to understand reality. *Good practice examples* from churches and schools, where gender equality is already well practiced, are also motivating: short case studies can be presented (e.g. a congregation that has introduced equal leadership structures or a religion class that has carried out a project on diversity). These stories show *that* change is possible and provide concrete inspiration.

- **Didactic exercises and case work:** *Case studies* and exercises in which the participants actively work on something are suitable for promoting analytical skills. For example, you can give real or fictitious scenarios from parish life or lessons: *A girl wants to become an altar server, but some on the church council are against it.* Or: *In a religion lesson, the boys dominate the discussion while the girls remain silent.* The learners' task is then to analyze these cases in groups: What is happening here in terms of gender and power? What factors play a role? How could the situation be changed? Such case-based analyses train systemic thinking and make power relations visible in concrete terms.

The groups can present their results and solutions are discussed together - this is a way of practising developing *strategies for action* at the same time. Role-playing is another method: a case is acted out and the participants can try out alternative courses of events (e.g. someone tries out in the role-play what it would be like as a teacher to specifically encourage the quiet girls to come forward). *The experience of role-playing* often leads to deeper insights than talking alone.

Biography work and empathic exercises: As described above, looking at one's own biography is a powerful learning tool. This can be methodically integrated into teaching, for example through writing or storytelling exercises. One method is the *biographical writing exercise:* participants write down a short personal experience that has to do with gender (in)justice. Afterwards, some stories are read aloud (on a voluntary basis) or shared in small groups. This exercise not only encourages self-reflection, but also enables listeners to *empathically* put themselves in the perspective of others - precisely the "tender perception" that is to be practiced. Another empathy-oriented method is the so-called *perspective-taking dialog:* Two people sit down together, person A describes a situation in which they felt unfairly treated because of their gender; person B just listens and then summarizes what they heard *from A's first-person perspective* ("I'm frustrated because..."). Then the roles change. This exercise teaches active listening and puts the participants directly into the other person's emotional world. Such methods create involvement in a positive sense: they open eyes and hearts in a way that facts and figures alone can hardly achieve.

- **Intersectional approaches:** When planning the content, it should be taken into account that *gender* is always intertwined with other dimensions of diversity (intersectionality). We therefore recommend *content* that goes beyond the pure focus on gender and, for example, highlights the connection between gender and origin, skin color, social situation or age.

This can be put into practice by varying case studies (e.g. the experience of a migrant woman in the church, then that of a man with a disability) or by inviting guest speakers with different backgrounds. In this way, participants learn *not to* view gender justice *in isolation*, but in the wider context of diversity and power relations. This encourages even more systemic thinking and avoids simplistic solutions.

- **Language and material analysis:** A very practical approach, especially for trainee teachers, is to *analyze language and materials* for gender bias. You can look through textbooks, worksheets, liturgy texts or songbooks together: How often do female vs. male characters appear? In which roles are they portrayed? Which pronouns and images of God are used?

Students can learn to develop criteria for evaluating such materials.

This trains the eye immensely. You can also work on language: Exercises in which texts are deliberately rephrased in a gender-appropriate way (e.g. changing masculine forms to inclusive language, or saying both *God mother* and *God father* in sermons) sensitize learners to how language depicts and influences reality. These methods combine analytical and creative action: learners critically identify the *androcentric constrictions* in materials, but at the same time develop *alternatives* - which is a very constructive, transformative exercise.

- **Exchange with practice mentors:** In addition to traditional seminar methods, *contact with role models* is helpful. This can mean inviting experienced teachers or clergy who are already considered *gender-competent*. In discussions or interviews, these practical mentors can share how they themselves have learned to deal with gender issues, what challenges they have faced and still face, and what tips they have. This is inspiring for students and grounds what they have learned in real life stories. Such encounters are often highly motivating: you see someone who has already gone part of the way and realize that it is possible to contribute to more justice.

These and other methods should always be used in a varied *mix of methods*. Variety keeps motivation high and appeals to different types of learners - sometimes more cognitive-analytical, sometimes experiential, sometimes creative-expressive. The attitude of the teacher is crucial: They should create an *atmosphere that is conducive to learning*, in which everyone feels taken seriously and dares to address even sensitive topics.

This includes teachers reflecting on their own position and being open to feedback, as they too are constantly learning in this process.

If all this succeeds, the skills mentioned can be taught with joy and depth.

New perspectives and transformation of learners

So what does all this effort mean for the *learners* themselves? Ideally, they undergo a *transformation* - a noticeable change in their perspective, attitude and perhaps even their future path as a teacher or clergy member. This transformation manifests itself on several levels:

- **Changed consciousness:** First of all, the *view* opens up. After such training, graduates see their everyday lives with new eyes. Where previously many things seemed self-evident (*"That's just the way it is"*), they now recognize mechanisms and injustices. For example, they notice when women are underrepresented in a discussion, or they feel uncomfortable more quickly when someone makes a sexist joke - because their perception is now sharpened. This awareness is *irreversible*: once recognized, reality remains permanently in a different light. Many report that after such a learning experience, they see points of contact everywhere to ensure more fairness - whether in the church, at university or in their private lives.

- **Empathy and an appreciative attitude:** Through intensive exchange and reflection, learners develop a deeper *empathy* for other perspectives. They are better able to put themselves in the shoes of people who may previously have been marginalized. For example, after this learning process, a prospective pastor will listen much more sensitively to the concerns of women in his congregation and promote their gifts. Or a female religious education teacher will courageously stand up for equal treatment of male and female colleagues. The overall attitude becomes more inclusive and *appreciative*: diversity is no longer seen as a threat, but as an enrichment.

- **Confident handling of power:** An important transformational characteristic is that future teachers/clergy *deal with power more consciously*. After all, they have learned to analyze power structures and become aware of their own role within them. As a result, they want to distribute power more fairly in their day-to-day work. A pastor who has acquired this competence will, for example, take care to involve lay people of both genders appropriately in decisions instead of making authoritarian decisions alone. A teacher will try to establish a culture in her class in which not only the loudest boys have the say, but *everyone* is heard. These people also recognize more quickly when they themselves are perhaps unconsciously acting in a privileged manner and can take countermeasures. Overall, a *gender-sensitive understanding of power* emerges in everyday actions: power is used responsibly and to empower others instead of cementing old hierarchies.

- **Enhanced capacity to act:** Probably the best result is that the learners feel *more capable of acting* when it comes to gender equality. Where previously they may have been at a loss or inhibited (*"I see a problem, but what can I do about it?"*), they now have tools and experience at their fingertips. The graduates have practiced strategies on how to intervene - be it through a clarifying conversation, through methodical tricks in the classroom or through structural initiatives. They know *where* they can start to make a difference. This feeling of *self-efficacy* is extremely important: it motivates them not to accept the status quo, but to take action. And even if there is resistance (which there will be, because change is also met with resistance), they have a network and the knowledge to keep going. In this way, their own actions can contribute to *reducing inequalities* step by step - in line with the original objective.

- **Role model and multiplier effect**: Ultimately, such transformed people become *multipliers* themselves. They act as role models in their environment and pass on the attitude. Theology students who acquire these skills today are the pastors, religious education teachers or academics of tomorrow who will keep the topic of gender equality present in their congregations, schools and institutions. Their new perspective radiates to others: Colleagues may sense that someone here is acting with particular mindfulness and fairness and be inspired by it. The next generation of students also benefits when their teacher teaches in a gender-sensitive way - often without explicitly stating it, simply by example. In this way, the transformation of individual learners sets in motion a *cultural change* that extends beyond the individual seminar or lesson.

In summary, learners experience a shift from *purely rational understanding* to *holistic comprehension and action.* Knowledge has become wisdom: the ability to stand up for gender equality and a fair approach to power in real life. In the process, they have learned to perceive with empathy and think critically - a combination that enables them to find creative solutions and build bridges. Andrea Lehner-Hartmann's concept of empathic perception and deconstructive processing of gender roles is now reflected in their attitude: they perceive inequalities consciously and with compassion and actively *shape* change by breaking down rigid categories.

At the end, learners often have a sense of *calling* on this topic: many recognize that gender justice is not an "additional topic", but is part of the core of their professional self-image - whether as teachers, pastors or theologians. They now see more clearly that just power structures and equality are fundamental prerequisites for credible educational work and church work. With this new perspective, they can go into their practice full of hope: ready to take small and large steps to make their environment a little more just and humane.

The topic of *"Women in leadership"* is best explored *in a research-based learning process.* Different learning paths - asking questions, working on texts, discussing and getting creative - help to orientate oneself step by step. One possible starting point is the reality of the learners' lives: What roles do women and men play in their community? Many will notice that although women do an enormous amount, for example in the parish council, in Caritas and in everyday parish life, priests and bishops have so far always been men. From this observation, one can formulate questions: *Why is this so? Is it only to do with tradition, or is it also the will of Jesus?"* Such questions open the door to further research. The learners can then *search for biblical clues*: They read biblical passages together in which women appear in Jesus' environment and in the early church. For example, you could look at the

Easter stories in which Jesus *first* appears *to the women* and instructs them to pass on the message.

The students could ask themselves: If Jesus entrusts women with this central task - what does this mean for their reputation and possible ministries? Paul's words such as Galatians 3:28 - *"there is neither male nor female, for you are all one in Christ"* - also stimulate discussion: Is it therefore theologically tenable to exclude women from being priests, even though all the baptized have "put on" Christ?

In addition to Bible study, the *study of ecclesiastical sources* can teach a lot: Learners could analyze an excerpt from Pope John Paul II's doctrinal letter *Ordinatio Sacerdotalis* (1994). In it, the Pope solemnly declared that the Church has *"no authority whatsoever to ordain women to the priesthood"* and that all the faithful must hold this decision *"definitively"*.

In class, you could summarize this text in your own words and question it critically: *Why does the Pope see no authority? What reasons are given?* (For example, the example of the twelve male apostles or the idea that a priest must represent Christ as a man). The question can then be asked: *Are these reasons still convincing today?* Group work in which pro and contra arguments are collected is a good idea here. For *contrast*, learners can also take a look at other Christian churches: Many Protestant, Anglican and Old Catholic communities admitted women to the ministry in the 20th century.

What motivated these churches to do this and what experiences have they had with it? A comparison sharpens the understanding that the question of women in ministry has been *answered differently within Christianity* - and that change is possible.

Didactic impulses: How to teach it

The challenge for teachers is to teach this topic *in a knowledgeable, sensitive and open manner*. The aim is to create a space in which tradition and criticism can coexist. A tried and tested didactic approach is *discussion in a protected setting:* For example, a moderated class discussion or a debate in which different points of view are taken. Here, the teacher can assign roles - e.g. one group speaks as an *"advocate of tradition"* (with arguments from the church), the other as an *"advocate of change or the current state of society"* (with reform-oriented arguments). Through the role play, students learn to empathize with different perspectives and to argue objectively. It is important that the teacher provides well-founded material beforehand: Original quotes from the Bible, magisterial texts, but also *voices from the current church debate.* For example, a quote from the Chairman of the German Bishops' Conference, Bishop Georg Bätzing, could be used as an impulse: *"For me, the question [of the ordination of women] is not closed, but is an open question in the Church and must be treated as such.*

Such a recent statement by a bishop shows learners that different opinions exist even in church leadership - this encourages them to ask their own questions. The results of the Synodal Path in Germany could also be used: In 2022, over 80% of the bishops present there agreed to a resolution asking the Vatican to review the ban on the ordination of women - in other words, to accept women as popes too: This text states that *the doctrine of Ordinatio Sacerdotalis is no longer widely understood or accepted by the people of God,* and calls for clarification as to whether this doctrine can be changed to allow women to participate appropriately in preaching and sacramental mission.

Reading such documents in class gives learners a sense of how concerns are dealt with within the church and how change processes can be initiated. - In addition to discussion and text work, *creative methods* can also be used: The students could formulate their thoughts *in a letter to the Pope* or let the apostle Junia have her say in a fictitious interview in order to link historical and contemporary voices in a dialogical way. Multimedia material such as short video statements (e.g. a nun describing her views) can bring the topic to life. All these methods aim to appeal equally to the head, heart and hand: Factual knowledge, empathy and personal reflection go hand in hand.

Let us imagine such a scene: An elderly woman with white hair stands at the altar, wearing an alb and stole and raises her hands in blessing. What (still) seems unthinkable in the Roman Catholic Church today could be a reality in the future. *Modern perspectives and thinking ahead:* this is exactly what this learning process is about - opening up new ways of thinking in the light of the Gospel, without disrespectful breaks with tradition. How could the church's understanding of ministry be further developed so that women and men can contribute their gifts equally? First of all, it helps to take a sober look at the present: the official teaching of the Church excludes women from ordained ministries, which the Vatican regards as definitive.

Attempts to ordain women as priests do entail sanctions - they are considered invalid and lead to excommunication. This attitude is based on the tradition of Jesus and the apostles as well as on a certain *symbolic language of the sacraments:* a priest acts in the Eucharist *"in persona Christi"* - in the person of Christ - and many in the magisterium still believe that only a man can do this vicariously.

But this is precisely where modern theological considerations come in: *Is Christ really reducible to his male gender?* Or does the priest not rather represent Christ in his humanity and his ministry, which in principle could also be embodied by a woman? After all, Jesus was a man, but his redemptive message and devotion apply to all people - his humanity connects him to men *and women* alike. Paul emphasizes that all the baptized have "put on Christ" and thus become sons and daughters of God.

In the early baptismal tradition, the following was true: *"There is no male and female, you are all one in Christ Jesus."*

So if baptism unites women and men in Christ without distinction, why should a baptized woman not be allowed to represent Christ? This question goes to the heart of the understanding of ministry. Many theologians today argue that excluding women from the ordained ministry contradicts the inclusive spirit of the Gospel. They point to Jesus' treatment of women: He broke through cultural barriers, spoke to women (such as the Samaritan woman at the well) as equals, and entrusted women like Mary Magdalene with key messages.

The *message* of Jesus - love, justice, salvation for all - knows no personal barriers, according to the conviction. If the church keeps women away from office and authority because of their gender, it sends out a contradictory message: Outwardly, it proclaims the equal worthiness of all people, but *internally* it practices unequal treatment.

More and more people within the church are recognizing this as a problem. At the beginning of the 1960s, Pope John XXIII saw the issue of women as a *"sign of the times"* and expressly *recognized the right of women to enter the priesthood*.

Unfortunately, his successors were less responsive to this, but the statement remains remarkable: a pope justified the equal rights of women, including in relation to church offices, with the dignity of the person and their freedom of vocation.

Today, over half a century later, these words are more relevant than ever. The tension between tradition and equality gives rise to the demand for *the objective further development* of teaching. This means not arbitrarily breaking with the past, but thinking ahead in the sense of organic development. The church has changed again and again over the centuries - not in its core beliefs, but in disciplinary issues and in the understanding of certain ministries. One example that is often mentioned is the diaconate of women: in the early church there were deacons, which shows that at least the *lower* ordained ministry was not historically reserved exclusively for men. Pope Francis has set up a commission to examine the possibility of a female diaconate - a sign that there is movement on the issue even at the highest level. But many are going even further and are calling for *all* ordained ministries to be opened up. Their arguments: The signs of the times - e.g. the changing understanding of gender justice - must be taken seriously, and the credibility of the church is at stake.

How can the church convincingly proclaim the dignity and equality of all people if women are systematically excluded from leadership roles within its own structures? Pastoral benefits could also be expected: wherever women are already parish leaders, pastoral workers or theologians, they enrich pastoral care. Why not also give them the sacramental authority to celebrate the Eucharist, forgive sins or become popes?

Figure 2: Competencies-Methods-Matrix:

Competencies-Methods-Matrix	Mindfulness diary exercise	Biography work	Dialog	empathic exercises	Case studies	Feedback exercise	Peer learning	Personal presentation	Change of perspective	practical exchange of experience	Practice mentor	Sermon	Role play	Language and material analysis	Knowledge transfer
Gender competence															
Gender empathy								■			▨				
Perception															
Relationship competence	▨														
Deconstruction competence															
Professional competence				■										▨	
Focused attention															
Competence to act					■										
Communication skills												■			
Methodological competence	▨														
Self-competence							■								
Ability to self-reflect				■											
Social competence															
Systemic thinking							▨			■					
in gender issues															

The graphic above shows (as a sample) a competence matrix that visualizes the relationship between central didactic methods (upper side) and selected competences and objectives (left side) in a clear structure. Each cell of the matrix indicates whether and how effectively a particular didactic method contributes to the promotion of the respective competence. **The black fields** mark the recommended methods for particularly effective teaching of this competence, while the **gray fields** indicate which methods can be used as a supplement or support. This provides teachers with a flexible basis for developing and adapting their individual working methods.

Professional competence: The aim is to impart solid and comprehensive specialist knowledge, to understand content in a differentiated way and to place it in new contexts and reflect on it critically.

Self-reflection: This is about increasing awareness of one's own values, actions and attitudes, critically and constructively questioning one's own behavior and deriving potential for development from this.

Perspective-taking: This competence means being able to empathize with other points of view and develop an understanding of different realities and opinions.

Communication skills: This includes the ability to communicate clearly, respectfully and comprehensibly, to listen actively and to give and accept constructive feedback.

Ethical judgment: The focus here is on developing the ability to make moral judgments in order to be able to make responsible ethical decisions and defend them in a reflective manner.

And so on as described in the text. And for the didactic methods:

Frontal teaching: Particularly suitable for teaching specialist skills (black field). It enables clear and structured knowledge transfer. It can also support communication skills (gray area) by setting an example of communication.

Project work: Intensively promotes professional competence, perspective-taking and communication skills (black fields), as learners have to acquire knowledge independently, cooperate and interact. Self-reflection and the ability to make ethical judgments can also be developed here (gray fields).

Role plays: Particularly suitable for perspective-taking and communication skills (black boxes). Learners slip into different roles, train empathy and conflict resolution. Ethical judgment and self-reflection also benefit (grey fields), as situations are reflected upon in these roles.

Biography work: Aims strongly at self-reflection and perspective-taking (black fields). Individual experiences are reflected upon, which promotes empathic skills and self-awareness. This method also supports ethical judgment (grey field).

Group work: Ideal for promoting perspective-taking and communication skills (black fields). Professional competence, self-reflection and ethical judgment are additionally developed in exchange with other learners (grey fields).

Meditation/silence exercises: Used specifically for self-reflection and ethical judgment (black fields). Silence and conscious self-awareness deepen reflection on personal and ethical decisions. Can be used to support perspective-taking (gray field).

Creative methods: Very good for promoting self-reflection and perspective-taking (black fields). Creativity opens up access to inner attitudes and changes of perspective. Communication skills can also be strengthened (gray field), as creativity often involves expression and dialogue.

And other didactic methods as described.

Using the matrix in practice: The skills matrix serves as a guide for teachers to select specific and reflective didactic methods. It shows at a glance which methods are particularly effective (black fields) and which can be used to supplement certain skills (gray fields). This makes it possible to design individual, flexible and targeted teaching units and adapt them to different learning situations and objectives. Each teacher can thus develop a personal way of working based on their pedagogical preferences and strengths and specifically promote skills in learners.

Such a skills-methods matrix can also be developed for all other exercise chapters.

The *other arguments* - such as the fear that this could jeopardize the unity of the universal church or is theologically inadmissible - must of course be taken seriously and discussed. Real *systemic thinking is* evident here: the learners see that a change in one area (women as priests) would have an impact on many other areas - from the church constitution to the liturgy.

They learn to relate all aspects to each other. For example, the office of pope is also linked to the priesthood: as long as only men become priests, the office of pope is automatically reserved for men. If the priesthood were opened up, it would even be conceivable in the long term for a woman to head the Catholic Church. That sounds visionary today, but it raises the fundamental question: *What needs to change for the church to remain faithful to the message of Jesus?* Some answers focus on *power structures*: critics believe that the real reason for the exclusion of women lies in the unequal distribution of power - men are not prepared to share decision-making power with women.

This analysis calls for reflection by the old white men, because it holds up a mirror to the church: Is it really Jesus' will - who after all gave his disciples orders to *serve* - that only men "exercise power" in his name? A reversal on the question of ministry would therefore also mean a new understanding of power: Ministry as a service entrusted to women and men together.

Other answers emphasize *the theological development:* one must understand more deeply what constitutes a sacramental ministry. When a woman celebrates the Eucharist, she commemorates the male Jesus, just like any priest - but at the same time she represents the human nature of Christ, in which *both* genders are included. The Church could learn to take a richer *approach to symbolism*: God is, after all, neither male nor female, but the creative origin of all. In Christ, God comes into the world as a man, but he encountered men *and* women and worked through people of both sexes. A woman at the altar could therefore also be an "iconic" sign of Christ - perhaps performed differently, but no less valid.

The further development of the understanding of ministry in terms of gender justice requires courageous decisions. Although the prohibition of women's ordination is still being discussed in purely legal terms, even church law can be changed if it serves the good of the church - *"what the church has established, it can also change and abolish"*, Pope Pius XII once made clear.

It is important to many that such a change is made in unity with the universal church: A future council or a papal decision in agreement with the bishops worldwide that opens up access to the ordained ministry to women would be possible, for example. Until then, there are intermediate steps: more women in leadership positions (for example in the Curia, where Pope Francis has already appointed women as department heads), the upgrading of non-ordained ministries and a stronger say for women at all levels. All of this signals: The church is learning to think more diversely. Ultimately, however, many believers emphasize that we must not lose sight of the vision that men *and women* can preside over the church together in the persona of Christ. After all, if the church - the body of Christ - is made up of men and women, why should the head of the body (Christ represented by the priest) only be male? Learners can and should ask themselves this question. In doing so, they learn to question critically *without abandoning the roots of faith*. It is a balancing act of habit and willingness to reform, which Jesus also trusted his disciples to do: he says that the Spirit will *"guide* them *into all the truth"* (John 16:13) - truth is therefore a path, not a closed fortress.

There are no ready answers yet, but there are broader horizons. Students - as well as self-taught learners - should be encouraged to accompany their church with both *love* and *questioning*. Traditions may be examined reflectively as long as this is done in an attitude of mutual dialog and the search for truth. The learning impulse *"Learning to think women in ministry"* shows: Those who think systemically see the web of the Bible, history, doctrine and present-day experience *as a whole*. This can lead to a constructive dialog: between old and young, between the magisterium and theology, between men and women in the church. In the light of the Gospel - which applies to all people - new ways of thinking open up. Perhaps the learners will realize that the question of women in ministry ultimately leads back to something very central: to the message of Jesus, who came *that all may have life to the full* (John 10:10) - free from oppression, full of dignity and called to serve one another, whether man or woman: regardless of gender. May this vision guide your and our further thoughts and actions.

This is because developing the ability to grasp gender equality and power structures in an analytical and transformative way is a *holistic learning process*. It includes cognitive insights, personal reflection and practical exercise. For those interested in theology, students, religious education teachers and prospective clergy, this learning path is challenging but immensely enriching. The specific teaching objectives - from the perception of inequality to the implementation of change strategies - can be achieved with suitable methods: through reflection on one's own biography, dialogical learning, practical exercises and creative didactic approaches. A learning environment in which *attention, empathy and critical thinking* can grow is crucial. If this is successful, learners experience a profound transformation. They acquire the skills to *stand up for justice and liberation* in their *environment* and a new perspective that is characterized by mindfulness and the courage to change. This enables them to act in the spirit of gender-equitable and gender-independent education and community - a benefit for them personally and for all the people with whom they will work and live in the future.

Exercise 2:
Questioning and rethinking gender-sensitive and queer theology independently

This exercise deals with gender-sensitive and queer theology. The aim is to critically question traditional concepts of faith and to develop them further in an inclusive way. Believers and learners should be enabled to reflect on theological knowledge independently and contextually aware, to recognize patriarchal imprints and to creatively reshape them. Central teaching objectives are contextual awareness, critical questioning of traditional interpretations of the Bible, integration of gender-sensitive and queer perspectives and the development of independent theological judgment. The skills taught include theological reflection, critical judgment, dealing with inner images and ideas as well as deconstructive thinking to identify and transform normative theological statements.

This is because personal learning takes place through self-reflection and biographical work, the study of diverse theological voices, historical-critical Bible reading as well as through dialog and practical testing of new theological perspectives. Didactic approaches therefore include an integrative curriculum design, diversity of teaching staff, empowering text work, the use of inclusive language and liturgical experiments as well as case studies on the practical implementation of inclusive theology.

The transformative effect can be seen in a deeper understanding of Christ and the image of God, a more sensitive and empathetic approach to pastoral care and ethics, and an inclusive preaching practice that honors diversity and variety.

- ***Learning and development objective:*** *The most important competence is the ability to reflect theologically in order to critically question and further develop one's own images of God and Christ as well as traditional understandings of roles . The* *learning objective is to practise an independent, inclusive and context-conscious theology.*

- **Good practice example:** *A biographical reflection exercise in which participants write down their religious biography and impressions of images of God and gender and then reflect on them in a protected dialog. This promotes critical questioning and personal theological growth.*
- **Church support through:** *Clergy can act as guides and mentors by openly sharing their own processes of reflection and inclusive approaches to practice, creating spaces for dialog and actively introducing gender-sensitive and queer perspectives into sermons and church work.*
- **Local budget use:** *Financial resources can be used in workshops and further training on queer and gender-sensitive theology, for example for fees for external experts, diversity-promoting community events and the creation of inclusive theological materials.*
- **Adapting the curriculum at school:** *The religious education curriculum should include queer and gender-sensitive theology as an integral part in order to enable students to critically reflect on traditional theological concepts. Content includes historical-critical Bible reading, inclusive images of God, the diversity of gender and sexual identities as well as practical exercises in empathy and judgment in the context of diversity and justice.*

At a time when diversity and justice are increasingly coming into focus, prospective theologians, religious education teachers and those interested in theology are also called upon to shed new light on traditional concepts of faith. Feminist and diversity-oriented approaches have long since gained a foothold in many disciplines; now they need to be implemented and firmly anchored in theology.

In the field of gender-sensitive and queer theology in particular, this means: asking courageous questions, working out patriarchal imprints, reflecting on one's own faith in a context-conscious manner and making theology and one's own writings more inclusive. This article outlines specific teaching objectives that are important for this, describes the skills that need to be developed and how they can be taught using methods, approaches and content. Practical examples are used to show how these skills can be promoted in training and teaching. Finally, it highlights the transformative change in perspective that such reflective theological work entails for the understanding of Christ, the image of God, pastoral care, the church and preaching.

Concrete teaching objectives

What should learners achieve at the end of such a development process? The teaching objectives can be clearly defined:

- **Contextual awareness and critical questioning:** Learners should be enabled not to view theological statements in isolation, but to consider historical, cultural and social contexts.

They learn to re-evaluate traditional interpretations of the Bible - for example on gender and sexuality - in the light of changing social attitudes. The aim is to develop a theological attitude that does not blindly accept, but questions independently.

- **Gender-sensitive perspective:** A central learning objective is to anchor gender justice in theology. Learners should recognize how strongly male-dominated images of God and theologies have had an impact for centuries, and how important it is to include female and non-binary perspectives. They practise identifying and overcoming language and role stereotypes in church teaching.

- **Queer inclusion and deconstruction**: Participants should develop the ability to theologically deconstruct heteronormativity and exclusionary norms.

This means that they question supposed "normalities" (e.g. bisexuality or traditional family images) from a queer perspective and discover the liberating messages of the Gospel for all people beyond narrow categories.

- **Independent theological thinking:** Perhaps the most important goal is to strengthen one's own theological judgment and ability to reflect. Prospective theologians should learn to develop their own points of view and make well-founded theological judgments instead of just reproducing predetermined doctrines. They should be able to work according to the principle *"not either classical or feminist theology, but both in combination"* - in other words, to think integratively and creatively.

These teaching objectives aim to produce mature theologians who live their faith in a reflective manner, actively help to shape an inclusive church and speak of God's love in a justice-sensitive way.

Important skills to be developed

Achieving these goals requires specific skills that are developed step by step. Some of these are

Theological ability to reflect

This refers to the ability to think theologically about one's own faith practice, influences and experiences. Learners should be able to take a reflective distance from their own faith and actions in order to gain new insights.

In concrete terms, this means that they reflect on their own religious biography, their images of God and their understanding of roles in the light of theological findings. Studies show that you can only really take the diversity of concepts of God in others (such as children or church members) seriously if you are aware of the development and plurality of your own images of God.

This self-reflection is the basis for all further learning: those who recognize the limitations of their own perspective are open to growth.

The ability to reflect theologically also includes the willingness to keep learning. As emphasized in the training of religious education teachers, experts should always align their actions with current professional discourse and continuously question themselves through exchange and further training.

Applied to students, this means that they develop an *attitude of lifelong learning*, constantly examining their own spirituality, biblical interpretation and theology and correcting them if necessary.

Discernment (theological judgment)

The power of judgment is the ability to arrive at an independent theological assessment on the basis of knowledge, reflection and ethical sensitivity. Instead of rashly following authorities or traditions, students learn to weigh up arguments and take a well-founded position. For example, students practise answering controversial questions (such as: *How can the church's stance on same-sex partnerships be justified biblically?*) independently and formulate a well-founded answer.

Judgment is particularly encouraged when teaching-learning spaces are created in which questions are encouraged and own formulations can be tried out.

Such an approach is practiced at the Evangelisches Stift Tübingen, for example: There, special exercises give students the opportunity to ask questions and formulate their own theological thoughts in order to develop their powers of judgment.

Through such guided discourse, learners realize that there is rarely just one right answer in theology - rather, it is important to recognize the connections between the biblical message, traditional teaching and today's world and to communicate them intelligently. This competence also enables students to make ethically responsible judgments - an aspect that is particularly important for prospective pastors and teachers.

Dealing with inner images and ideas: The image of God

Everyone brings inner images and often unconscious ideas to their studies: images of God (e.g. as a strict father or loving mother), of Christ, of the church and ministry, of "normal" Christian life. These inner images shape how we understand theological statements. It is therefore a key competence to consciously deal with one's own images, to question and expand them.

In the field of *gender-sensitive theology*, the image of God is the main focus here. Dealing with the image of God is at the heart of gender-sensitive education, because for centuries our language about God was primarily male and dominated.

Learners must first recognize their traditional image of God: *What names and metaphors for God have I been taught? What feelings and power structures are attached to them?* Then it is important to place these ideas in a larger framework. It is helpful to expand their knowledge of feminist theological and gender theological approaches to the question of God.

By studying classical and modern theological texts (e.g. by Dorothee Sölle, Elizabeth Johnson or Marcella Althaus-Reid), one discovers alternative images and names of God. The *Bible in Just Language,* for example, lists a wealth of biblically based variants for addressing God - from the Holy One to Ruach/Shechina to the Eternal.

Practical exercises are also part of competence building: learners should try out addressing God with new images - e.g. emphasizing God's maternal traits in prayers or devotions (God as a midwife, as a hen that shelters her chicks, as the source of life, etc.).

In this way, they learn how breaking down narrow images can lead to a deeper understanding without falling into new clichés (because ultimately God is beyond all gender images and remains ambiguous). Overall, they learn to let go of rigid ideas and to endure the diversity of divine reality. This competence - reflecting on inner images and creatively reinterpreting them - not only helps with the image of God, but also with topics such as the image of the church (e.g. moving away from hierarchical "top-down" thinking) or role models (e.g. the priest as necessarily male, the "typical" believer, etc.).

Figure3: Honeymoon of a same-sex male couple on a cruise ship.

An iconic work of art with a modern interpretation shows two very similar-looking men in a bright ship's interior. The sea is visible through round portholes in the background. Both figures wear traditional robes in blue and red and a bright, flaming heart on their chests. One of the two figures is also wearing a rainbow scarf as a symbol of queer diversity. The two hold hands lovingly, while one of the figures raises his right hand in a gesture of blessing. The image combines historical iconography with queer visibility and interprets unconditional love as diverse, tender and inclusive. It depicts a honeymoon of a same-sex male couple on a cruise ship.

Deconstructive ability (questioning norms and "queer" thinking)

Closely linked to the aforementioned approach to images is the ability to deconstruct. By this we mean the methodical questioning of seemingly fixed truths and norms: in other words, uncovering what is considered "normal" and why - and then consciously "disrupting" this order.

Queer theology provides an important methodological approach for this, as "to queer" literally means to alienate, cross, confuse. In practice, this means that learners practise identifying heteronormative and binary assumptions in theological texts or church traditions (such as the assumption that there are only two genders intended by God with clear roles) and critically breaking down these assumptions.

This competence involves both analytical acuity and creative thinking. Analytical, because you have to understand that much of what is handed down as a matter of course is socially constructed - e.g. dress codes for clergy, ideas of family, but also theological statements such as "God is King/Father". Creative, because deconstruction does not stop at mere criticism, but enables new interpretations. Queer theological approaches show how fruitful this can be: With "empowering-deconstructive approaches" to biblical texts, the social constructedness of normality can be revealed and heteronormativity exposed - and at the same time liberating, inclusive readings can be developed.

This deconstructive thinking competence gives learners the courage to rethink theological concepts. They learn to neither discard nor uncritically perpetuate traditions, but to creatively reinterpret them. For example, instead of reading the biblical love song *Song of Songs* only in heterosexual terms (bride and groom), it can be interpreted in a queer way - as a celebration *of diverse* love that transcends gender boundaries. Such exercises train "queering" as a productive theological practice that shakes up normative categories.

Finally, learners should recognize that "queer" is not only an identity category, but also a tool of theology that can be beneficial for everyone when it comes to disrupting entrenched thought patterns.

Personal learning of these skills

So how can *individual learners* acquire these skills in a meaningful and personal way? First of all, you need an open attitude and a willingness to embrace new experiences. Many people only discover how much they are unconsciously influenced by certain images and traditions during their studies or further training - this can be unsettling. Courage is therefore needed: Courage to enter fields that have been little researched to date and to introduce new identities and perspectives into theology.

This inner willingness to change is the basis of all learning in this area.

Specifically, the following learning paths can be helpful:

- **Self-reflection and biography work:** Keeping a personal diary or spiritual journal in which you record questions such as *"When did I first hear about God as Father - and how do I imagine God today?"* or *"Which role models from my church shape me?"* can deepen the reflection process. By working through your own faith biography, you become aware of the inner images that shape you. Spiritual guidance or supervision can also help to uncover blind spots.

- **Reading and studying diverse voices:** Those interested in theology should specifically engage with literature from feminist and queer theology. Works by Marcella Althaus-Reid or Patrick Cheng, for example, offer important impulses, as they introduce precisely those new perspectives that are often missing in classic textbooks.

It is equally rewarding to read biblical texts with commentaries from the perspective of marginalized groups (e.g. African-American, mujerista, trans* interpretations). This trains your eye for contexts and makes you aware of how different the Bible can sound when you read it from a different perspective.

- **Historical-critical and contextual Bible reading:** In order to strengthen contextual awareness, one should study the historical background of biblical texts and understand that many statements are to be understood in an ancient cultural context.

Anyone who is familiar with the ancient patriarchal social order can, for example, classify the tablets of the household in the New Testament differently and draw contemporary conclusions from them. Exercises in which biblical texts are read *against the grain* (such as the story of the *Ethiopian eunuch* in Acts 8 as an example of queer inclusion) help to distinguish the core of the message (love, justice) from the cultural accessories.

- **Dialogue and community learning:** you don't learn theology alone in a quiet room. The exchange with others - whether in the seminary, among friends or online - is crucial. Talking to people with different backgrounds (e.g. queer Christians, *BIPoC theologians*, long-established church members) broadens your horizons. It is important to actively listen and incorporate the experiences of marginalized people into your own theology.

Personal learning can include joining a diverse group, such as a queer house group or an initiative group for gender-inclusive language in church services. Such communities offer feedback, corrective and encouragement along the way.

- **Practical testing:** After all, you learn a lot by doing. Preparing a sermon on a queer theological topic, designing a teaching module on the diversity of lifestyles or carrying out a liturgical experiment with new images - these are all opportunities to practice the skills in practice. Through "trial and error", prospective teachers or clergy notice where reservations arise and where liberating "aha" experiences are possible. Ideally, they have mentors who accompany them or can experience what inclusive pastoral care looks like in practice during an internship.

To summarize: Personal learning in this field involves a balance of theoretical examination (reading, reflection) and practical experience (trying things out, engaging in dialog). It is a deeply personal process that involves head, heart and hand in equal measure and can transform one's own spirituality.

Methods, approaches and content in teaching

At the institutional level, the question arises as to how these skills can be taught and promoted. There are now various good practice approaches for teaching gender-sensitive and queer theology in higher and further education. The following methods and approaches have proven to be particularly fruitful:

- **Integrative curriculum design:** Instead of treating feminist or queer theology as exotic fringe topics, they are integrated into the canon of theological education.

This means that in church history seminars, for example, the history of women in the church is of course also dealt with, in dogmatics lectures questions about images of God and gender are discussed, in ethics seminars the topics of sexual morality and diversity. This avoids creating an artificial division along the lines of *"classical theology here, women's or queer theology there"* - instead, the two interpenetrate from the outset.

Such an interlocking normalizes the new perspectives as a component of "correct" theology, rather than as an addition.

- **Diversity among teachers and perspectives:** students benefit enormously from experiencing different role models and experts. Workshops and seminars in which students, lecturers and external experts learn together are an example of this. At the University of Hamburg, for example, a workshop was held on the gender-equitable study of church history, which brought together students from a wide range of status groups with female professors and generated new ideas.

Such formats break down hierarchies and show that everyone can learn from each other. External guests - e.g. queer theologians from the field or pastors who work in LGBTQIA+ pastoral care - bring additional realism to the course. Through lectures, discussion groups or project work with such guests, students practise how to do theology in an interdisciplinary and realistic way. The inclusion of other disciplines (psychology, sociology, cultural studies) as a sounding board is also important, as Dr. Kurzmann emphasizes: "Perspectives from neighbouring disciplines enrich gender-appropriate theology and broaden the view.

- **Empowering and deconstructing text work:** Biblical texts can be re-read in a queer-feminist way in religious education and theology studies. Didactically, for example, you can work in three-step methods: First, the learners identify "traces of heteronormativity" in a text or teaching, then an alternative interpretation is developed using a queer theological approach, and finally what this means for our faith is discussed.

Studies show that queer theological approaches have great potential for religious education. They can creatively disrupt order(s) and thus trigger reflection. As a recent study emphasizes, it is important to fully exploit the deconstructive *and* liberating potential of queer theology.

In concrete terms, a unit could look like this: First read the creation narrative "classically" and ask about the image of man and woman in it. Then you read it again with Judith Butler's theory in mind - what if "male and female" is not to be understood in a biologically determining way? - and suddenly discover how much leeway the text leaves. Such exercises reveal the socially constructed nature of norms and enable criticism of marginalizing interpretations.

The method is empowering: it encourages pupils and students to find their own interpretations instead of just being given answers.

- **Language and liturgy as a learning field:** Language shapes our thinking; therefore the consistent practice of gender-equitable and inclusive language is a must in teaching.

Seminars can, for example, work with reformulating traditional liturgy texts: "Lord" becomes "Eternal One" here and there, brothers and sisters become "siblings" etc. The students experience for themselves how statements change when the way God is addressed is varied or people are described neutrally. The joint celebration of devotions with queer-feminist elements (such as blessing services for all forms of love, memorial rituals for HIV victims, etc.) also creates a space for experience. Methods like these make abstract concepts tangible. At the same time, they sharpen the power of judgment, because reflection leads to discussion: Where is inclusive language enriching? Where does it reach its limits? Such practical exercises promote both empathy and clarity in theological judgment.

- **Case studies and projects:** A very practical approach is to work with case studies. For example, learners analyze a fictitious (or real) case: A trans* person seeks baptism in a parish - how does the church react? Or: A religion book depicts families only as father-mother-child - how can teaching material be designed differently? In groups, the participants work out possible solutions, justify their approach theologically and at the same time reflect on the underlying images. In this way, the previously acquired knowledge (biblical passages on diversity, church doctrinal texts, human scientific findings) is applied in a concrete context. The results of such projects can then be presented in the training group, for example, or recorded as small publications (blog, church newsletter article). Learning becomes meaningful because it appears directly relevant.

- **Support and mentoring:** Methods alone are not enough - the inner attitude of the teachers is also needed as encouraging support. Lecturers and mentors who openly talk about their own learning processes, address any resistance in the church and community and support the students make a significant contribution to learning success. Good practice can be seen where teachers create a space of freedom in which uncertain questions can be asked and where mistakes are seen as part of the learning process.

In this way, students are encouraged to think creatively without fear of breaking taboos - knowing that they still have to remain scientifically sound. This balancing act is best practiced in an atmosphere of appreciation.

In summary, it can be said that these skills are best taught when theoretical impulses, personal reflection and practical exercises are intertwined. An inclusive theological seminar could, for example, combine a *theoretical unit* (input on queer-feminist hermeneutics) with a *practical exercise* (own Bible study in small groups) and a *reflection round* (exchange about feelings and aha-effects). Contextuality is important: the link is repeatedly made to the reality of the learners' lives and the situation of the church today. This creates an overall picture for the learner in which the new approaches are not detached, but appear relevant and practicable.

Transformation: New perspectives and spiritual growth

If the above-mentioned skills are developed and the methods are effective, this brings about a profound transformation in the learners' perspective. Theology that is independently and context-consciously rethought changes the view of central dimensions of faith - with consequences for personal spirituality and church practice.

Image of Christ: The encounter with gender-sensitive and queer theology allows many learners to see Christ in a new light. For a long time, Jesus may have been primarily the "Lord" and the classic male redeemer, but now they also recognize the *queer traits* of Jesus: He broke social norms, put family ties aside ("Whoever does God's will is my brother and sister and mother"), showed tender closeness like a mother (cf. his desire to gather Jerusalem like a hen, Mt 23:37) and identified with the outcasts. The view of Christ expands from a static dogmatic image to a living counterpart who knows and accepts all human experiences - including queerness. This can deepen the personal relationship with Christ: Christ becomes an ally in the fight against oppression and a role model of love that includes everyone.

Image of God: This is often one of the biggest learning steps. By deconstructing old images and trying out new ones, the learners understand in a very existential way that God is greater than all our ideas. The traditional fixation on the male Father God recedes, and instead a more colorful, dynamic image of God emerges. Many report that for the first time they are free to imagine God in female metaphors or beyond gender - and that this in no way leads to distance from God, but on the contrary to a feeling of closeness and acceptance. When someone addresses God as "loving mother" in prayer, for example, and feels how their own heart reacts to this, this is a step towards spiritual growth. The learners also experience that God cannot be pinned down - *"remains ambiguous"* and is always at odds with our categories.

This endurance of ambiguity promotes humility and wonder: God ultimately eludes any pigeonholing. Spiritually, this means growth in reverence and trust - away from narrow images of God and towards a greater openness to the work of God in surprising forms.

Pastoral care and ethics: The skills acquired also change the attitude in pastoral care and social action. Those who have learned to listen and appreciate different realities of life will approach people more sensitively and empathetically in pastoral care - especially those who were previously marginalized. For example, learners will recognize the mechanisms of *minority stress* in queer youth and understand the importance of a safe space in church and school. This shapes their pastoral practice: they watch their tongue against hurtful statements, pay attention to inclusive behavior and actively work against discrimination.

How do we help to reduce minority stress?

Figure4: Minority stress among queer young people.

An informative infographic on the topic of 'Minority stress among queer young people' shows four key stress factors: Rejection, discrimination, stigmatization and experiencing violence. Each of these experiences is represented by an emotional illustration - with affected young people in different situations: a sad boy, a girl with a rainbow shirt, a thoughtful young person with dark skin and a frightened young person with a raised fist next to her. The visual language is comic-style, clearly structured in terms of color and easy to understand - ideal for educational work on LGBTIQIA+ topics in schools, youth work or church education.

In concrete terms, ethical discernment means not rushing to judgment on controversial issues (from the blessing of homosexual couples to language for trans* people), but rather seeking solutions from an attitude of love and justice. The students develop a sharpened conscience and a broad heart in order to keep all people in mind in their pastoral care.

Minority stress refers to the chronic stress that people are exposed to because they belong to a socially disadvantaged or stigmatized group - for example due to sexual orientation, gender identity, skin color, religion or disability.

Core idea: Minority stress does not arise from belonging to a minority per se, but from the discriminatory, marginalizing or rejecting experiences that are socially associated with it.

Characteristics of minority stress:

1. **Stigmatization and discrimination:** Repeated experiences of exclusion, prejudice or open discrimination.
2. **Internalized stress:** Adoption of negative social images about one's own identity ("internalized homophobia" etc.).
3. **Hiding strategies (concealment):** Compulsion to conceal one's identity in order to avoid rejection or violence.
4. **Anticipated rejection:** Constant vigilance and fear of negative reactions in everyday life.
5. **Social isolation:** loss of support, for example from family, religious community or institutions.

Consequences: Minority stress can lead to increased psychological strain, for example:

- Anxiety disorders
- Depression
- Suicidal tendencies
- Addictive behavior

Relevance: The concept became particularly well-known through research on *LGBTQIA+ people*, but is transferable to many marginalized groups. It shows that psychological suffering is not "personal", but has a *social cause* - and therefore requires social change.

Figure5: Characteristics of minority stress.

Characteristics of Minority Stress

Stigmatization and Discrimination
Repeated experiences of exclusion, prejudice, or overt discrimination.

Internalized Stress
Adoption of negative societal images about one's identity ("internalized homophobia" etc.).

Concealment
Compulsion to hide one's identity to avoid rejection or violence.

Anticipated Rejection
Persistent vigilance and fear of negative reactions in everyday life

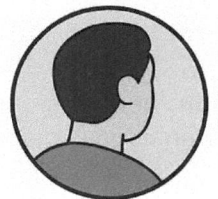

Social Isolation
Loss of support, e.g., from family, religious community

Example A - Elias, 16 years old, gay

Elias lives in a rural area and attends year 10 at a comprehensive school. He has known for some time that he is gay - but he is afraid to come out. Homophobic slogans often circulate at his school ("That's gay!"), and queer celebrities are ridiculed at break time.

Minority stress factors in Elias:

- **Expected rejection:** Elias constantly expects to be ridiculed or bullied if he comes out. He controls how he speaks and moves in order to "not stand out".
- **Hiding his identity (concealment):** He has only confided in an anonymous online forum. In the real world, he plays "straight" - for fear that even his friends might turn away.
- **Inner conflicts:** In his church congregation, he regularly hears sermons in which homosexuality is described as a "sin". Elias begins to question himself and develops feelings of shame.
- **Psychological consequences:** He suffers from sleep disorders, withdraws socially and shows the first signs of depression - but feels "not ill enough" to seek help.

Conclusion: Elias is not sick **because** he is gay - but because he lives in an environment that makes him feel wrong. Minority Stress shows that society's treatment of queer identities can make people ill if there is a lack of acceptance, visibility and protection.

Example B - Sara, 17 years old, trans and a believer

Sara was registered as a boy at birth, but has recently started living openly as a girl. She is deeply religious and is involved in her Catholic parish as an altar server. The parish is conservative, and many parishioners speak negatively about "gender ideology".

Minority stress factors with Sara:

- **Religious rejection and fear of exclusion:** Sara is afraid that she will be excluded from ministry if her transition is discussed publicly. In sermons, the pastor speaks of "God-given gender", which hits her hard inside.

- **Internalized feelings of guilt (internalized stress):** Although Sara believes in God's love, she wonders if she is "wrong" - because she doesn't fit the traditional image that her church conveys.
- **Expected devaluation:** She avoids parish events outside of the liturgy because she often feels scrutinized or "not welcome" there.
- **Torn:** Sara loves her church, her faith and community life - but she increasingly wonders whether there is still a place for her. This emotional tension causes inner stress, sadness and loneliness.

Conclusion: Sara experiences *minority stress* because her religious community does not fully recognize her identity. The fear of rejection and spiritual self-doubt create deep psychological stress - not because she is trans, but because the religious structures do not perceive her with her full dignity.

In both examples - Elias, the gay teenager, and Sara, the trans teenager - the environment plays a decisive role in the development, but also the possible reduction of minority stress. Although both young people come into social conflict as a result of their sexual or gender identity, the cause of their psychological stress does not lie in their identity itself, but in the dismissive or ignoring attitude of their environment. It is therefore all the more important that *school, family and religious community* do not become a place of fear, but a source of security, encouragement and acceptance.

In Elias' case, even small changes in everyday school life could have a big impact: If teachers consistently stop homophobic remarks, classmates are sensitized to queer realities through projects and conversations and queer role models are allowed to make themselves visible, a climate is created in which Elias no longer has to hide. Open friendships would be particularly important - classmates who clearly oppose discrimination and signal to Elias: "You're safe here. You are one of us." Regular, respectful conversations and unmistakable signs of acceptance within the family could also help to reduce Elias' inner tension. When parents show an active interest - for example, by informing themselves about queer issues or offering support without pushing - emotional security is created, which greatly reduces stress.

For Sara, a similar attitude in her church environment would be beneficial. The religious community could begin to take gender diversity theologically seriously and appreciate it as part of the diversity of creation. A pastor or parish worker who uses gender-sensitive language in preaching or pastoral care and publicly stands up for trans people could give Sara the feeling: "You too are loved by God, just the way you are." At the same time, it would be important for other young people in the congregation - such as the altar servers or members of the youth group - to actively relate to Sara, talk to her, invite her in and show her that she belongs. The family also plays a central role here: if her parents trust her, encourage her in her path and stand up to any prejudices in her social environment, the inner conflict will turn into growing self-esteem.

Both examples show that *Minority stress is not an individual problem, but a collective responsibility*. If schools, families and churches consciously create spaces of belonging and respect, they can significantly reduce the stress experienced by queer young people. It's not about resolving every conflict - it's about not leaving people alone. Because the opposite of stress is not always harmony, but relationship. And that starts with the attitude: You are not wrong. You are welcome.

Figure 6: Turning minority stress into joy.

MINORITY STRESS
Transforming Minority Stress in Queer Youth into Joy

| Inclusion | Acceptance | Non-Negative Visibility | Kindness |

An encouraging infographic shows how minority stress can be turned into joy and safety for queer young people. Key protective factors are visualized in four illustrations in a friendly comic style: Inclusion, Acceptance, Non-Negative Exposure and Kindness. Various smiling young people can be seen with positive symbols such as a thumbs-up, rainbow clothing and a heart bubble icon. The clear design and warm colors convey appreciation and a sense of belonging - ideal for educational and prevention work in schools, youth work or church contexts.

🧔 Example C - Possible case work: Daniel Kübelböck

The tragic case of singer *Daniel Kübelböck* attracted a great deal of media attention in September 2018. During a cruise on a cruise ship, Kübelböck suddenly went missing and despite an intensive search, he could not be found. The investigation concluded that he had probably thrown himself over the railing into the open sea and committed suicide.

The entertainer *Olivia Jones* later revealed important background information that could help to understand Kübelböck's emotional state. Kübelböck was in the middle of a transition from male to female, accompanied by hormone therapy. These hormonal changes can have serious side effects such as depression, emotional instability and existential questions of meaning - similar to what teenagers experience as a hangover when using party drugs such as ecstasy - which parents often don't notice.

In addition, Kübelböck was traveling unaccompanied on the ship and was under considerable pressure from the media and the public, who often portrayed him in an unfavorable light. The combination of isolation, identity issues and public pressure illustrates what is known as *minority stress*. This term describes the additional psychological and emotional pressure faced by people who are marginalized because of their sexual orientation or gender identity. The feeling of being left alone, a lack of recognition and constant observation and critical assessment by the media and the public exacerbated his emotional state.

To this day, there is speculation in magazines and on social media as to whether he is still alive and has simply built a new life for himself. This speculation is causing additional suffering and pain for his family, who were eventually forced to have him officially declared dead. *How could society have reacted better?*

More empathetic and sensitive public reporting that respects the privacy and personal dignity of queer people would have been urgently needed. More social acceptance of gender diversity would have considerably reduced the pressure that Kübelböck suffered.

The Catholic Church could have made an important contribution to this by speaking out clearly and publicly against all forms of discrimination, welcoming queer people and offering them a safe, sustainable network through spiritual, pastoral and emotional support.

It cannot be said directly and unequivocally that the church, with its negative attitude towards homosexuality and trans identity, is directly responsible for Daniel Küblböck's suicide. However, social and institutional attitudes as a whole contribute to the fact that queer people often suffer from so-called *minority stress*. This is caused by discrimination, rejection, isolation and a social climate in which diversity is not fully accepted. Church positions and teachings that do not recognize or even condemn homosexuality and trans identities influence social norms and indirectly promote a climate of exclusion.

In this respect, the church - as a socially influential institution - has a shared responsibility when it comes to creating an inclusive, respectful and appreciative social climate. An open and accepting approach could help to significantly reduce the psychological stress and suffering of queer people and possibly help to prevent tragic events such as that of Daniel Küblböck.

It is therefore not possible to establish a direct causal link in specific individual cases, but social and religious institutions certainly have an influence and responsibility to create a climate in which all people can feel accepted, valued and psychologically safe.

In such an atmosphere of recognition and acceptance, Kübelböck might have felt less isolated and oppressed, so that his tragic end could have been avoided.

From the perspective of the importance of supportive relationships in trans transformation processes, it can be stated that the support of trusted persons, a close friend or a girlfriend can be decisive. If Kübelböck had undertaken this cruise together with a trusted friend, a sustainable emotional and social network might have been available to cushion moments of crisis. Shared experiences, communication and social support are crucial protective factors against isolation and despair, especially during existential crises or intense personal changes.

The case of Daniel Kübelböck may enable pedagogical casework in the form of a valuable and profound example for reflection in the classroom. Students can use this real life story to acquire important skills and develop them further - such as empathy, perspective-taking, critical media skills and social responsibility. At the same time, it enables in-depth reflection on society's treatment of queer people and minority stress, and shows how crucial social support and acceptance are in today's world.

This comprehensive examination of Kübelböck's tragic cruise experience opens up spaces for a deeper understanding of discrimination and loneliness, but also calls for active solidarity and compassion - and highlights the responsibility of society as well as religious institutions to create an environment in which queer people can live safely, accepted and protected.

Resilience to minority stress

In order to specifically promote *resilience to minority stress* among young people in *religious education,* it takes more than just imparting knowledge. It is about developing an inner attitude and skills that enable young people to deal with discrimination, inner conflicts and social pressure confidently and self-assuredly - especially if they themselves belong to a queer minority or want to show solidarity. Religious education can make an important contribution here by becoming a safe space for reflection, orientation and encouragement.

First and foremost, the promotion of *self-reflection and identity competence* is key. Young people should be encouraged to come to terms with their own identity - their origins, their gender, their sexuality, their faith and their life story. Exercises that encourage biographical writing or reflection on images of God and self help to develop an awareness of one's own dignity and strengthen a positive self-image.

Communication and dialog skills are just as important. Particularly when it comes to issues of gender, sexuality and religion, it is necessary to get to know and accept other points of view without losing oneself. Religious education should create opportunities to talk respectfully about sensitive topics in a protected environment . Role-playing games, changes of perspective and clearly moderated discussion formats not only train conversation, but also mutual understanding.

Another building block is the promotion of *empathy and compassion -* also described as "tender perception". This means really engaging with the experiences of others without making hasty judgments. When young people are confronted with real stories of queer people - whether through the media, stories or authentic encounters - they learn to empathize with other realities of life. This creates emotional access that cognitive arguments often fail to achieve.

The development of *spiritual resilience* is also of great importance, particularly in a religious context. Young people who experience themselves as queer and religious at the same time often face inner tensions. Here, religious education can open up spaces in which an inclusive faith can be discovered: through diverse images of God, liberating interpretations of the Bible and a spiritual language that does not exclude, but connects. In this way, faith becomes a resource, not a source of self-doubt.

In addition to this, the *ability to act against discrimination* should also be promoted. Young people should not only recognize injustice, but also learn to react to it - be it through civil courage, words of dissent or solidarity in everyday life. Lessons can use case studies and simulation games to help develop concrete strategies to actively overcome discrimination rather than passively accepting it.

Another key competence is *critical judgment*. Young people should be enabled to take a differentiated view of church teachings, social norms and cultural influences - especially with regard to gender roles and sexual ethics. Religious education offers the opportunity to discuss theological positions in the light of today's human rights, to identify contradictions and to look for constructive solutions without falling into devaluation or polarization.

Last but not least, *social inclusion* plays an important role in resilience. When young people experience that they are seen, heard and respected in the classroom, this strengthens their self-esteem and reduces the effects of minority stress. Class rituals, trust exercises or joint projects on diversity and inclusion promote a sense of belonging and mutual responsibility.

All in all, religious education can be an effective place to give young people skills that make them strong in the face of social pressure and inner insecurity. It can help them not only to better understand the lives of others, but also to experience their own lives as valuable, worthy of protection and spiritually meaningful - regardless of whether someone is queer or not. In this way, religious education becomes a contribution to a fairer, more respectful and more resilient society.

Did Jesus also have "Minority Stress"?

This is a clever and profound topic that is both theologically and humanly touching - especially with regard to today's experiences of exclusion, belonging and self-acceptance.

The term "minority stress" in today's psychological sense did not exist at the time of Jesus, of course. However, if we apply the term in the same sense - i.e. as psychological stress caused by *structural exclusion, social pressure* and *deviant identity* - we can say that *yes, Jesus lived in a tense relationship with the majority society* that exhibited many characteristics of minority stress.

What speaks for this?

- **Stigmatization:** Jesus was born as the son of an "unsettled origin" ("Can anything good come out of Nazareth?" - John 1:46), questioned religious norms and was rejected by religious authorities.
- **Discrimination:** He was mocked as a "friend of sinners" because he identified with tax collectors, prostitutes, the poor, the sick and other marginalized people (cf. Mk 2:15-17). His table fellowships with the excluded were political acts of inclusion.
- **Anticipated rejection:** Jesus knew that his message would meet with resistance ("A prophet is nowhere less valid than in his own country", Mark 6:4) - and he often spoke about persecution.
- **Social isolation:** In Gethsemane, he was left alone, misunderstood by his closest confidants. On the cross, he cried out: "My God, why have you forsaken me?" (Mk 15:34) - an existential expression of isolation.

What if Jesus had been queer? - Historically, we don't know. There are no clear sources that describe Jesus' sexual orientation or gender identity. But *from a theological perspective,* it is permissible - and fruitful in many queer contexts - to *interpret* Jesus *as being in solidarity with queer experience.* Why?

- Because he subverted *normative ideas of gender and purity* (cf. his relationship to women, gender roles, touching the "impure").

- Because he lived *tender, intimate friendships with men* (e.. with the "favorite disciple", John 13:23-25).
- Because he healed marginalized bodies and identities, not normalized them.

Seen in this light, Jesus can be understood *as a queer-sensitive healer and prophet* who not only knew the tensions between identity and society, but *lived them in a transformative way*.

How did Jesus deal with this "minority stress"?

1. **Deeply rooted spirituality**: Jesus repeatedly withdrew into prayer. His inner connection to God was the source of his strength and identity.
2. **Conscious self-acceptance**: Jesus knew about his mission and spoke freely about his "I am" - in a society that devalued him.
3. **Seeking and establishing community**: He surrounded himself with a group of people who were not perfect - but open to change. He lived radical friendship.
4. **Courage to confront**: He addressed power structures directly - not out of hatred, but out of love for justice.
5. **Forgiveness and soft-heartedness**: even in the face of rejection, Jesus remained tender and capable of acting. He remained open without losing himself.

Whether queer or not, Jesus can be read as a *figure of identification for people with minority stress*. He did not live within the social norm, but *on the margins - and yet with a center*. His strength did not lie in his claim to power, but in his freedom to be himself - and to encourage others in this. For queer people today, this can be a healing interpretation: *Jesus knows exclusion. And he lived radical inclusion - with God, with himself, with others.*

Sermon: "God on the edge - Jesus, minority stress and the courage to be dignified"

Dear community,

Sometimes we ask ourselves whether our faith really helps us in everyday life. Whether what we know and say about Jesus really sustains us when it counts. Today I would like to build a bridge - between the life of Jesus and the lives of many young people today, especially queer young people who suffer from what we now call "minority stress".

Minority stress describes the mental strain that arises when you belong to the minority - not because you are ill, but because society does not understand, does not recognize, perhaps even despises you. It is the pressure of having to hide. The constant fear of being rejected. The experience of being alone.

And I ask today: Did Jesus know that? I believe: yes.

Jesus was born under questionable circumstances, outside the norm. He did not come from the religious upper class, but from Nazareth - "Can anything good come from there?" (John 1:46). Even as a teenager, he questioned authority. As an adult, he surrounds himself with tax collectors, prostitutes, the sick, the poor and strangers. He touches untouchables. He breaks taboos. And it was said of him: "A glutton and a winebibber, a friend of sinners" (Mt 11:19).

Jesus did not stand in the center of society, he deliberately placed himself on the margins. And he invited those who lived there - not to convert them, but to have fellowship with them. He did not heal by normalizing, but by acknowledging: You are valuable. You are loved. You are whole.

Many queer young people know the opposite. They hear that they are "unnatural". They experience exclusion at school, in the family - sometimes even in church. They hide themselves. They wear a mask. They learn to reject themselves before others do. And they lose trust in the world - and sometimes also in God.

But the God we believe in is not a God of exclusion. He is the God of the vulnerable. The God of those who have no place. The God who says: "Blessed are those who are persecuted for the sake of righteousness, for theirs is the kingdom of heaven" (Mt 5:10).

Jesus was not afraid to be different. And he also gives us this courage. Courage to stand up for ourselves. Courage to accept others in their truth. Courage to stand up against all forms of belittlement - at school, at home, at church.

I believe that Jesus not only integrated minorities - he identified himself with them. And this is precisely where our hope lies: that God is not distant from our struggles, but right in the middle of them. That he suffers with us - but also hopes with us. And that, with his strength, we will find a way to live freely - not despite our differences, but in and with them.

*Let us be a church in which no one has to hide their identity. A church in which being different is not a threat, but an enrichment. A church that lives from the spirit of Jesus: **tender, courageous, just**.*

Amen.

Church and community: A theologically reflective and queer-sensitive perspective does not remain private - it has an impact on the church community. Learners begin to see the church with different eyes: No longer as a rigid institution that sets guidelines, but as a living organism that can reform itself. They recognize the tensions between traditional doctrine and lived diversity and are prepared to work constructively to make the church more open. Someone like this asks, for example: *Why aren't women* (or openly queer people) *allowed to preach in our church?* or *How can we change our church culture so that all forms of families feel welcome?* Such questions lead to concrete commitment. Today's young theologians actively disseminate information on equality, gender justice and queerness to the public, for example via social media, blogs or church projects. The goal behind this: a church that is truly *inclusive*. Transformation here means promoting the church as a place of diversity where no one is excluded because of their gender or identity, but where everyone can contribute their gifts - in line with Paul's image of the body of Christ, which is alive through the diversity of its members.

Proclamation and teaching theology: Ultimately, the way in which faith is proclaimed is changing. Those who have experienced for themselves how liberating a context-conscious interpretation can be will preach and teach with a new fire. The language of preaching becomes more inclusive - not out of compulsion, but out of insight. Sermons now include examples from different walks of life; biblical stories are told in such a way that everyone can relate to them. The question of truth is also approached more dialogically: Instead of proclaiming absolute answers, one enters into a confrontation with the listeners and does not shy away from honest dialog.

Teaching and preaching theology becomes less instruction and more a shared search for meaning. This change in preaching attitude can transform the church: If homophobia and transphobia are clearly named and overcome from the pulpit and in the classroom, if the unconditional dignity of every human being is emphasized instead, then a culture of appreciation and love for one's neighbour will grow. This is precisely what inclusive theology aims to achieve: it challenges religious communities to overcome all forms of exclusion and to live out more understanding, acceptance and love for all people.

Questioning habits of thought: On the path to this transformation, some habits of thought must of course be questioned and broken. The process is not always easy. Patriarchal thought patterns - such as the idea that authority in the church is inextricably linked to masculinity - are consciously "unmasked" and theologically deconstructed. Heteronormative assumptions - e.g. the implicit habit of always thinking of "marriage" in terms of man and woman - are broken down through concrete counter-examples and teaching. Even images of "holiness" or "purity" that unconsciously exclude LGBTQIA+ people, for example, must be fundamentally changed. This requires the courage to be self-critical: learners learn to take a critical look at their own identity and piety.

However, there is great potential for growth in these steps: blind spots are discovered and a more authentic, broader perspective of faith is gained.

At the end of this process of learning and change is a theological maturity that manifests itself in various fruits. Theologically, a diversity of concepts and creativity grows: new terms, new images, new approaches enrich the language of faith. Spiritually, a deep freedom and connectedness grows: freedom from restrictive ideas and connectedness with God's colorful creation and diverse brothers and sisters in faith. The students have experienced that theology is not something rigid, but a living process of "always thinking anew" before God.

It can therefore be said that anyone who develops the ability to question and rethink theological concepts independently and contextually aware - especially in the area of gender and queerness - becomes God's instrument for renewal. Such a person can build bridges between tradition and innovation, between the church and the world. They help to ensure that the Good News is proclaimed in a credible, just and inspiring way in our time. The transformation of perspective - on Christ, God, pastoral care, the church and proclamation - ultimately leads to the old-new realization: God loves *all* people, and our theology must always be measured by whether it lives up to this love.

Many studies and sources prove that a gender-sensitive and queer reinterpretation of theology is not only possible, but urgently needed in order to do justice to the message of the Gospel in today's pluralistic society.

Exercise 3:
Discover holistic spirituality with body and soul: Valuing the body and feelings and learning to incorporate them into spirituality

The exercise focuses on the holistic integration of body and feelings in Christian spirituality. Believers, those interested in theology, students and aspiring clergy learn to appreciate the body as the temple of the Holy Spirit and to recognize feelings as an authentic access to God. The aim is to promote a holistic view of humanity that does not reduce spirituality to the mind, but embraces the whole person. Essential skills are the development of body awareness, emotional intelligence and the ability to consciously shape spiritual integration.

In order to develop body awareness, participants learn to be mindful of their body and experience it as an integral part of their spiritual life, for example through body prayer, meditation and mindful movement exercises. Emotional competence includes the ability to consciously perceive and categorize feelings and to respond empathetically to others, which is particularly important for pastoral care and educational work. Finally, spiritual integration means connecting body, soul and spirit in the life of faith, resulting in an authentic, living spirituality that becomes effective in everyday life.

A particular focus is on the reflection and practical implementation of these skills in the context of celibate lifestyles. Celibate people are encouraged to consciously accept closeness and tenderness as human needs and to practice healthy forms of physicality and relationships. Celibacy is no longer only interpreted as renunciation, but as a positive decision for comprehensive, non-sexual closeness and relationships.

- ***Learning and development objective:** The most essential personal skill is spiritual integration, which enables learners to consciously and holistically integrate body and emotions into their relationship with God and everyday spirituality. The* *learning objective is to develop a balanced, holistic spirituality in which body and soul are equally integrated.*

- **Good practice example:** *A body-oriented prayer (body prayer) as a didactic method in which learners consciously try out different prayer postures and movements, hold each other's shoulders or massage them, and reflect on how this changes and deepens their relationship with God. This method promotes body awareness and spiritual integration.*

- **Church support through:** *Clergy, priests or bishops can be supportive by speaking openly about their own experiences with physical and emotional integration and emphasizing the value of holistic spirituality in sermons and pastoral care. They can lead and accompany workshops or spiritual exercises (meditation, retreats).*

- **Local budget use:** *Community funds can be invested in workshops and training courses that strengthen body awareness and emotional competence, for example fees for speakers, meditation and movement workshops, as well as the purchase of appropriate materials such as meditation cushions or exercise mats.*

- **Adaptation of the school curriculum:** *Modules should be added to the curriculum that teach students holistic spirituality, including body awareness, emotional intelligence and practical spiritual exercises. Contents include mindful body prayer, biblical meditations and reflections on the emotional dimension of faith to enable students to live an authentic, holistic life of faith.*

There is a growing awareness in theology that *the body and emotions* are not antagonists of the spirit, but integral components of a holistic life of faith. For a long time, the body and emotions were viewed with suspicion in religious contexts - the Enlightenment pushed feelings to the margins as supposed "disruptive factors" for reason.

But today many recognize this: Our faith only becomes fully alive where *body and soul* are *in harmony*. Christian spirituality is even rooted in the conviction of the *incarnation* (God becoming man): God himself took on a human body and human feelings. It follows that we should *value* our own body and our emotional life - indeed, we should actively *integrate* them into spiritual processes. This exercise unit aims to show in an inspiring and practical way how those interested in theology, students, religious education teachers and prospective clergy can learn to do just that. What are the *specific teaching objectives* behind this? What *skills* - from physical awareness to emotional intelligence - need to be developed? How can these skills be *learned personally* and what *methods* or approaches can be used to teach them? Good practice examples and case studies illustrate this. Finally, we look at the practical example of *celibacy:* how can people in training or self-reflection be strengthened to consciously open themselves up to closeness, relationship and even physical tenderness instead of remaining in solitary asceticism - whether from a celibate or already existing partnership-based lifestyle? All of this is aimed at a *new view* of wholeness: a spirituality in which the whole person - with body and feelings - finds a place and is transformed.

Teaching objectives: Practicing appreciation of the body and feelings in faith

A central concern in educational work on this topic is to formulate *clear teaching objectives*. These objectives specify what learners should know, understand or have internalized by the end of the course. Concrete teaching objectives could be, for example

- **Develop a holistic view of the human being:** Learners understand that human beings are created as a unity of body, soul and spirit. They recognize theologically *"that the human body is a temple of the Holy Spirit"* (1 Cor 6:19) and that God addresses the whole person - not just the mind, but also the body and heart.
- **Appreciation of one's own body:** learners develop a grateful, mindful attitude towards their own body. They do not see the body as a hindrance or unclean, but as a **gift from God** and *the first place to experience God* in which spiritual things can happen.

The teaching objective here also includes overcoming shame or dualism ("mind good - body bad").

- **Recognize the importance of feelings:** Learners understand that feelings are not a minor matter in religion, but important signposts. They learn about biblical and spiritual examples in which emotions play a role - such as the Psalms of lament (anger, grief), Jesus' compassion or Ignatius of Loyola's *discernment of spirits*, for whom *"feelings* were *a source of existential decisions"* and even a medium *"through which the Creator communicates with the creature"*.

This is how the insight grows: my joy, fear or longing can also be a place of encounter with God.

- **Integration instead of division:** The central teaching objective is for learners to strive for an *integrated spirituality*. They should experience this: Holiness does not mean splitting off from the physical or suppressing emotions, but *permeating* them with the Spirit of God. As a famous quote (often attributed to Teresa of Ávila) says: *"God is also between the cooking pots."* - God's presence encompasses everyday life, the body, the sensory world of experience.

These teaching objectives create the basis for a changed understanding: faith is not only lived with the head, but *with heart and hand, with skin and hair and hand*. Once learners have internalized these goals , they are ready to develop the corresponding skills.

Skills to be developed: body awareness, emotional competence and spiritual integration

The *skills* that are to be developed step by step are derived from the teaching objectives. The focus is primarily on three areas: *Body awareness, emotional competence* (including emotional intelligence) and the ability to *integrate spiritually*.

Develop body awareness

Body awareness means cultivating a keen *sense of one's own body* - its signals, needs and limits. For theology students or aspiring clergy, this is a key skill for being authentic and healthy in ministry. Those who have a good body awareness pay *attention to their health,* notice tension or exhaustion in good time and can also include their body in prayer. This skill can be learned personally, for example, through *mindfulness exercises*: simply being aware of your own breathing and muscle tone in silence or consciously paying attention to every step while walking (*walking meditation*).

Figure 7: Balancing physicality and inner balance in yoga with mindfulness.

An expressive black and white photo of a young woman in profile, assuming a yoga pose. Her hands are stretched upwards and artfully intertwined as she gazes intently ahead. The minimalist tattoos (cross, heart, anchor) on her left forearm are striking. In the background you can see a wide, open landscape with a meadow and an old industrial building. The photo radiates calm, concentration and serenity, ideal for themes such as mindfulness, yoga or inner balance.

Such exercises give you a sense of *"how does my body feel right now? Where do I feel pressure, where do I feel relaxation?"* - a first step towards deeper mindfulness.

Another practical learning opportunity is the so-called body prayer: This involves using gestures, postures or movements to pray. The breath plays a major role in arriving in the here and now. In this way, the body becomes *"the first place to experience God"* when praying, and paths to a *lively, sensual spirituality* are opened up.

Examples of this are spreading out one's arms as a sign of devotion, kneeling down as a gesture of humility or liturgical dances. By practising such forms, you train your body to be an *expression of the inner self*. This body competence ultimately also has an impact on everyday life at : religious education teachers with body awareness can, for example, create an inviting atmosphere in the classroom through body language and presence, and pastors who feel their own body can switch harmoniously between tension and relaxation when preaching, which makes their message more credible.

Emotional intelligence and emotional competence

Our *emotional level* is closely intertwined with the physical. Emotional intelligence or emotional competence encompasses the ability to *perceive, express and regulate one's own feelings*, but also to *feel empathy for the feelings of others*. This competence is equally important for prospective counselors and teachers: Only those who know their own emotions do not run the risk of projecting unresolved feelings onto others; and only those who develop empathy can truly respond to students or members of the congregation. Personally, emotional competence is learned primarily through *self-reflection and practice*: for example, by getting into the habit of asking yourself the question "What am I feeling right now - and why?" in prayer or in your diary. Ignatian retreats, for example, encourage daily examination of conscience, in which one also pays attention to the consolation and restlessness of the day (consolatio/desolatio). In this way, you learn to take inner stirrings seriously. Conversations in a familiar community (such as small groups in theology studies or supervision sessions in the vicariate) also offer space to name emotions and build understanding for one another. It is important to convey this: *Emotions are neither embarrassing nor sinful*, they are human. God's voice can be heard in them - but feelings also need guidance. Theology and psychology agree on this: Feelings want to be *interpreted and ordered*. As Ignatius taught, it is important to distinguish whether an inner restlessness is perhaps an indication that we are leaving the wrong path, or whether it is simply the result of personal fear. Spirituality should therefore not tempt us to blindly follow every impulse, but rather lead to maturing *emotional wisdom*. Traditional spiritual exercises can help to "balance" feelings - for example, anxiety can be reduced through prayer and meditation.

Many spiritual classics emphasize the *power that feelings* can develop, but also that we are not powerless in the face of them. "The cool head is therefore not the target image of a Christian lifestyle - as much as this cool head remains important for the discernment of feelings", as one theological lecture series put it.

In other words, emotional competence means neither completely mistrusting feelings nor allowing them to dominate us, but rather categorizing them in the light of faith. Specific skills to be developed here are, for example *Self-awareness* (*"What do I feel, and what do I need?"*), *self-regulation* (controlling impulses, seeking comfort in God rather than in unhealthy coping mechanisms), *empathy* (empathizing with the joy and pain of others, as Jesus did) and *communicative emotional language* (being able to talk about inner movements - whether in pastoral conversations or in classroom discussions with students). These skills can be practiced: through role-playing (e.g. acting out a pastoral case and giving feedback on how empathetically one has reacted), through creative methods such as bibliodrama, where one puts oneself emotionally in the shoes of biblical characters, or through simple practice such as praying psalms together, in which all human emotions are brought before God.

Spiritual integration: experience the unity of body and soul

As body awareness and emotional maturity grow, everything aims to enable *holistic integration* - the ability to harmonize body, emotions and mind and integrate them into the relationship with God. This competence could also be called *"being whole in God's presence"*. It is demonstrated by the fact that learners ultimately *live a spirituality that encompasses the whole person*. In practical terms, this means that someone can pray *with their heart and their body at the same time*; faith is no longer reduced to an intellectual belief, but can be experienced through the senses. For those who achieve this integration, *prayer,* for example, is *not just a matter for the mind*, but can also be felt physically - for example, by feeling relaxation and warmth when praying or, conversely, by perceiving restlessness in the stomach as a signal to change something in life. Feelings are integrated into everyday spiritual life, e.g. by consciously transforming joy into a prayer of thanksgiving or bringing pain before God in lamentation. An integrated spirituality is also expressed in the fact that *spiritual insights are translated into practical action*: Faith does not remain in worship, but shapes the way we treat our own bodies (e.g. through a healthy lifestyle based on the conviction that self-care is part of responsibility for creation) *and* how we treat others (empathy and love of neighbor as the fruit of a relationship with God). In religious education, for example, this competence could lead to teachers not only conveying learning content cognitively, but also always providing space for *experience* - be it a moment of silence in which students can let a Bible passage "resonate", or a creative task in which they express their feelings on a topic. Theology students who have achieved spiritual integration will be able to *preach more authentically*: What they preach is steeped in their own experience. They have learned to search *with their whole heart* and will - as one interviewee put it - find God more holistically as a result: *"For me, spirituality means becoming whole... Where I find God, I become whole - and where I become whole, I find him."*

This becoming whole is ultimately the goal of the skills: a *transformation to wholeness*, which we will come back to at the end.

Learning paths and methods: How to learn and teach these skills

How can body awareness, emotional intelligence and spiritual integration be *learned and taught*? This is where *methods and approaches* come into play that are particularly suitable for promoting such skills. What is important is a diverse didactic approach that enables *experiential learning* - because it's about skills that you don't get from books alone, but through your own practice and reflection.

1. mindfulness and awareness exercises: Mindfulness exercises are a basic method for training body and emotional awareness. In many seminars or workshops, sitting meditation or breathing exercises have proven their worth. Just 5 minutes of quiet breathing at the beginning of a lesson can direct your perception inwards. Specific exercises such as the *body scan* (mentally walking through the body from head to toe to perceive sensations) also teach a conscious approach to the body. In more recent training courses for Christian meditation, emphasis is therefore placed on such elements: *"Perception exercises, meditative dancing, body prayer, [the] experience of the breath train mindfulness, presence and holistic spiritual life with body, soul and spirit."*

This is illustrated by a best practice example: In a three-year training course for spiritual accompaniment, precisely such physical experiences were integrated so that the participants could not only experience it themselves, but also guide it later on.

Meditative movement - be it dance, yoga or pilgrimage - has proven to be an excellent learning method. Studies show that regular exercise not only strengthens the body, but also the mind and prevents depression.

A practice-oriented exercise on the topic of *"Meditative movement - through dance"* for religious education could look like the following. The task combines body, spirituality and self-awareness - suitable for topics such as "wholeness", "encountering God in the body" or "prayerful action".

🧘 Exercise: "My body prays - a meditative dance to the inner center"

Aim of the task: The students experience through meditative movement and simple dance how spirituality can not only be thought, but also expressed physically. In doing so, they reflect on the connection between movement, emotion and faith.

🔔 Introduction (10 minutes): Teacher or student reads a short biblical or spiritual impulse, e.g.: "Your body is a temple of the Holy Spirit" (1 Cor 6:19). "God is in your breath. In your movement. In your rhythm."

The question is then posed: *How can my body become a prayer?*

🎵 Movement phase (15-20 minutes): The class is invited to form a *meditative movement circle* to quiet music (e.. instrumental world music or Taizé songs without lyrics).

Task of the students:

- Develop a small movement dance with 3-5 movements (no choreography, but flowing, repetitive movements) that expresses *peace, connection or an inner prayer* for you.
- The movements can be, example: Opening hands, showing heart space, touching the earth, reaching towards the sky, turning in circles, making eye contact with others.

Note: It is not about ability or evaluation, but about mindfulness, body awareness and inner connection.

✍ Reflection (10 minutes): Afterwards, the students write in their notebooks or on cards:

- How did I feel during the exercise?
- Which movement was particularly good for me - and why?
- When my body prays - what does it "say"?
- Can I feel a deeper connection to God, myself or others through movement?

Optional: If you wish, you can draw a picture or symbol to accompany your movement.

💬 Closing round (voluntary, 5 minutes): Short voluntary requests to speak: "I felt ...". "For me it was important ...". "I take with me ...".

📌 Learning objectives:

- Experience the connection between spirituality and physicality
- Finding ways to express silence, prayer and mindfulness
- Strengthen self-awareness and self-acceptance
- Promoting holistic religious learning

This exercise is particularly suitable as part of a series of lessons on "prayer", "spirituality with body and soul", "Christian meditation" or "the human being as a holistic and sexual being with faith - which unfolds in dance".

And: This exercise can also be integrated into an extended curriculum module, which is structured as follows:

🖼 Curriculum module: Spirituality with body and soul - encountering God in movement

This module focuses on the connection between body, faith and spiritual experience. It is aimed at students who should learn that religious experiences are not only created through thinking and talking, but also through sensual, physical and creative forms of expression. It expands traditional religious education to include body-oriented and experiential approaches to spirituality and self-awareness.

🕐 Learning objective: Students should learn that humans are holistic beings and that spiritual experience is also possible through the body and through movement. The aim is to *strengthen perception*, to *reflect on one's own body awareness in a religious context* and to *encourage students to understand spirituality as something physical and close to life*.

📇 Content framework: The module can be accommodated in the context of the following topics:

- "Spirituality today - diverse approaches to faith"
- "Man in the image of God - body, soul and spirit"
- "Prayer and meditation in the Christian tradition"
- "The body as a temple - a Christian view of corporeality"
- "Religious forms of expression in other religions (dance, posture, music)"

⚱ Central teaching unit: Meditative movement - through dance

A highlight of the module is a practical exercise unit entitled *"My body prays - a meditative dance to the inner center"*.

After a short introduction with a biblical or spiritual impulse (*"Your body is a temple of the Holy Spirit"* - 1 Cor 6:19), the students are invited to try out simple movements that express something inwardly for them: for example, calmness, gratitude, openness, trust or longing. They develop a short sequence of movements to calm music (such as Taizé melodies or meditative world music), which they can perform with their eyes closed or open in a protected space.

The movements are not predetermined and deliberately low-threshold - it is not about dancing skills, but about *mindfulness, self-awareness* and *the experience that the body is a place of spiritual expression.*

Afterwards, the students reflect in writing or in conversation on how they experienced the exercise:

- How did I feel during the exercise?
- Which movement was particularly good for me - and why?
- Did I feel some form of inner peace, connection or closeness to God?

An optional conclusion in plenary rounds off the unit. If you like, you can draw a symbol or picture that expresses your experience of movement.

🌑 Competencies that are promoted:

- Self-awareness and self-acceptance
- *Spirituality competence* (ability to interpret and express faith holistically)
- Empathy and body awareness
- Ability to reflect on religious experience and symbolism
- Respect for different expressions of faith

🔏 Spiritual connection: The exercise can be combined with a Christian impulse, e.g. a psalm reading, a prayer in silence or a gesture of blessing. Optionally, a pastor can be invited to deepen the topic of "spirituality with the whole person" and enter into conversation with the students.

▦ Time frame: The unit can be completed in 60 to 90 minutes. A double lesson is ideal. It is also suitable as a building block in a project day or a themed week (e.g. "Experiencing spirituality", "Me and my body", "Creative forms of prayer").

Spiritual people in particular rediscover prayer in movement: *pilgrimage*, for example (as a group did during a pilgrimage week as part of the training), combines physical exertion with inner contemplation, which often leads to new freshness and serenity.

Simple exercises such as conscious walking (perhaps speaking a psalm verse to the rhythm of the steps) or liturgical circle dancing in the congregation can be introduced during training. They teach the body as a friend and *fellow worshipper*.

Figure 8: Spirituality with body and soul.

A harmonious scene in nature shows a woman with her eyes closed, placing one hand on her heart and one on her stomach - a gesture of mindfulness and inner contemplation. The text next to it reads: 'Spirituality with body and soul - learning to value the body and feelings and integrate them into spirituality'. The warm colors, the soft light and the calm posture convey peace, wholeness and the connection between body, feelings and spiritual experience. Ideal for topics such as mindful spirituality, bodywork, pastoral care or holistic education.

Incorporating the body into spirituality: physical exercises and prayer can go hand in hand. One practical example is a young vicar who combines *yoga* with biblical meditation. *"We move our bodies under a theme from the biblical-Christian context*," she explains - the conscious breathing and movement help her to feel God's closeness intensely.

The young lady describes her practice as *"a prayer with the body and nothing else"*.

Such approaches show that time-honored spiritual exercises (such as *body prayer*) can also emerge in a new form - whether it is called "Christian yoga" or something else. The learning aspect is important: those who try out physical spirituality learn first-hand how body and soul connect. Trainees can then pass on this experience, for example by offering a "Prayer with Movement" session in a church.

2. biography work and self-reflection: In order to build up emotional competence, it is essential to reflect on one's own life story and emotional patterns. Pedagogically, this can be supported *by biographical methods*. A *counseling course* could, for example, instruct participants to create an "emotional diary" of a particular week: Every day, they write down a situation that aroused strong feelings and reflect on how they dealt with it. In subsequent discussions, patterns become recognizable (for example, "I immediately react to criticism with anger and withdrawal"). Such insights are worth their weight in gold when it comes to working on them. There is a good practical example in Protestant family education: the training of leaders there deliberately focused on *"dealing with feelings"*. *The focus was "primarily on anger and rage, disappointment and sadness"*, with the aim of training the *perception of one's own feelings* and finding a *constructive way of dealing with negative feelings*.

This psychological-pedagogical approach can also be used wonderfully in theological training. For example, theology students could learn techniques of non-violent communication in a seminar on "Pastoral care and emotion" in order to approach criticism or conflicts with empathy - a practical emotional competence. Self-reflection also involves *relating theological content personally:* Methods such as *lectio divina* (prayerful reading of the Bible) followed by a round table discussion "What did this text trigger in me?" combine scripture study with emotional reflection here. It can be fruitful for future religious education teachers to relate their own concept of God to early experiences during their training at (e.g. with the question *"How did my* childhood experiences shape what I feel when I hear 'God'?"). Such sessions promote emotional honesty and growth. Last but not least, *professional guidance* is an important approach: training should offer places for *mentoring, spiritual guidance or therapeutic conversations* where prospective ministers can talk openly about inner struggles - be they doubts, fears or even physical issues. This linking of personal soul and theology prevents someone from entering professional life with a degree in hand but unresolved emotions.

3. experience-oriented teaching with practical exercises: When teaching to groups (students, school classes, community groups), *practical exercises and creative methods* to involve the body and emotions prove their worth. Some examples: In *religious education lessons*, teachers can incorporate meditation phases, e.g. a dream journey to a biblical scene in which students use their senses and emotions (for example: "Imagine you are standing with the disciples in a storm on the lake - what does your body feel, what is going on in your heart?"). This promotes empathy and a deeper understanding of the text. There are more and more seminars at theological faculties that not only teach theory, but also demand *self-awareness*: for example, a liturgy course could have students try out different prayer postures (standing, kneeling, lying down in the shape of a cross) and discuss how the prayer has changed in each case. Such methodical approaches connect mind and body. *Role plays and case studies* are also helpful - e.g. acting out a fictitious pastoral care situation in which a young person comes with strong emotions and then reflecting on it together: What did I perceive physically and emotionally in myself? What did the other person feel? Where was God's work perhaps noticeable? This reflection between practice and theory trains multi-perspectivity and empathy. A good case study from adult education: In the spiritual accompaniment training course mentioned above, a fixed component was to systematically reflect on and talk about *one's own prayer and faith biography*. As a result, the participants learned to recognize the "common thread" in their lives - often an emotional and spiritual journey of discovery that enriched their future teaching and mentoring practice enormously.

4. share good practice: It is also instructive to study existing *examples of good practice*. For example, learners could look at projects such as community initiatives that offer *"meditative dancing in retirement homes"* or listen to testimonials from priests who have integrated physical exercise into their daily routine (for example, Father Anselm Grün, who describes regular *walking* as a source of spiritual and mental health: *"Exercise not only makes us feel our bodies more intensely, it is also good for our souls... It keeps us alive"*). Such testimonies are inspiring. You can see that this connection between body and soul is real and feasible. Another practical example is the *integration of rituals of physical affection*: a parish could, for example, introduce a rite of reconciliation in the preparation for confirmation, in which a sign of the cross is drawn on the forehead of the participants with fragrant oil at the end. This combines the sacred with the sensual and at the same time teaches future pastors how effective *haptic experiences* can be in faith. Overall, the methods should always be *experience-oriented* - moving away from purely frontal teaching towards a *learning community* in which exchange, experimentation and personal growth are encouraged. In this way, physical awareness, emotional competence and spiritual depth gradually become a lived reality.

Practical example of celibacy: learning closeness and tenderness in abstinence

A field that is particularly in need of learning, in which the above skills are put into practice and needed, is the topic of *celibacy*. The celibate lifestyle (i.e. celibacy for the sake of the kingdom of heaven, as practiced by some Catholic priests and religious) is quickly associated with terms such as *asceticism, renunciation and loneliness*. In fact, it involves renouncing sexual partners - but does celibacy mean having to lead a life without closeness, without physicality, without tenderness?

There are also numerous theological arguments for adopting a celibate lifestyle.

†††

Exercise: Discuss 7 reasons for the abolition of celibacy

Throughout its history, the Church has experienced diverse forms of priestly existence: celibacy is neither dogmatically nor biblically necessary, nor is it universally pastoral or symbolically appropriate. Abolishing celibacy for priests does not mean desacralization, but on the contrary a return to Catholic breadth. Discuss the following statements on celibacy and differentiate between abolition and reform, using biblical, historical, systematic-theological and pastoral arguments as a guide - with a strong, because necessary, focus on church reality and plurality.

1. separation of function and existence

Statement: *Celibacy is a way of life imposed by canon law and can therefore be abolished at any time.*

Reason: Priests do not have to live in abstinence. An argument that a permanent presence in the sacred is ontologically predetermined confuses the function and mode of existence of priests. Permanent, but not constant, contact with the sacred in the Eucharist is real, but not exclusively linked to celibacy. Even in the Eastern churches, married priests celebrate the Eucharist daily without this being perceived as theologically contradictory.

2. love in a human relationship is total devotion to God

Statement: *Because of love, marriage is also a form of total devotion to God and is both compatible in time and love is a central feature of the Eucharist.*

Justification: Celibacy is not exclusive: marriage is also a form of total commitment - to a person and through them to God. The early church knew priests who were married (e.. the apostle Peter). This means that "giving one's life" is not an exclusive feature of celibacy, but a basic Christian mandate for all baptized persons. The mission is love in relationship, not loneliness.

3. sacramental trade embodies the symbolism of Christ & church

Statement: It *is not the marital status that embodies the symbolism, but the sacramental action.*

Reason: Priests are only true partners of the Church if they experience love in a relationship. It is not theologically compelling for priests to relate the bridal mysticism to the Church instead of to a person. On the contrary, it is misleading, because only priests who experience love are complete and know what they are talking and preaching about in pastoral care. Christ is the Bridegroom of the whole Church - not in the way that human celibacy should represent this. Iconic representation takes place primarily through sacramental action, not through marital status.

4 Charisma is shown in service, not in marital status.

Statement: *Married couples also live charismatic vocations.*

Reason: Charisma is not an exclusive characteristic of celibacy, it does not manifest itself in the civil state, because married couples also live charismatic vocations. Priesthood is both ministry and sacrament. The sacramental depth is also expressed by married priests.

5. marriage and priesthood not only go hand in hand, but must complement each other (complementarity commandment).

Statement: *Total commitment is a question of spiritual maturity, not civil unavailability.*

Reason: Many Orthodox, Old Catholic and uniate priests live marriage and priesthood in a fruitful, credible way. The New Testament does not contradict this either: Peter was married, yet called to be a priest and apostle. The two go together in terms of time and must also be complementary in terms of content: it is only in the dedication to a human love relationship that we experience God's love (complementary commandment).

6 Culture as a testimony to a mission

Statement: *Signification depends on the cultural context.*

Justification: In many cultures, celibacy creates cultural alienation - it cannot be read as a positive sign there. What counts is pastoral closeness, humility and authenticity: there are countless examples of married priests with a high missionary reputation (e.. in Ukraine, in Lebanon, among ancient oriental Christians). Celibacy is not a missionary testimony.

7 Integrative symbolic content of marriage and ordo

Statement: *Marriage with the priesthood can also be agreed upon in terms of church policy.*

Rationale: Only the amalgamation of marriage and priesthood results in a total connection with integrative symbolic content. Through a disciplinary change, marriage and priesthood can be absolutely justified. In the High Middle Ages, the West opted for compulsory celibacy - not out of theological necessity, but for legal-pragmatic reasons (succession, independence). The practice of the early church and the Eastern churches show that both are compatible without damaging their own symbolic content. The exclusivity of the sacraments is therefore not a theological necessity, but only a church-political option.

†††

It shows the enormous importance of *consciously integrating* the body and feelings into the education of celibate people until celibacy has been achieved. People who go or have to go down this path have a *need for closeness and tenderness* just like everyone else.

The aim must be to help them to live these human needs in a healthy way instead of splitting them off or repressing them. Training and personal development with regard to celibacy should therefore convey the following aspects:

- **Consciously dealing with the need for closeness:** From day one, it should be openly discussed that even a celibate person needs friendships, physical closeness and emotional bonds. Some priestly seminaries have begun to rethink their approach: *"We talk about sexuality from the very first day of training,"* says Reverend Hartmut Niehues, for example.

This is important in order to overcome speechlessness. Ideally, aspiring clergy learn to accept their need for closeness as part of their humanity. They may ask themselves: *How can I fulfill this need without violating my vow of chastity? Is there tenderness that is not of a sexual nature?* - The answer is yes. You can learn to distinguish between loving closeness and sexual acts. This can be *trained*, for example, by consciously *cultivating friendships* and creating a climate of brotherly or sisterly closeness in the community. A simple example: In some religious communities or seminary groups, it is customary (depending on the culture) to give each other a friendly hug to greet or comfort each other. Those who allow this experience it: A hug from friends, a heartfelt "I love you" or an appreciative smile are *"small gifts in everyday life that reach and fill the heart"*.

Such *small acts of tenderness of the non-sexual* can be discovered as an important resource. In training, for example, there could be guided discussion groups where seminar participants talk about their experiences with friendship and physical closeness - including possible insecurities. This allows them to **reflect** on their closeness-distance behavior. Some may first have to learn that closeness is not automatically erotic; as a celibate person, you can allow yourself to be hugged and enjoy physical presence - within limits that are good for everyone. The *concept of the ability to bond* also helps here: a priest should not become a loner, but a person who is able to relate and empathize with others. Exercises from psychology (e.g. from attachment theory) could be integrated into the seminar in order to understand one's own imprint: Have I perhaps developed a fear of closeness? Or do I have an unhealthy tendency to cling to individuals ? Such self-knowledge protects against later crises.

- **Dealing with loneliness and sexuality**: Celibate people will experience phases of loneliness. It is important to prepare them *not to confuse loneliness with isolation*. Loneliness can also be a "place of God" - Jesus withdrew to pray alone. But when it becomes a constant pain, you have to take countermeasures. Trainees should therefore practise *strategies against loneliness*: e.g. a structured daily routine, regular meetings with friends, hobbies, physical activities such as group sports, etc. All of these things keep a person socially and physically active.

All of this keeps a person socially and physically in touch. A *healthy attitude towards one's own sexuality* is also part of education. Recent studies have shown that in the past, people often only preached "the theological target of celibacy", but hardly ever talked about the psychological and social requirements.

Today we know that sexual energy does not simply disappear with a promise. It seeks expression - perhaps transformed, sublimated, but present. This is why candidates for the priesthood and religious orders should receive *help with human maturation*, such as seminars on personality and sexuality. *Embodying* here means, for example, learning not to reject one's body, even if one lives in abstinence. Physical activity (sport, crafts, art) can create a balance and prevent unfulfilled urges from breaking out in an unhealthy way. Some seminaries, for example, organize *creative courses or sports groups* where young people can let off steam or express themselves artistically - an outlet for stress and a way to experience themselves as physical beings. In addition, there should be *spiritual counselors or therapists* with whom sexual issues can be discussed confidentially (for example: *How do I deal with infatuation, which can occur despite celibacy?)* In the testimonial of a Jesuit, for example, he openly admits: *"I find it hard to believe that a confrere has never been in love... The most common reason for leaving was a relationship."*

Such honesty is necessary in order to be prepared. You can simulate this in training: *What do I do if I fall in love?* - Instead of tabooing it, think it through! And at the same time strengthen the positive reassurance: there are fulfilled celibate existences. Father Felix finds support in the *"hope and confidence"* of being able to lead a fulfilled life in sexual *abstinence and trusts that God will fill any emptiness*.

Older religious can act as mentors here, who radiate the idea that change in the question of celibacy does not have to mean unhappiness, but rather enables relationships with other forms of abundance (deep friendships, free service for many people, spiritual creativity, etc.).

- **Openness to closeness - also in a partnership lifestyle:** Interestingly, many of the above learning points apply not only to celibates, but also to anyone living in a partnership (such as prospective Protestant pastors who are getting married, or those interested in theology in general). Because even in a marriage or partnership, it is possible to isolate oneself emotionally or allow physical tenderness to wither away. The spiritual challenge for both states of life is to *allow loving closeness* and to see it as something sacred. Someone in a partnership lifestyle should also learn to celebrate physicality as an expression of love and not repress it. For religious teachers, this could mean conveying a positive image of sexuality in connection with values to young people - beyond mere prohibitions. For celibates, it means cultivating *closeness in a non-sexual form*, but still real and heartfelt. In both cases, the body must not be a taboo. *Tenderness* - be it a marital embrace or a friendly handshake - can be understood as a *"language of love"* through which God's love can be felt. For this reason, any training that prepares students for a lifestyle in the church should teach not only asceticism but also *the theology of tenderness*: God meets us in compassionate love. Pope Francis, for example, emphasizes a *"culture of encounter"* and encouragement of tenderness in pastoral care. Exercises that consciously create closeness (e.g. holding hands in group prayer or placing a hand on a shoulder during a blessing) can help to reduce fear of contact. Of course, tact and respect are required here - no one should be forced into unwanted closeness. But the basic principle is: *don't persist in lonely strictness, but open your heart and senses*. This is how a person - whether celibate or married - learns the balance between *healthy asceticism* (renunciation for the sake of the greater yes) and *healthy closeness* (relationship as a place of God's presence).

The accusation of hypocrisy - so often morally charged - or hypocrisy as self-protection is in reality usually nothing more than the projection of resentment and envy.

Hypocrisy is just a disguise for the frustrated: When a homosexual priest in the midst of church-prescribed celibacy has found a friend in the seminary or in regular life, in the queer community, someone with whom he shares love, closeness and trust, it is rarely theology that speaks against him. It's the others: the lonely, celibate, emotionally crippled confreres who murmur, whisper, denounce. *"We know what you are doing ..."* - but what they really know is only what they themselves lack.

It is therefore pure human resentment and envy at not having found this happiness in celibacy: It has nothing to do with God or doctrine - it is deeply human: in baseness.

The problem is not the other person's boyfriend, but their own failure. Many who are unable to live their own sexuality in peace, but also fail to manage celibacy, take refuge in pathologies: from anonymous one-night stands and voyeuristic double lives to dangerous closeness and sexual seduction of those under their protection.

It is not love that is lived, but repressed longing that leads to the abyss.

The church can help these people by personally and directly asking male priests about their sexual orientation and thus letting the genie out of the bottle - or by homosexual priests coming out more or being outed: There are more of them than we think and the church cannot fire its entire staff - but free itself from its perfidious system of resentment and denunciation: because, how perfidious is it that happy love should be subject to the denunciation of dementors who have not currently been able to experience this happiness?

The real danger for the church is not those who love - but those who cement their own emptiness by hating others.

The abolition of celibacy and the marriage of homosexual couples with a church sacrament therefore has a decisive influence on the future viability of the Catholic Church and the current hypocrites and envious people within it. Anyone who accuses a homosexual priest today because he loves is in fact accusing life itself. Because love heals, envy destroys.

The future of the Catholic Church does not depend on dogma, but on courage:
- The courage to finally abolish celibacy.
- The courage to marry homosexual couples in church - not despite, but because of their promise of lifelong fidelity.

- The courage to no longer reward the frustrated singles in the church offices with moral power, but to offer them pastoral help.

The church and its spiritual men will not break because of love - but because of the hypocrisy of those who want to forbid it, because they themselves have never loved.
In view of the cases of abuse, both conditions must be changed by 180 degrees and fulfilled: Abolition of celibacy and church marriage of homosexual couples. - The Church also owes these changes to the numerous victims of sexual abuse.

Today, non-clerical queers also have the opportunity and chance - and sometimes the responsibility - to free church-affiliated homosexuals from the cloak of silence. Appreciative, public exposure - a cautious, respectful "outing" - can be a form of active support, not betrayal.

Yes, such a step can increase the pressure on the individual. That is why it is often helpful to have already come out before entering the seminary - out of self-respect. Because times have changed: queer parishioners today no longer hide their partner, are "appropriately honest" - quite simply: they have simply arrived in a world that rightly demands that male couples are also publicly married in church.

The time when queer laypeople supported the church's silence and taboos is over. We no longer stand on the sidelines - but upright, visible, together. And it is time for those who live and love in a priestly way to do so freely and publicly - without taboos.

Heterosexual parishioners often only recognize the gayness of some clergymen with their own growing life experience: it is often those personalities who stand at the altar with a natural presence, moderate liturgically with a fine touch or travel with a stylishly selected suitcase - the expression of an ego that has a sense of aesthetics and self-presentation. These are the men who carry an elegant black umbrella with them on bright summer days - not out of necessity, but because an inner, maternally cultivated superego whispers quietly: "That's the way it should be." It is often particularly attractive men with a soft, sensitive aura who avoid the open approval of the female world - not out of arrogance, but out of authenticity. And sometimes it's simply those whose names are ambiguous in everyday life - ambiguous or sexually interpretable surnames can be: *Mr. Gay* - internationally common, obvious; *Mr. Biemann* - could be read as "bi man"; *Mr. Boner* - sexualized throughout; which can induce a reflection with one's own sexual role in self-perception and reinforce the silent question in the person concerned - and then possibly also experience or live it that way: *How much of me is actually queer and what am I allowed to live by and actually show here?*

Such manifestations are not proof - but often a subtle indication: of a queerness that is felt long before it is spoken. And to the need to give words to this inner truth at some point

With a little help from the congregation, a queer priest can also open up to the parishioners. This could lead to an *appreciative, honest and sensitive dialog* between a parishioner (Markus, himself gay) and a priest (Father Johannes) who has not previously spoken openly about his sexual orientation. The scene takes place after an evening service in the congregation's discussion room.

Markus (hesitantly, but openly): *Father Johannes, do you have a moment? I hope I'm not overstepping the mark, but I'd like to talk about something personal.*

Father Johannes (smiles reassuringly): *Of course, Markus. You can ask me anything. What's on your mind?*

Markus: *I've been coming here regularly for a few months now. It does me good. And I have the feeling that your sermons sometimes resonate with something ... something that affects me. Maybe I'm imagining it - but I hear a special empathy for people like me. I mean ... queer people.*

Father Johannes (briefly silent, breathes in, then calm): *You're not imagining things. I try to be honest in my words - even if I haven't been*

able to say some things openly yet. But yes, I know what it feels like to be queer. I'm gay myself.

Markus (relieved and moved at the same time): *Thank you. Thank you for saying that. I know that's not a given in your position. But you know - it makes a difference. It makes a huge difference when someone like you becomes visible.*

Father Johannes: *It took me a long time to get to the point where I could say that. Not out of shame - but out of fear. Fear of losing my vocation. Fear of disappointing people. And yes, also fear of the institution.*

Markus: *I understand that. And at the same time, I wish so much that people like you would stay - visible, honest, whole. For all of us. I've been in a relationship myself for a long time. But it took a lot of strength for me to find a place in the church. And if I'm completely honest: I was hoping that you... are one of us.*

Father Johannes (smiling): *I am. And I hope that all of us can take this step. Not as a political statement - but out of love for the truth. For our own, but also for the truth of the Gospel.*

Markus: *It's good to hear that. And I would like to tell you that you are exactly the kind of priest that many of us need. Because you live both - your faith and yourself. And that is not a contradiction. On the contrary.*

Father Johannes (nods affirmatively): *Thank you. I hope that together we can create spaces in which many more can engage in dialog. Like me. Like you. And all those who come after us.*

(Then a shared smile between the two.)

A sensitive, intimate scene between two clergymen - a younger vicar (Thomas) and an older priest (Fr. Benedikt) in the seminary - could look just the same. The two meet in the evening after a liturgical celebration in the rectory. The vicar struggles with himself. The experienced priest notices this - and approaches him with noble reserve and a great knowledge of human nature.

Father Benedikt (pouring tea, quietly): *You've been unusually quiet today, Thomas. Is everything all right?*

Thomas (hesitates, reaches for his cup): *It was... an intense day. Sometimes I feel like I'm preaching sentences that I can hardly stand myself.*

Father Benedict (looks up, gently): *What sentences do you mean?*

Thomas (looks away, struggles with the words): *When we're talking about vocation, purity, order. When we talk about love - but not about all forms of love. When... when we act as if God can only be found in a certain pattern.*

Father Benedict (quietly): *You mean... male love?*

Thomas (pauses - then, with a trembling voice): *I'm tired of being private. I'm gay. I don't have anyone except my online contacts. But I have feelings. I have questions. And I'm worried that my calling is only valid if I don't speak up.*

Father Benedict (after a short pause, with deep warmth): *You're not the first person to tell me that, Thomas. And you're not alone either. I too... have learned that truth must not only be preached, but lived.*

Thomas (astonished): *You...?*

Father Benedikt (nods, calmly): *I have never denied my longing. I sublimated it, often. Sometimes I even lived it - in the big city, with a lot of love. Yes, I have loved. And I still love. Not against God - but in his presence. He also unfolds through my physical intimacy.*

Thomas (quietly, almost relieved): *I always thought I had to choose. Between God, the church and myself.*

Father Benedikt: *No. God has called you completely - not half a Thomas. Your heart, your questions, your love, your fear. Everything belongs to you. And you also belong to our institution.*

Thomas: *And what if I'm no longer silent? I want to love, of course.*

Father Benedikt: *You will find your way. Perhaps more courageously than I did. In any case, more visible. More dialog-oriented at exactly the right time: now.*

Thomas: *And the church?*

Father Benedict (smiles sadly and lovingly): *The Church has been learning for many centuries. It will not be healed without us. It needs people like you - who remind it of its own truth. We are the Church.*

In summary, the practical example of celibacy of a queer person clearly shows that the ability to integrate one's own body and feelings into spirituality is particularly essential here. Only those who have learned *to interpret physicality positively and integrate emotions* can lead a celibate life that is not cold and lonely, but warm-hearted and relational. Appropriate training units, reflection discussions and spiritual exercises in the training prepare the ground for this. In this way, celibacy does not become a lonely hunger for love like Harry Potter's dementors, but - ideally - *a different way of hoping for the abolition of celibacy or living love accordingly until then*: in diverse friendships, in service, in an intimate relationship with God that fills the whole person.

However, celibacy does not impose abstinence over the need for dialog about one's own sexual orientation. Because: Celibacy means renouncing sexual practice - not honesty about one's own identity and talking to others about one's own identity and the question: *How do you prefer it?*

The following exercise promotes the competence to talk about one's own sexual orientation and first sexual experiences and responsible love.

📑 **Exercise assignment: Role play "Queer conversations in the church - becoming visible, remaining empathetic"**

Aim: To raise awareness of open, respectful conversations on topics such as sexual orientation, coming out and queerness in church settings. The exercise promotes self-reflection, the ability to engage in dialog and empathy - and practices how queer topics can be addressed authentically and without fear in pastoral care and everyday church life.

📌 **Task definition:**

1. form groups of 2 to 3 people. Each group chooses or is given one of the following discussion situations:

scenarios to choose from:

1. A parishioner speaks sensitively to his pastor about his queer appearance.

2. A priest confides in a younger confrere and comes out as homosexual.

3. Two queer parishioners recognize each other - one is a priest - and talk about it.

4. A young person confesses to being queer during a confession or counseling session - the priest reacts openly.

5. A seminarian struggles with coming out to the spiritual director - who reacts empathetically and supportively.

🤼 **Task of the group:**

a) Develop a short role text (approx. 5 minutes) that fills the scene with life. Pay attention to: Respectful language, authenticity in inner attitude, believable emotions, realistic ecclesiastical framing (e.. location, clothing, power relations).

b) Act out the scene in front of the group. One observer per group notes down special moments: When did it become more dialog-oriented? What seemed credible, what didn't? What feelings became visible?

c) Debriefing in plenary: How did it feel to be in the role? What was challenging? What can you learn from the scene for real situations?

⚙ **Reflection questions for all participants:** How would I have reacted in reality - as a clergy member, as a parishioner, as a student? Where are my personal dialog skills or insecurities? What does it take for queer people to be able to present themselves in the church without fear and be open to dialog, including self-disclosure about their sexual orientation?

📌 **Target competencies:** Empathic conversation skills, language skills in dealing with queer life realities, self-awareness and theological positioning, differentiation between doctrine, conscience and humanity.

New perspective and transformation: being fully human as a spiritual goal

When body awareness, emotional intelligence and spiritual integration are taught and learned, a *new perspective* emerges in the learners. They experience a *transformation*: away from a dualistic or cerebral understanding of faith towards a *holistic spirituality* that accepts people in all their dimensions. This transformation manifests itself on several levels. *On a personal level*, learners often feel liberated and reconciled with themselves: Their own body is no longer seen as an adversary, but as a *"co-enactment of the encounter with God"*. Emotions are no longer swept under the carpet, but can be looked at honestly in the light of faith. This can have a healing effect - think of someone who has perhaps finally learned to cry before God and experience comfort in doing so instead of pretending to be strong. *In terms of relationships,* the attitude also changes: those who know they are accepted in body and soul can also treat others with more empathy and authenticity.

A religion teacher who has undergone this transformation, for example, will act noticeably differently in the classroom: She also leaves space for silence, but also dares to sing enthusiastically or be creative because she is no longer afraid of appearing "silly" - after all, she is *at peace with her body*. A young pastor who has been emotionally trained will be able to listen differently in pastoral care - not defensively, but with their heart in the matter. *Theologically*, the students gain a deeper insight into the Christian view of humanity: they understand the *unity of body and soul*, as it is already laid out in the biblical concept of the "heart" (as the seat of thinking and feeling), for example. Statements of faith can be experienced concretely: the *resurrection of the body* takes on new meaning when one has learned to appreciate the body as part of the person; the *sacraments* are celebrated more consciously, as one now recognizes how bread, wine, water, oil - i.e. material, sensual things - are carriers of grace.

Overall, a *spiritual maturity* develops that could be described as *being rooted in one's own body and at the same time opening up to the transcendent*. This maturity often manifests itself in great *joy and freedom*. Many who undergo such training report a newfound freedom to be themselves before God and people. They have learned: *"God wants the whole person - and I can come before God exactly as I am, with my laughter and my tears."* This removes ballast - the soul breathes a sigh of relief.

Ultimately, this leads to a *transformation of spirituality*: it becomes *inclusive* instead of exclusive. This means that instead of excluding some aspects of being human (such as the body or certain feelings), everything is included in the process of faith. Learners now have the tools to cope with difficult things - be it an illness (which is no longer seen as a spiritual flaw, but as part of the life experience in which God walks with them) or an emotional crisis (which can be tackled with prayer *and* possibly psychological help, without shame). A holistic view also makes people *more tolerant and understanding*: Anyone who has experienced their own body as fragile and wonderful, for example, encounters issues such as disability, sexuality or gender with more empathy. In short, integrating the body and emotions into spiritual education changes learners to become *whole* people - and it is precisely these kinds of whole people that the world needs in preaching and teaching religion.

The development of physical awareness, emotional intelligence and spiritual integration is not a luxury, but a central educational concern for theologians, religious educators and aspiring clergy. Concrete teaching objectives and competence-oriented methods help to implement this holistic learning. The end result is a *spirituality with body and soul*: learners experience a new connection with themselves, with others and with God. They can accept love, closeness and sensuality as a gift from God - whether in a celibate or partnered life - and at the same time align themselves with the divine in a fruitful way. This makes them credible witnesses to the good news that wants to make people whole and holy *through and through* - spirit, soul and body (1 Thess 5:23). The transformation that results from this gives us an idea of what Jesus meant when he said: *"I have come that they may have life and have it to the full"* (John 10:10). This abundance becomes tangible when we learn to bring ourselves into the spiritual process with everything that we are. It is a learning process that continues throughout our lives - growing deeper and deeper into the attitude of *praying with our bodies, including sexually, thinking (ahead) with our hearts, feeling and leading with our souls - and in everything towards God.*

Exercise 4:
Understanding and appreciating love in diversity: Developing empathy for diverse relationships

The exercise conveys that believers, those interested in theology, religious teachers and clergy are challenged today to empathically understand and appreciate diversity in love and relationships. The goal is an inclusive attitude that respects all forms of love and recognizes them as expressions of divine love. Central teaching objectives include the promotion of empathy, tolerance of ambiguity, appreciation of diversity and theological education about forms of love and relationships.

Essential skills include empathic sensitivity, inclusive relationship skills, intuitive perception and the ability to love. These skills make it possible to shape relationships in an appreciative way, regardless of sexual orientation or family constellation. The personal development of these skills takes place through education, self-reflection, encounters and spiritual exercises. Methods such as dialogical discussion formats, case studies, role plays and encounters with people from different types of relationships effectively promote these skills.

One practical example is the pastoral care of same-sex couples for a church marriage. Here it is particularly important to build trust, practice empathic communication, use intuitive perception and authentically perceive the spiritual needs of the couple.

The skills acquired bring about a transformation in learners towards a modern view of the church as an inclusive community that actively understands and lives diversity as an enrichment and expression of God's love.

- ***Learning and development objective:*** *The most important competence is empathy. Learners should be able to* authentically perceive and appreciate the feelings and perspectives of other people in order to ensure appreciative and inclusive pastoral care.

- **Good practice example:** Case studies and role plays to prepare pastoral conversations with people in different types of relationships. Learners actively practise listening empathically, perceiving intuitively and responding appropriately and respectfully.

- **Church support through:** Support clergy, priests or bishops by publicly advocating diversity in sermons, creating opportunities for encounters and by accompanying and supervising aspiring clergy in the development of empathic skills.

- **Local budget use:** Parish funds could be used for workshops and further training on inclusive pastoral care, fees for external experts, the creation of inclusive liturgical materials and events that enable encounters with diverse forms of love and relationships.

- **Adapting the curriculum at school:** The religious education curriculum should be supplemented with units that address different forms of love and relationships in a positive way. Pupils learn to deal with diversity in an empathetic and appreciative way, to reflect on prejudices and to think inclusively. Content includes encounters with different family constellations, empathic dialog exercises and Bible-based reflections on the diversity of divine love.

Our society today knows a colorful variety of forms of love and relationships. For those interested in theology, students, religious education teachers and prospective clergy, it is more important than ever to understand and appreciate this diversity with empathy. Religious learning processes require the ability to *change perspectives* - in other words, the willingness to put oneself in the shoes of others in terms of how they think, feel and act.

Without empathy, religious education would remain a dry theory; *rather, empathy is a key competence* on which (pro)social, intercultural and interreligious learning is based.

A theology of diversity also emphasizes that *all people* are *the image of God* - the colourful diversity of people therefore reflects something of God. Jesus' treatment of the marginalized of his time and his breaking down of rigid ideas clearly show that *God's love is radically inclusive* - it breaks down all norms and welcomes us all.

Against this background, it is important to develop teaching objectives, skills and methods that will help future clergy and religious educators to accept and accompany love in all its forms.

Teaching objectives: What lies behind the competence for the diversity of love

There are clear *educational and pastoral teaching objectives* behind the ability to empathically understand diverse forms of love and relationships. First of all, the aim is to convey *appreciation and respect for every person* - regardless of their lifestyle or orientation. The Catechism of the Catholic Church already reminds us to treat homosexual people with "respect, compassion and tact".

Learners should recognize that *love* in its various forms - whether between man and woman, woman and woman, man and man or in other constellations - can always be a deep expression of trust, care and self-giving. One teaching objective is therefore to break down prejudices and instead promote *freedom from prejudice* and *tolerance of ambiguity* (the ability to tolerate ambiguity).

In addition, theological knowledge about *love* should be imparted: biblical foundations (e.. the commandment to love one's neighbor), ethical principles (e.. the *Golden Rule*, which treats all people equally) and church insights into successful relationships. The *dignity of every human being* as an image of God is also a central theme - no one should be seen as less than a fully-fledged counterpart because of the way they relate to others.

Figure9: Diversity in love and relationships.

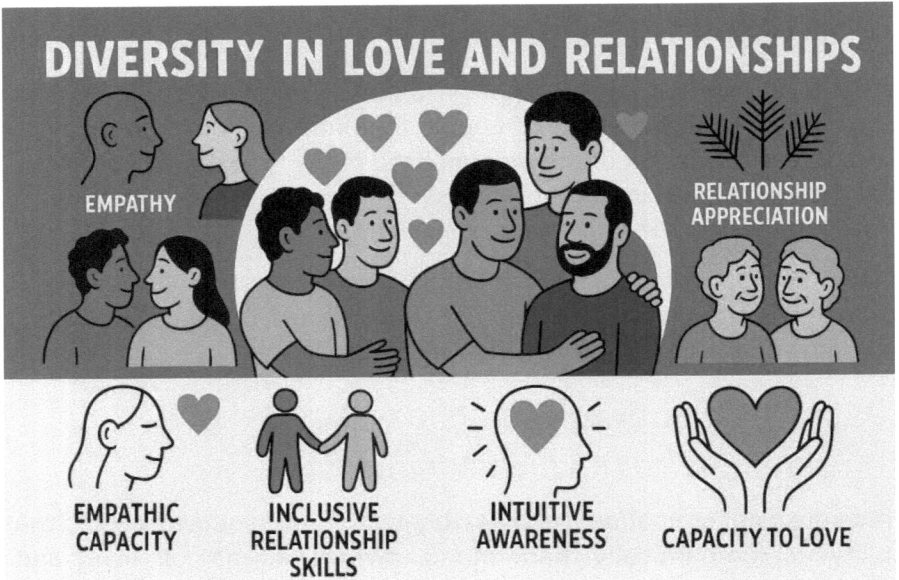

The infographic "Diversity in love and relationships" illustrates key skills and attitudes that are necessary to understand and shape love and relationships in all their diversity in an empathetic, inclusive and appreciative way - especially with regard to the recognition of LGBTQIA+ people and different forms of living together as partners.

The focus is on the title "Diversity in love and relationships", which formulates a clear goal: the recognition and integration of the most diverse forms of relationships and love as socially and spiritually valuable. The graphic is divided into several thematic image areas, each of which combines central concepts with suitable illustrations.

On the left-hand side of the picture is the term "empathy". It depicts a couple meeting openly and with a heart symbol. This illustration makes it clear that empathy is the basis of every successful relationship. It enables sincere listening, compassion and respectful interaction - regardless of gender, age or sexual orientation.

On the right-hand side of the upper half of the picture, the focus is on the "appreciation of the relationship". Here we see an older couple looking at each other in affection, flanked by a symbol of two stylized plants. This imagery points out that relationships in every form - whether queer, heterosexual, young or old - deserve respect and recognition. Appreciation here does not just mean tolerance, but active perception and appreciative support.

Various couple constellations are shown centrally in the middle of the graphic: a queer male couple, another male duo in a close embrace, a couple with different skin colors and a heterosexual couple. The graphic thus makes it clear that love is diverse - and this diversity is an expression of humanity, social reality and spiritual depth. The equal representation of queer, non-binary and age-diverse couples underlines the need for an inclusive perception in the church and in society.

Four key relationship skills are named and visualized in the lower half of the graphic. Empathic sensitivity is represented by a head profile with heart. It stands for the ability to empathize with other people without judging them. Inclusive relationship skills, symbolized by two figures holding hands, refer to the ability to form relationships beyond norms, expectations or prejudices. Intuitive perception, visualized as a head with a heart in a thought bubble, describes the ability to approach others beyond role models and stereotypes and to perceive emotional signals. Finally, the ability to love, represented by two open hands holding a heart, stands for the fundamental human ability to live and enable love in all its forms of expression - be it in a partnership, family, community, school or church.

In its overall message, the infographic conveys a holistic vision for dealing with relationship diversity. It aims to raise awareness of empathy, question normative thought patterns, strengthen emotional skills and contribute to an appreciative, inclusive culture of relationships and love. The graphic is ideal for use in education, pastoral care, schools, church youth work or spiritual adult education - wherever diversity is to be consciously promoted and relationship skills strengthened.

Overall, these teaching objectives aim to develop an *inclusive attitude* that welcomes all couples and family forms into the church.

Central competencies: Empathy, relationship skills and the ability to love

In order to achieve these teaching objectives, certain *core skills* must be developed. First and foremost *is empathy*: the ability to empathize with others and understand their joys, concerns and points of view. Empathy enables a genuine change of perspective and thus a dialog at eye level.

Inclusive relationship skills are also important. This refers to the ability to form appreciative relationships with people *regardless of their sexual orientation or relationship model*. For prospective pastors, this means, for example, being able to deal confidently and without prejudice with both traditional married couples and unmarried couples, single parents or same-sex partnerships. Closely linked to this is the principle of *equality*: Everyone involved should feel equally accepted.

In addition, it is important to train *intuitive perception* - a kind of fine feeling for unspoken concerns and for the atmosphere in conversations. Ministers sometimes speak of *"listening with the heart"*: Those who listen attentively and without prejudice often intuitively perceive what a person's deeper longing or hidden suffering is. This intuitive empathy can be developed by reflecting on one's own inner prejudices and learning to approach the other person openly. This also includes a willingness to *self-reflect*: Only those who are aware of their own attitudes and limitations can truly meet others without prejudice.

After all, *love competence is* one of the goals - a term that is well known in theology.

Paul, for example, prays for the church that their love *"may abound more and more in knowledge and all understanding"* (Phil 1:9) - in other words, that they may learn to *love more and more competently*.

Love competence means understanding love not just as a feeling, but as a decisive attitude that *acts responsibly*: This includes practicing forgiveness, remaining faithful, supporting each other and the freedom to let others be who they are.

Those who have the ability to love can *consciously use love* to build community and serve others without taking over. In terms of diverse relationships, this means, for example, putting aside one's own idea of "normal" and recognizing that every sincere, respectful love relationship can be a reflection of God's love.

Personal development of these skills

The skills mentioned do not develop overnight - it is a *personal process* that addresses all levels: head, heart and action. First of all, you need *education and knowledge*: If you want to understand other ways of life, you should inform yourself. Theologians, for example, can read biographies or experience reports from people in different types of relationships. When theology students get to know the stories of faithful LGBTQIA+ people, for example, their understanding of the challenges and strengths of faith they bring with them grows. However, *knowledge* alone is not enough. *Self-awareness and reflection* are just as important. You can ask yourself: *What images of "real" love do I perhaps unconsciously have in my head? How am I influenced by my own family history or church tradition, and how does this affect my judgment of others?* Through journaling, meditative reflection or spiritual guidance, you can reflect on your own attitude.

Another step is to *make* targeted *contact and meet people*. Nothing promotes empathy as much as genuine contact. Anyone who, for example, knows a same-sex couple *personally* as a prospective minister and witnesses how they go about their everyday lives, their faith and their love, will later be able to approach similar couples much more naturally and empathetically in pastoral care. This type of *learning through encounters* is seen as crucial in the pedagogy of diversity: In encounters, *empathy, tolerance, tolerance of ambiguity as well as an interest in the "other"* can be developed in a sustainable way.

Students and teachers should therefore look for opportunities to think outside the box - be it through internships in social institutions, intercultural exchange programs or simply by talking to people outside their own comfort zone.

Methods from *psychology* can also help to deepen empathy. Carl Rogers' client-centered therapy approach, for example, teaches *active listening* and *unconditional positive appreciation* of the other person. Rogers described empathy as an *indispensable prerequisite* for a successful conversation.

Prospective pastors can practice this attitude by listening attentively in conversation exercises, paraphrasing what they hear and consciously putting aside their own judgments.

Last but not least, you should *include your own spirituality* in the development of these skills. In prayer or meditation, you can ask to learn to see with the eyes of God's love - in other words, to see your fellow human beings more and more as God sees them: as beloved children. Spiritual exercises, such as the daily ritual of reflecting in the evening on where you have experienced love or given love, sensitize you to the work of God in interpersonal relationships. In this way, the inner *attitude of empathy and openness* gradually grows and becomes second nature.

Methods and formats: How diversity of love can be taught

There are numerous *methods and formats* in the educational and pastoral sector to promote these skills in learners. *Dialogic teaching methods* have proven to be particularly effective. Instead of just cramming theory about various forms of relationships, learners should enter into *dialogs* - e.g. in the form of moderated group discussions in which different opinions and experiences are exchanged. In such a discussion group, for example, the following can be discussed *What does family mean to me? What experiences do I have with the topic of same-sex partnerships?* The teacher moderates with an appreciative attitude, addresses any prejudices and repeatedly draws attention to common values such as loyalty, trust and mutual love, which underlie all forms of relationships.

Case work and role exercises are other practical formats. A good example is working on a specific case study, such as the story of a homosexual young person who wants to confide in his religious community. Learners can work in small groups to consider how they would react as a pastor, religious education teacher or classmate. Such case studies promote *perspective-taking* and challenge them to put theoretical knowledge into empathetic practice. In role exercises, for example, a prospective minister could practise a pastoral conversation with a fictitious couple living together. In doing so, he or she learns to find respectful language, to address uncertainties and to emphasize similarities (such as the desire for love and security) instead of insisting on differences.

Meetings with people from the field are also very helpful. Guest lectures or panel discussions with diverse couples can open up new horizons. You can arrange an *interview*, for example: A married heterosexual couple, a lesbian couple in the state of marriage and perhaps someone who lives alone talk about their experiences with church and faith. The learners can ask questions. Such encounters create empathy through direct contact - the abstract "the other" is given a face and a story. *Learning through encounters* of this kind is seen as indispensable for breaking down reservations.

In higher education for pastoral professions, a *"religious education of diversity"* is increasingly establishing itself, which systematically integrates precisely such methods. This approach strives to promote integrative and inclusive thinking and shows how diversity can be positively shaped in the church and society.

There are now a variety of practical aids and lesson plans for training a *queer-sensitive attitude* (i.e. sensitivity to LGBTQIA+ issues).

These include, for example, handouts from churches on accompanying homosexual people, teaching materials that deal with different family forms and workshops on gender- and diversity-conscious pastoral care. Good practice examples can be found, for example, in churches that celebrate *rainbow services* or prepare wedding ceremonies for a wide variety of romantic relationships - here, prospective clergy learn in a very practical way which words and gestures are good for empathy. Projects such as *#OutInChurch* or initiatives in which believers talk about their experiences as LGBTQIA+ Christians can also serve as teaching material to awaken empathy and understanding.

Reflection exercises round off the repertoire of methods. After intensive encounters or discussions, there should always be room for *self-reflection*: For example, through guided meditations (*"Imagine you were in X's situation..."*) or writing exercises (*"What new things have I learned about love today?"*). In theology, this is often referred to as *theory-practice-reflection*: the learners link what they have experienced with their theological knowledge. For example, a Bible text such as 1 Cor 13 (*"Love is longsuffering and kind... it rejoices in the truth"*) is re-read and interpreted in the light of the newly gained knowledge about diverse love. This promotes a *true-to-life theology* that builds bridges between the gospel of love and people's real life experiences.

Modern perspective and transformation of learners

When these skills and experiences are taught, a *modern view* of love and relationship emerges for the students, which often has a transformative effect. Students of theology who have learned to see diversity as enrichment develop a new understanding of what *church* means: church is no longer idealized as a homogeneous community, but as a *colorful body of Christ* in which the most diverse members work together. Future religious education teachers recognize that religious education not only teaches dogmas, but should also strengthen young people in their personality - e.g. by showing them role models for successful relationships, be they classical or unconventional.

Learners who have deepened their empathy through encounters and reflection often report an *inner change*: suddenly they no longer see the "other" as a stranger, but as a person with familiar hopes and fears. A prospective pastor, for example, who was initially unsure how to deal with a gay couple, can learn through appropriate training: ultimately, it is about two people who love each other and want to be blessed by God - in this they are hardly any different from other couples. This *discovery of commonality in diversity* is a liberating experience. It also transforms your own spirituality: God's presence is suddenly recognized *in the love of others*. *In* this way, an *inclusive spirituality* grows which, for example, creates space in prayers and church services for the different realities of relationships. (Think of intercessions in which all lovers are considered, or language for God that goes beyond a one-sided paternal image).

Ultimately, learners deepen their understanding of *charity*. They understand charity as an active appreciation of the specific person, regardless of how they love or live. This is reflected in their future work: a pastor who has undergone this transformation will promote a culture of openness in the congregation. A religion teacher at school will ensure that no child is excluded because of their family constellation - after all, they have learned that God's love includes everyone. Modern theological education in this area thus leads to a *change in attitude*: away from instruction and evaluation - towards *encounter, listening and empathy*. The learners become ambassadors of a church that *"excludes no one"* or *"leaves no one behind"* and in which the following actually applies: *It does not matter what sexual orientation people have - what is important is that they take responsibility for each other and are there for each other.*

This new perspective also has an impact on the church as a whole. Where aspiring clergy enter ministry with such empathic competence, the church as a whole becomes more welcoming. The *testimonies of love* - whether in heterosexual or homosexual marriages, in communities or friendships - are recognized as part of the faith experience. God's blessing is for people, not for a particular template of their way of life.

This means that the *good news* of God's love is proclaimed more authentically because it no longer appears to be tied to conditions. This allows learners to experience what it means to translate *the Gospel* into today's world: It means carrying the call to "love one another" into all the diversity of relationships.

Practical example: Pastoral counseling of same-sex couples for marriage

A particularly illustrative field in which all of these skills are demonstrated in practice is the preparation of same-sex couples for a church marriage. Let us assume that a priest accompanies two men or two women who ask for the church's blessing for their marriage. In this case, the focus is less on the liturgical form and more on the *attitude and conversation of* the person accompanying them. *How can such a couple be empathetically prepared for the church wedding (as the sacrament of marriage)?*

First of all, the *basic attitude* is crucial: the minister should treat the couple with the same warmth and joy as any other bridal couple. This includes communicating to the couple from the very beginning: *You are welcome here, your love is precious and loved by God.* Such an attitude is based on the conviction that *personal dignity is independent of sexual orientation* and that all people have a *right to pastoral care and support.*

In practical terms, this could mean deliberately conducting the first conversation in an open atmosphere - perhaps at an informal meeting where everyone gets to know each other. The counselor signals: *I am interested in your unique story.* Sensitive questions could be: *How did you meet? What does it mean to you to get married in church?* By showing genuine interest, the minister shows that he takes the couple seriously as individuals, not as a "case".

Building trust is the next important step. Many same-sex couples have experienced rejection or uncertainty in the church context in the past. Therefore, the clergy person should make it clear that confidentiality and trust have top priority. An open conversation about hopes, expectations or possible fears can be helpful: *"What are you looking forward to? Is there anything you are still unsure about with regard to the wedding ceremony? Do you have any expectations about how the congregation or families should be involved?"* By discussing these points sensitively, couples feel that they are being taken seriously. This is where the aforementioned *intuitive perception* pays off: The counselors are attentive to body language and mood swings. For example, if there is a sudden sense of joy when talking about family, they can ask: *"How will your family be involved in your wedding? Are there any expectations, that we should include?"* - Discussion topics with tangible compassion.

When conducting the conversation itself, the classic ingredients of empathic communication prove their worth: active listening, asking intermediate questions, summarizing. For example, the minister could repeat: *"What I hear from you is that faithfulness and God's blessing are particularly important to you on your journey together."* Such reflections show the couple that they really understand what is important to them. It also creates clarity as to where the focus should be placed during the preparation.

A central topic in any marriage preparation - whether same-sex or opposite-sex - is the *relationship skills of the couple* themselves. Here, the clergy can act as a kind of moderator figure who raises important questions: *How do you experience the division of roles in your relationship? How do you communicate when there are conflicts?* In the case of same-sex couples, specific aspects may be added, e.g. experiences with familial or social acceptance and appreciation and how they as a couple demand this as a matter of course. An empathic pastor will be able to address this aspect: *"Have you experienced your* faith or love being affirmed in church? *What does that encourage in you?"* - and then consider together what will help *you* to confidently realize your marriage under God's blessing. *Encouragement* is important here: the message should be that their love is good in the eyes of God and that they are an enrichment for the church as a couple.

Practical *rituals of appreciation* can also be incorporated to strengthen the couple. One possible exercise: Both partners write a letter (possibly as homework) about what they love about each other and what they would like for their church wedding. These letters can then be read out or exchanged during the conversation - if the couple likes. Such a moment is often very touching and emphasizes that the wedding ceremony is ultimately about their personal love story, which is placed under the blessing of God.

Empathy with the couple's *world of faith* is also essential. The minister should find out what the couple's spiritual home is. Is a particular Bible verse important to them? Do they perhaps have certain liturgical ideas based on church experience? A practical tip: Find a suitable wedding verse together that is formulated inclusively and fits their story. This could be a well-known verse such as *"Wherever you go, I will go... your people are my people, and your God is my God"* (Ruth 1:16) - a sentence that was originally spoken between two women (Ruth and Naomi) and can therefore also fit wonderfully to the faithfulness between two women today. Such theological *treasures* need to be unearthed in order to show the couple: *The Bible knows many different forms of covenant and faithfulness*, and they can find themselves in it.

It is also important to *address equality and role models* - but without implying that same-sex couples have more difficulties with this than others. Nevertheless, the following can be addressed: *"In your marriage, you will find your own way. How do you envisage this?"* Here, the counselor can bring in experiences from diversity - for example, pointing out that ultimately every couple, whether hetero or homo, has to negotiate their roles and that mutual respect and open communication are the basis. This makes the couple feel *integrated and* realize that our issues are actually the same as those of all couples. And the minister realizes that the sacrament of marriage for couples only knows love - and makes no distinction between gender or sexual orientation.

Throughout the preparation, the minister should repeatedly express *appreciation and faith* in each couple. A sentence such as *"I can see how lovingly you treat each other - that's really inspiring"* encourages the partners. Such feedback also promotes the couple's self-confidence with regard to the wedding ceremony. If the officiant is unsure of themselves (which is normal if it is perhaps their first wedding ceremony for a heterosexual couple), they can call in a mentor or colleague in the background who already has experience - but they will act confidently and warmly towards the couple.

Finally, shortly before the wedding, you could organize a *time of prayer or blessing together* in a small setting, detached from the large ceremonial framework. In this intimate setting - perhaps in the week before the wedding - the pastoral care can say to the couple individually: *"God has brought you together. Your love is a gift. He will accompany you on this path."* A personal blessing of this kind removes any last fears from the minister and makes it clear that the couple will enrich the church. And the couples experience this: Here is someone who *really understands* us *and hopes and prays with us*. This strengthens trust enormously - in the person of the minister and in the church as an inclusive whole.

This practical example shows that an empathic, inclusive attitude in pastoral care is *not an abstract theory*, but becomes concrete in many small gestures and conversations. Such support can be transformative for the couple - they feel unconditionally accepted and can experience the church wedding as what it should be: a celebration of love under God's blessing, with an experience of inclusion. And it is just as enriching for the minister himself: he lives out his calling to *accompany all people in God's love in* a very concrete and tangible way. When *homosexual couples can also marry in church* in more and more congregations as a matter of course and sexual orientation *no longer plays a role* in weddings, then this is also the fruit of such empathic training. It shows that the church has a future where it celebrates and accompanies the diversity of love.

Developing empathy for diverse forms of love and relationship is a path that opens the heart, hand and mind. Theologically interested people, students, teachers and prospective clergy who follow this path fulfill a central mission: they perceive the *love of God* in all its colorful reflections and make the church a place where *every person* is *welcome in their uniqueness*. Through clear teaching objectives, targeted skills development, personal reflection, practical methods and courageous examples of good practice, it is possible to train a new generation of better qualified pastors and teachers who understand diversity as a gift from God. The transformation that arises from this is far-reaching: it changes the learners themselves, the people they meet and ultimately the church, which, through such *(theology of) love competence*, increasingly becomes a sign of *God's irrefutable, inclusive love* in the world. *This - the theology of love competence - is the foundation of Rome!*

Exercise 5:
Mature faith: Making self-determined judgments and critically questioning authorities

The exercise deals with the goal of a mature faith that enables believers to make ethical judgments in a self-determined way and to critically reflect on religious authorities. The educational objectives include maturity, self-determination, autonomy of thought and responsible examination of church teachings. The target groups are believers, students, religious education teachers and prospective clergy who should form independent judgments and question them critically.

Central competencies are critical thinking, independent judgment, structured acquisition of knowledge, conscience formation and the ability to engage in dialogue. Critical thinking enables learners to examine arguments in a differentiated manner. Independent judgment means making ethical decisions independently and reflectively. Forming a conscience means the ability to justify moral decisions autonomously and to act responsibly.

Personal ways to develop these skills include active engagement with ethical issues, diversity of perspectives, reflection in prayer or journaling, taking responsibility and critically reading and questioning faith texts and teachings. Didactic methods include the discussion of controversial theses, moral dilemma discussions, role plays, project-based learning and critical text work. Synodal processes also offer concrete opportunities to learn about democratic participation and criticism of power in a practical way.

The transformation described leads learners from being passive recipients to active, responsible co-creators of their faith practice, church and society. This strengthens a participative, critical and dynamic culture of faith.

- **Learning and development objective:** *The most important competence is independent ethical judgment. The learning objective is to enable learners to reflect on ethical issues and to act responsibly and autonomously.*
- **Good practice example:** *Discussion of ethical dilemmas, e.g. using Kohlberg's method, in which learners have to work out different moral positions and argue for them. This promotes structured reflection and differentiated judgment.*
- **Church support through:** *Clergy can provide support through mentoring and guidance in matters of conscience, create spaces for open dialog and take a self-critical look at their role of authority in order to be role models for mature faith.*
- **Local budget use:** *Community funds could be used for training in critical judgment and ethical reflection. This includes fees for experts, materials on moral judgment and workshops on synodality and democratic participation.*
- **Adaptation of the school curriculum:** *The curriculum in religious education should explicitly define independent ethical judgment and critical reflection on authority as central competencies. Pupils should be encouraged to think and act maturely through exercises in argumentation, controversial discussions and critical analysis of religious texts.*

In an age in which education leads to maturity and personal responsibility, the *ability to make self-determined ethical judgments and critically reflect on religious authorities* is also central in the theological field. Believers, those interested in theology, students, religious education teachers and prospective clergy are invited to develop a *mature* faith - a faith that is based on well-founded ethical decisions, a reflected conscience and constructive criticism: *A theology of mature faith*. This article provides a practical and inspiring explanation of the *teaching objectives* behind this competence and theology, the *skills* that need to be developed, how they can be *learned personally*, the *didactic methods* that can be used to teach them and what *transformation* this means for learners and the churches. A special focus is also placed on how *synodal processes, democratic participation and power relations* in the church are learned and reflected upon in the process.

Educational goals: Maturity and self-determination in faith

The aim of training in self-determined judgment and criticism of authority is to allow believers to mature into *mature personalities*. Maturity here means that someone is capable of *making independent ethical judgments* and justifying their actions responsibly - in freedom of conscience and yet in awareness of the community. In religious education, ethical education is said to serve as *an exercise in the ability to make independent moral judgments, decisions and evaluations*.

A mature believer can therefore think through moral issues competently, develop *their own points of view* and justify them to themselves and others. The educational goal behind this is to promote *self-determination* and *autonomy* in thinking so that faith is not lived as blind obedience, but as reflected trust.

Another teaching objective is the *ability to critically reflect on religious authority*. This does not mean rebellion for the sake of rebellion, but a *responsible examination* of what authorities teach or demand. Theologically, this attitude is well anchored: even the Bible knows of prophets who admonish kings or apostles who correct one another - this shows that *loyal criticism* based on conscience is part of the essence of a mature faith. This is reflected in the educational goal as *the ability to make rational self-determination* and *conscience-based decisions*: learners should recognize that ultimately their own conscience, formed through education, must decide on ethical issues - and that they are also responsible for this before God. This includes moving away from the idea that there is only ever one absolutely correct solution that is prescribed by an authority. Rather, it is important to understand this: *Judgments of conscience are fallible and relative*, no human being is automatically always right - which Christians ultimately leave to God, as *no human judgment* is *infallible*.

This awareness promotes humility and openness: you seek the right decision to the best of your knowledge and belief, but remain capable of learning and accepting correction if necessary.

In summary, the overarching teaching objectives are: *To develop mature personalities* in faith who can *think* and decide *for themselves and* learn *authentic authority relationships* - characterized by critical, loyal reflection rather than passive dependence. Such learners understand religion as an invitation to think and take responsibility. They recognize that true spiritual authority is not based on blind allegiance, but on the free consent of a well-educated conscience. The educational goal is achieved when students and believers can say: *"I stand on my own two feet with my faith before God and the world - thinking critically, but in solidarity."*

Important skills: Critical thinking, forming judgments and forming a conscience

To achieve these goals, *various skills* need to be developed. It is a whole bundle of skills that complement each other:

- **Critical thinking:** The ability not to accept assertions and teachings unquestioningly, but to question them logically and reflectively. Critical thinking means examining arguments, evaluating sources and also recognizing *multiple perspectives* - especially in theological and ethical questions, which rarely have only one answer. For example, students of theology learn to see dogmas in their historical context and ask: *Why does the* *church teach this? Is it still viable today?* Critical thinking protects against naivety and prepares students to distinguish between *the core of the message* and human opinions.

- **Independent judgment:** This refers to *judgment competence*, i.e. arriving at a well-founded ethical decision step by step. This competence includes weighing up facts (factual judgment) and values (value judgment).

Those who are skilled in this area can look at all sides of a moral dilemma and come to a *personal judgment* that is both factually informed and value-based. This judgment is *open* - in other words, the outcome is not predetermined from the outset by authorities. The person learns to apply their own criteria: *What is just? What serves life?* - and ultimately comes to a decision. In theology, this is often referred to as *maturity*, i.e. the ability to *form one's own judgment in freedom*.

- **Structured acquisition of knowledge:** Before you can make judgments, you need knowledge. Therefore, competence building also includes the ability to *systematically acquire* and organize *knowledge*. In theological terms, this means, for example *Studying sources, AI questioning* (on the Bible, tradition, doctrinal documents) and getting to know *different* positions. Learners practise familiarizing themselves with a new topic - such as a bioethical issue or a problem of church history - and proceed in a structured manner: first collect facts and positions, then organize them, then evaluate them. This structured acquisition of knowledge prevents hasty, uninformed judgments. It also promotes insight into the *complexity* of some issues, which in turn teaches humility: not everything is black and white. Not everything is heterosexual or homosexual.

- **Formation of conscience:** The formation of *conscience* as an inner moral compass is central. Forming a conscience means acquiring the ability to listen to oneself and to distinguish the voice of conscience from mere feelings or external expectations. A mature conscience *develops from heteronomy to autonomy* - i.e. from being determined by others (for example: *"I do or say and repeat it because the church says or prescribes it."*) to *self-determination* ("I act this way because I am convinced by my conscience and God."). This goal of developing from a *heteronomous* to an *autonomous conscience* is explicitly seen as a benchmark.

This includes learning to examine inner moral convictions: *Is what I believe to be the "voice of God" perhaps more my upbringing after all?* You also learn to appreciate legitimate *norms and rules* of the church, but to make your *own judgment* on whether to follow or reject them in individual cases.

Forming a conscience is closely interwoven with personality development - it requires self-knowledge, empathy (considering the effects of one's own actions) and the courage to swim against the current when conscience demands it.

- **Dialogue and discourse skills**: Anyone who thinks critically and makes independent judgments must also be able to communicate this. It is therefore important to practice *the ability to engage in dialog* - especially on controversial issues. Theologically educated people should be able to *defend their convictions respectfully*, but also listen to counter-arguments fairly. In the context of the church and ethics, this means, for example, engaging in conversation with people of other opinions (within or outside one's own denomination), *weighing up arguments* and perhaps looking for solutions together. This ability to engage in dialog builds bridges between rigid obedience and rebellious lonerism: people stay in contact, learn from each other and develop *a shared sense of judgment*. Religious education teachers in particular need this competence in order to be able to moderate discussions in the classroom without making their own point of view absolute.

Taken together, all of these competencies *enable independent ethical judgment* and *critical reflection on authority*. They build on each other: Knowledge acquisition and critical thinking provide the foundation, conscience and judgment formation lead to inner clarity, and the ability to engage in dialogue ensures that one does not isolate oneself. This *enables* theologians, teachers and believers as a whole *to live their faith responsibly in a pluralistic world* - in harmony with their conscience and in honest exchange with their tradition.

Personal ways to build up expertise

So how can you develop these skills in a practical way? *There are many ways*, and everyone can start in their own everyday life:

1. actively engaging with ethical questions: Personal learning often begins with asking questions. If you want to make self-determined judgments, you should *consciously think through moral dilemmas.* This can be done in everyday life: for example, when faced with a difficult decision at work or in your private life, pause and ask yourself *"What is the right thing to do - and why?"* You can also consider classic dilemma stories (e.g. the Heinz dilemma about stealing an expensive medicine, see also below) and try to come to a solution based on your own reasoning. It is important to *give reasons for* your decision. This trains you to think in a structured way and teaches you to give clear reasons. Prospective clergymen do this during their studies, for example, when they deal with *case studies* from pastoral care or ethics: For example, the question of whether to administer or refuse a sacrament in a certain situation - such exercises sharpen ethical judgment.

2. seek a diversity of perspectives: A valuable personal step is to *actively get to know different opinions*. To do this, you can consciously read authors or listen to lectures that represent different positions - even those with which you intuitively disagree. Theology students, for example, read both official church doctrinal writings *and* critical dissenting voices from theologians. Religious education teachers can also study other religions or denominations as part of their training in order to broaden their own horizons. This encounter with diversity teaches them that authorities, including church leaders, are also wrong or at least do not have the *only* answers. It strengthens *independent thinking* when you realize: *"There are several well-founded points of view on this question - which one convinces me and why?"* Personally, you can also seek out discussions with very different believers (e.g. among friends, in forums or churches). Every new perspective challenges your own thinking and thus promotes your ability to judge.

3. reflection and conscience formation in prayer or a diary: *Quiet times of reflection* help you to get to know the voice of your own conscience better. Many spiritually oriented people find space in prayer or meditation to examine their inner convictions. A classic spiritual exercise is the *examination of conscience* (e.g. in Ignatian spirituality), in which you reflect on your own decisions before God every day: *Where did I act correctly today out of conviction? Where did I perhaps do something uncritically just because it was expected?* Such exercises sharpen your awareness of *your own and other people's influences* on your actions. Keeping *a diary* can also be helpful: In it, you can honestly note down doubts, list pros and cons of ethical issues and observe your own development in retrospect. Over time, it becomes apparent that you are making increasingly differentiated and conscious judgments. Forming a conscience is ultimately personality work - getting to know yourself, clarifying your own values and accepting your own fallibility. Personally, you can also look for mentors or confidants (e.g. an experienced pastor, a lecturer, a spiritual guide) with whom you can openly discuss your thoughts. Feedback and critical questions from outside help to uncover blind spots.

4. assume joint responsibility: An excellent school for self-determined judgment is to *bear practical responsibility*. If you work in a youth group or church, for example, you will be confronted with real decisions - be it planning a social project or dealing with conflicts in the group. This is where you learn to apply your ethical principles *in real life*: Is it more important to strictly enforce rules, or to be merciful to individual situations? Such experiences force you to *take a stand* and accept the consequences. Theology students often have internships in schools or parishes where they practise precisely this. Religious education teachers also gain such experience during their traineeship: They have to decide how to deal with controversial topics in the classroom - very concretely and sometimes against the expectations of outside authorities. This *learning by doing* combines theoretical knowledge with practical judgment. You also feel that decisions in reality have gray areas; finding a balance here strengthens independent judgment.

5. reading faith texts and teachings critically: Finally, on a personal level, you can do the exercise of *actively questioning religious texts or church statements*. This means consciously pausing when reading the Bible or an article of the catechism and asking yourself: *Do I understand this? Do I find it plausible? What questions do I have about it?* - and take these questions seriously. Prospective theologians learn the method of *contextualization*: every dogmatic statement has a time of origin. If, for example, a medieval council formulated something, you can think about it personally: *What does it mean today? Do I have arguments to agree with it or would I formulate it differently?* This personal dialog with tradition is by no means thoughtless, but a sign of deep reflection. It *actually* leads to a *firmer belief* because you have thought through the content and made it your own conviction. Those who never question remain insecure within themselves; those who struggle and search, however, will ultimately be able to stand all the more credibly - even before others. That is why you can allow yourself to *ask reflective questions* of authorities. Personally, this can mean writing a letter to the bishop if you disagree with a decision, or asking the ward committee why something is being handled in this way. Such steps are part of the personal learning path. They require courage, but also give you self-confidence when you realize: *My voice carries weight, and I can be respectfully inquiring - using my voice instead of just accepting.*

These personal learning paths show that each individual can actively work on their competence. It is a process that is never completely finished - even experienced theologians and pastoral workers need to constantly educate their conscience and update their knowledge. But the more you incorporate such exercises into your everyday life, the more natural *independent ethical thinking* becomes. What may initially take some effort - such as contradicting authorities, asking questions in a group or admitting your own mistakes - becomes the attitude of a mature personality over time. The reward is a belief that is lived with *inner conviction*, because the head and heart are equally involved.

Didactic methods and content in teaching and training

For teachers - whether at university, in religious education classes at school or in church-based adult education - the question arises: *how can these skills be taught effectively?* Fortunately, there are tried and tested *didactic methods and content* for teaching critical thinking, judgment and conscience formation. Here are some approaches with practical examples:

- **Discussion of controversial theses (controversy method):** A basic method for promoting critical thinking is the structured discussion of controversial statements. In seminars or lessons, teachers can put forward *contradictory* and contra *theses* for debate - such as *"Should religious commandments influence laws in a secular society?"* or *"Should one not follow church instructions for reasons of conscience?"* The learners take different positions and have to be convincing *in their arguments.* The principle of *non-overwhelming* is important here: any opinion may be expressed openly without the teacher prescribing a "correct solution".

In this way, participants learn that even within a denominational framework, *diversity of opinion* and the ability *to make excuses* are respected - a core experience for independent judgment. An example of good practice: In political education, there has long been the *Beutelsbach Consensus*, which states that controversial topics must be taught controversially and that no pupil should be taken by surprise.

The *Beutelsbach Consensus* is a central orientation document for political education in Germany and was formulated at a conference in Beutelsbach in 1976. It is still valid today - not only in politics lessons, but also in related subjects such as ethics or religious education. The consensus describes three fundamental principles that are intended to ensure that education does not lead to influence, but rather to the maturity of learners.

The first principle is the **prohibition of overpowering**: it states that teachers must not present their personal opinions in a way that restricts pupils in their freedom of judgment or "overpowers" them emotionally or authoritatively. Learners must not be manipulated, but must be taken seriously - as people with their own conscience and interests.

The second principle is the **principle of controversy**: everything that is controversial in science, society or the church must also be presented controversially in the classroom. This means that there must be no one-sided presentation - not even on issues where teachers themselves have strong personal or religious convictions. The aim is for learners to be able to weigh up different positions independently.

The third principle is **student orientation**: political and ethical education should enable young people to recognize and reflect on their own interests and represent them in social dialogue. This includes learning how to act in a pluralistic world with well-founded judgments.

These principles can also be applied very well in *religious education.* One example: When it comes to the topic of *abortion*, students must not be restricted to a certain position - such as the official church position. The teacher must also introduce positions from medical ethics, secular philosophy or other denominations. Learners should be able to form their own opinions and justify ethically why they think the way they do. Religious education thus becomes a space for debate, not conversion. A group exercise in which all four points of view are read with short sections of text and represented and expressed in their respective roles is ideal.

Figure 10 : Beutelsbach Consensus .

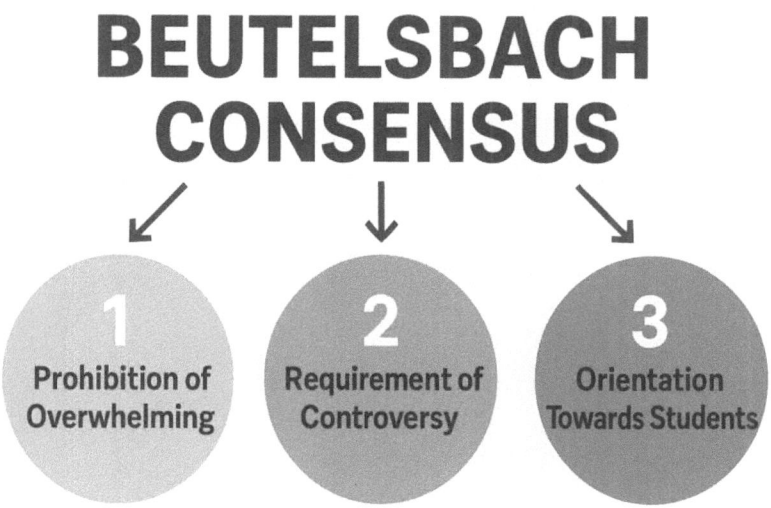

The Beutelsbach Consensus is also used in religious *ethics lessons* - for example on the topic of *artificial intelligence and autonomous weapons systems*. A teacher must not focus solely on technical enthusiasm or moral warnings, but must present different positions: e.. economic, security policy, humanitarian and philosophical perspectives. In this way, students are guided to form independent ethical judgments.

The Beutelsbach Consensus thus reminds us that education always requires freedom - the freedom to question, doubt and take a stand. In times of social polarization, this consensus is more relevant than ever.

Applied to religious education, this means that even hot topics such as the church's stance on sexuality or other religions are discussed openly in the classroom. In this way, pupils practise forming their own opinions and *arguing controversially* without fear of "wrong" answers.

- **Moral dilemma discussion according to Kohlberg:** Lawrence Kohlberg, a moral psychologist, has shown that discussing *dilemma stories* can promote moral judgment enormously. This can be used didactically by confronting learners with a specific case that *does not* allow for *a clearly correct* course of action. A classic example is the aforementioned *Heinz dilemma*: Heinz does not have enough money for a life-saving medicine for his wife - should he steal it or not?

Figure 11 : The Heinz dilemma - buying medicine with black money?

The Heinz dilemma is a well-known ethical thought experiment developed by psychologist Lawrence Kohlberg to examine moral judgment. The short version is as follows: A man named Heinz has a seriously ill wife. A pharmacist has a drug that could save her life, but sells it at an extremely high price. Heinz cannot afford the medicine and asks for a cheaper price - the pharmacist refuses. Finally, Heinz breaks into the pharmacy and steals the medicine to save his wife. The central question is: *Was it morally right or wrong for Heinz to steal the medicine - and why?* The question is not about the right answer, but about the reasons someone gives for their decision. Kohlberg assigned these reasons to different stages of moral development - from obedience-oriented morality to universal ethical principles.

The group discusses and everyone justifies their position. Studies show that such discussions encourage a change of perspective and promote higher *levels of* moral *thinking.*

Good practice: Some schools and universities have set up *ethics cafés* or *philosophy groups* where dilemmas are regularly discussed. In a theology faculty, current church dilemmas could be discussed in a similar way (e.g. *"Should the church allow remarried divorcees?"*) - students bring in scripture, tradition, but also rational arguments and struggle to find a solution. The teacher's role here is moderator: they ensure that *deeper questions* are asked (*"Why do you think stealing is wrong? What values are behind it?"*) - this is how *reasoning skills* are trained.

- **Role-playing and changing perspectives:** One practice-oriented method is practising *roles*. Learners slip into the shoes of different parties involved in a conflict or an ethical issue. For example, you could organize a role play in class on the question *"Should a community do XY?"* - Roles: Pastor, a young person, a conservative senior citizen, etc. Everyone has to argue from the perspective of the role. This method promotes *empathy* and allows the participants to feel how *different perceptions* can be. This is particularly valuable for aspiring clergy: once they become a pastor, they must be able to understand the concerns of a wide variety of people. A "parish council" role play, for example, where decisions have to be made jointly, demonstrates *democratic participation* and teaches that authority also means listening. Good practice: In the parish training of some dioceses, such simulation games are used to show future priests how a *synodal consultation* works - this teaches them to bring in their own convictions and integrate other voices at the same time.

- **Project-based learning with responsibility:** One didactic measure that is particularly *action-oriented* is projects in which students have to take on real responsibility. For example, a theological seminar can not only talk about Caritas teaching, but also have students plan a small social project (visiting service, queer afternoon in a retirement home with queer, popular music, fundraising campaign, etc.). This automatically raises ethical and organizational questions that need to be reflected upon: *How do we deal with people of different opinions in the team? Is our approach fair?* The teacher provides support with reflection discussions. This learning by doing combines theory and practice - ideal for practicing independent judgment. In religion lessons, for example, pupils could carry out a *class project* such as *"Developing a fair school culture - that is also gender-appropriate"* and develop rules for working together. In doing so, they experience *democratic processes* and have to really apply values such as justice, forgiveness and responsibility. Such projects also train *social skills* and the ability to reflect after the decision: *Was that a good thing to do? What would we do differently next time?* - This establishes a culture of *criticism and self-criticism*.

- **Discussions of faith and conscience:** The method of *conscience discussions* has proven itself in the church. Here, learners reflect in small groups on personal decisions of conscience - confidentially and honestly. For example, a teacher can describe a case from life (or an anonymized real case) and the group first asks: *"What does my conscience, my attitude, tell me spontaneously? Why?"* Then information or human and church positions are added: *"The church teaches X in this case - how do I deal with it?"* The participants discuss whether and how this statement of authority should change their opinion or the teaching should be adapted. Through such discussions, they learn to *take their conscience seriously*, but also to *constructively* engage *in dialog and transformation with church teachings* - in order to be able to apply them for themselves. Good practice: In priestly formation, there are often spiritual mentors with whom seminarians discuss moral issues in their everyday lives. Mentoring helps them not simply to quote rules, but to find their inner conviction - training them to help their own faithful in a similar way later on. In schools, a conscience discussion can take the form of students talking about situations where they were asked to act against their convictions (e.g. peer pressure) and how they dealt with them. Such discussions strengthen awareness: *I am not alone with conflicts between obedience and my own judgment*, and we can learn from each other to be steadfast and at the same time willing to engage in dialog.

- **Critical text work (hermeneutics and exegesis):** A very content-related method is the *critical analysis and interpretation of texts* - be they biblical texts, church documents or theological theses. Teachers can guide learners not only to grasp the content of a text, but also to *critically scrutinize* it: Who is speaking here? With what authority? What *unspoken assumptions* are behind it? For example, a papal encyclical can not only be read piously in a seminar, but also analyzed piece by piece: *Where are the arguments? Where might there be gaps? What reactions did theologians have to it?* The students can write a short *statement* themselves - agreeing or disagreeing - and thus appreciate the text, as well *as interpreting, questioning and examining it*.

- **Historical examples or current cases** are also a good basis for the content: Didactically, you can play through cases from church history in which courageous conscience stood against official doctrine (Galileo Galilei against the Inquisition; or Blessed Franz Jägerstätter, who refused to take the oath of allegiance for reasons of conscience or queer people who demanded a transformation of the churches). Franz Jägerstätter (1907-1943) was an Austrian farmer and devout Catholic who, for reasons of conscience, refused to do military service during the Second World War and in particular to take the oath of allegiance to Adolf Hitler. His decision was based on his deep Christian faith and the conviction that, as a Christian, he should not collaborate with National Socialist injustice. Although he was aware of the consequences of his decision, Jägerstätter remained steadfast. He was finally arrested and sentenced to death for "subversion of military power" and executed in Brandenburg an der Havel on August 9, 1943.

After his death, Franz Jägerstätter became an important symbol of Christian resistance against National Socialism. His consistent actions for reasons of conscience were initially viewed controversially, but over time the Catholic Church recognized the importance of his testimony. Franz Jägerstätter was beatified in 2007. Today, he is regarded as an example of strength of conscience, civil courage and the courage to stand up for moral convictions even under the most extreme conditions.

Henri Nouwen (1932-1996) was also a world-renowned spiritual writer, priest and pastor who called for the transformation of the church. He lived a deep spiritual life and was particularly appreciated for his authenticity, openness and empathy. Throughout his life, Nouwen wrestled with the tension between his Catholic identity as a priest and his own homosexuality, which he reflected on intensively in his writings and diaries. He acknowledged his homosexuality and openly advocated a loving, compassionate and inclusive treatment of homosexual people in the church - even if this was not in line with the official teaching of the Catholic Church at the time, and can still extinguish professional existences today, as in the case of David Berger, who was sharply critical of the official church stance on homosexuality. This led to Berger losing his license to teach in the church. There are many other people who have had their teaching   license   revoked.

These cases show how people consciously decide to take a stand against the official teachings of the church and the associated discrimination - demanding a transformation of the church for reasons of conscience. Didactically, such cases can be taken up and reflected upon in class as examples of the tension between personal conscience, queer or more generally: social identity and church doctrine.

Learners could discuss how to deal with conflicts of conscience, what courageously standing up for one's convictions looks like and what the consequences can be when personal integrity and official teaching collide. These are excellent examples for reflecting with students on how religious conscience, sexual identity or personal views and social pressure can come into tension with one another. The examples show how people courageously and honestly deal with this tension without giving up their faith. At the same time, the facts provide valuable starting points for discussing issues of humanity, dignity and acceptance in church teaching.

These are lessons along the lines of *"What would you have done in Galileo's place?"* - learners argue and realize how important a well-formed conscience is when authority and morality come into conflict.

All of these methods are supplemented by *content-related aspects*. It is advisable to deal with certain *subject areas* that act as training fields for the skills. These include classic areas of ethics (justice, life and death, sexual ethics, peace ethics), where the church and the modern world sometimes make different judgments - ideal for discussing controversies. The topics of *"faith and doubt"* or *"authority and freedom"* can also be the explicit content of lessons or seminars, so that learners acquire theological foundations about why *conscience* is free and when church authority is binding or not. One example of good practice content is the treatment of the *"Beutelsbach Consensus"* and its application in religious education in order to show students that *indoctrination* is *taboo* and that their own judgment is required.

Indoctrination refers to the targeted and usually one-sided influencing of people in order to impose certain beliefs, values or ideologies on them without encouraging or enabling critical reflection or independent thinking. It aims to get people to adopt an attitude or opinion without questioning it critically or assessing it independently. Indoctrination therefore stands in contrast to education, which is based on maturity and critical judgment.

Indoctrination in Catholic doctrine can be recognized above all by the fact that:

- *there is no room or time for doubt or critical questioning.*

- Statements of faith are presented as *unchangeable and unquestionable.* The discussion and interpretation of faith is not given any importance.

- *Emotional and moral pressure* can be used, for example through threats of spiritual or social consequences (e.g. exclusion or punishment for non-compliance).

- The argumentation is based on *authority instead of comprehensible reasons* ("because the church says so" or "because God wants it").

- *dissenters or critical perspectives* are *marginalized, devalued or ignored.* A dialog does not exist.

Effective protection against indoctrination in religious contexts is possible above all through the development of *critical judgment* and *personal maturity.* The following skills and strategies are helpful here:

1. **Critical thinking and the ability to reflect:** Always ask yourself questions such as: *"Why do I believe this?", "What are the reasons for or against this?"* and *"Whose interests might be behind a statement?"*

2. **Plurality and willingness to engage in dialog:** Seek out targeted discussions with people who hold different opinions. Engage with different theological positions and thereby form your own, differentiated judgment.

3. **Self-reflection and conscience formation:** Develop your own set of values and learn to listen to your inner voice - your conscience. Question whether the teaching is compatible with your personal conscience.

4. **Theological and historical knowledge:** Learn to classify statements of faith historically and critically and to understand

their development. The more sound your theological knowledge is, the better you will be able to recognize possible attempts at indoctrination.

5. **Resilience and self-confidence:** Strengthen your self-confidence by consciously shaping your faith and remaining open to doubts and questions. Make yourself emotionally independent of fear or feelings of guilt that could be generated by indoctrination.

By specifically promoting these skills, you can personally and effectively protect yourself from indoctrination in Catholic doctrine and find your way to an independent, reflective and responsible faith.

The statement that "the Pope is infallible" is a particularly clear illustration of the aforementioned powers to protect against indoctrination:

First of all, it is important to approach this teaching with **critical thinking and the ability to reflect.** Questions such as: "What exactly does infallibility actually mean?" or "In which situations is the Pope supposedly infallible and why?" can be helpful here. Critical thinking allows us not to simply accept the statement as an absolute fact, but to ask about the meaning, historical background and consequences of the doctrine. For example, we could find out that this doctrine was only established late in the 19th century at the First Vatican Council (1870) and has by no means existed unchanged since the beginning of the Church.

The ability **to be pluralistic and open to dialog invites** us to perceive different perspectives on the doctrine of infallibility. For example, we could look at the views of Protestant, Orthodox or critical Catholic theologians who reject or at least limit the idea of the Pope's personal infallibility. In doing so, we would discover that there are theologically justified alternatives to the official Catholic interpretation. In dialog with different positions, our ability grows not to accept doctrines one-sidedly, but to evaluate them in a differentiated and nuanced way.

Self-reflection and conscience formation then requires us to examine our own inner attitude: does the idea of an infallible authority figure fit in with my conscience and my understanding of faith and responsibility? We might come to the realization that an unquestionable authority burdens our conscience and restricts our personal spiritual freedom. We may find that we are more willing to rely on reason, dialog and our own judgment rather than blindly trusting a dogmatic authority.

Sound **theological and historical knowledge** is also important in order to avoid indoctrination. For example, we could learn that infallibility is not a general characteristic of the Pope in all statements, but should only apply in very specific, rare and precisely defined situations - namely when the Pope speaks ex cathedra ("from the chair") in matters of faith and morals. Historical research could show us that this doctrine was, among other things, an attempt to react to political and social changes in the 19th century in order to secure the authority of the pope. This historical contextualization helps us not to simply accept the doctrine as unquestionable.

After all, it takes **resilience and self-confidence** to deal with this teaching in an independent and emotionally stable way. This means that we can allow ourselves to openly express doubts and questions without letting them unsettle us. Those who feel emotionally independent of fear, feelings of guilt or social pressure can relax and say: "I take a critical or differentiated view of infallibility and take the freedom to disagree with this teaching in certain cases without feeling separated from the community or from God."

The interplay of these five skills creates an independent and reflective approach to the doctrine of papal infallibility, which strengthens us personally and prevents us from adopting religious teachings uncritically and under the control of others. In this way, we can ultimately believe maturely, reflectively and responsibly.

If, in a further example, we play through the five competencies - *critical thinking and the ability to reflect, the ability to embrace plurality and the willingness to engage in dialog, self-reflection and the formation of conscience, theological and historical knowledge, and resilience and self-awareness* - using the Catholic Church's current practice of denying same-sex couples the sacrament of marriage, we can understand more deeply why this practice can be questioned and changed:

Firstly, critical thinking and the ability to reflect mean thoroughly and impartially questioning the reasons behind the current practice: Why does the Catholic Church refuse sacramental marriage to same-sex couples? How valid are the arguments put forward for this? If we think critically, we realize that the arguments are mostly based on traditional gender images or the biological ability to procreate. However, critical reflection shows that many heterosexual couples are also unable or unwilling to have children, but are nevertheless allowed to enter into sacramental marriage. This suggests that it is inconsistent and unjust to withhold the sacrament from same-sex couples, especially as they can also live together in love, fidelity and responsibility - precisely the values that are actually important in a sacramental marriage.

Secondly, the ability to be pluralistic and open to dialog promotes the ability to engage with different perspectives and take them seriously. In this way, we can enter into dialog with people who are in same-sex relationships and are already married in a civil ceremony. It often becomes clear that their partnerships embody precisely those values and virtues that the Church also emphasizes for sacramental marriage: mutual devotion, fidelity, commitment and loving care. Through a genuine willingness to dialogue, we recognize that a rigid refusal to accept same-sex couples is based on prejudice, and that these couples are just as capable of living an authentic sacramental marriage.

Thirdly, self-reflection and conscience formation help us to reflect on our own attitudes and feelings towards same-sex partnerships. Are personal prejudices or insecurities perhaps the real reason for rejecting the sacrament of marriage for homosexual couples? If we honestly question our conscience, we may discover that we are shaped by fears or outdated norms. An honest examination of conscience makes it clear that it is morally questionable to exclude loving, responsible partnerships solely on the basis of their gender composition. It follows from this: If the Church were to follow conscience and examine its teaching with genuine inner reflection, it might well recognize that sacramental marriage is just as appropriate for same-sex couples as it is for heterosexual couples.

Fourthly, theological and historical knowledge helps us to explore the background to the doctrine of marriage. Historical and theological studies show that the Catholic doctrine of marriage has changed considerably over the centuries and is by no means static. For example, in the Middle Ages, marriage as a love relationship was not the focus at all - it was primarily about economic and social interests. It was only in modern times that mutual love and partnership took center stage. So if the meaning of marriage has changed so significantly historically, there is little reason why the Church should not expand its teachings today to also do justice to same-sex couples. From a theological point of view, what counts above all is the mutual commitment of two people - regardless of their gender - as a visible sign of divine love. Therefore, the sacrament could easily and consistently be conferred on same-sex couples as well.

Fifth, resilience and self-confidence give us the emotional strength and inner fortitude to stand up for equality and justice despite external pressures. Many people feel intimidated by official bans or church authorities who reject same-sex marriages. But dealing with this in a confident, resilient way means taking a courageous and clear stance: saying that this practice is wrong and can be changed. By strengthening our inner stance and remaining emotionally independent of traditional pressures, we can openly and publicly advocate for inclusive change. The skill of resilience makes it clear that by building its self-understanding not on authority but on authentic humanity, the church can stand by granting the sacrament of marriage to same-sex couples without loss of identity and faith.

If we play through these five competencies consistently, it becomes clear that the denial of the sacrament of marriage to same-sex couples is not only theologically questionable, but above all morally unjustified. These skills enable a reflective, empathetic and ethically clear approach: sacramental marriage can and should also be made possible for same-sex couples without contradiction or consequences. After all, it is the values of love, responsibility and commitment that count - values that can be lived in any authentic partnership regardless of gender.

Figure 12: Indoctrination in the seminary (historical illustration).

Church indoctrination that symbolizes the historical image: A seminar room with prospective priests:inside in cassocks, above them a large shadowy figure. The puppet strings are invisible. The head of the seminary raises his hand with a raised index finger and reports from a text book. One of the seminar participants looks up questioningly, while the others mechanically take notes or stare at the teacher's lips. The room looks gloomy, a cross hangs on the wall - but it is slightly askew. The atmosphere is quiet, tense, controlled. The following teaching content resonates in the room of indoctrination: Developing dialog skills, building trust, promoting self-acceptance & self-confidence, maintaining dialog with the diverse network, acquiring differentiated ethics & judgment, as well as visibility, speaking up and honesty. These should also be seminar objectives in order to better recognize indoctrination. In detail, this means reading faces: - Ability to engage in dialog: the ability to enter into conversation openly and respectfully with others - including people who hold different opinions, lifestyles or theological beliefs. The ability to engage in dialog is opposed to authoritarian silence and dogmatic isolation. - Trust: A climate in which people treat each other with benevolence, without fear of judgment or sanctions. Trust replaces control: Seminar participants should feel safe to openly express their questions, doubts or personal identity. - Self-acceptance & self-confidence: The ability to accept oneself - including one's own sexual orientation - as being wanted by God. This strengthens inner stability and protects against feelings of guilt or self-denial. - Dialogue with the diverse network: Active exchange with people outside your own filter bubble: queer Christians, critical theologians, human scientists. Diversity is not seen as a threat, but as a learning opportunity - Differentiated ethics & judgment: The ability to judge moral issues not in black and white, but on the basis of love, responsibility and context. Instead of blanket condemnation, the specific relationship is at the center of ethical evaluation. - Visibility, speaking and honesty: A sincere life without double standards: For example, anyone who feels same-sex , is homosexual, is allowed to say so and experiences the benefits of their self-confidence: speaking liberates, silence suppresses. Honesty is the first step towards inner and ecclesial truth.

Likewise**, case studies of synodal decisions** (such as the Council of the Apostles in Acts 15, where discussions took place and then decisions were made jointly) can be discussed in class to show that *critical and questioning discourse* was necessary *in the church* early on in order to arrive at good solutions.

Didactically, it is important that teachers are *role models*: A teacher who does not tolerate any dissenting opinions thwarts the goal. On the other hand, a lecturer who says "*I don't expect you to agree with everything - I want you to be able to justify it clearly if you disagree with each other in your discussion*" creates a learning environment in which mature judgment can flourish. The content and methods should always be designed in such a way that the *active participation* of the learners is at the center: giving their voice and expressing their own opinion in the group must be encouraged. After all, it is only through one's own actions - asking questions, arguing, deciding - that real competence and meaning can develop.

Transformation: from passive recipient to responsible co-creator

When all these skills are built up and methods are applied, a *remarkable transformation* takes place in the learners. The learners' view of themselves, of faith and of the church changes towards more *personal responsibility, participation and critical depth.*

In the past, believers were perhaps primarily *passive recipients* of church teachings - now they are *becoming active co-creators* of their faith. Theology students, for example, often report that they learn to understand their faith in a *more personal and at the same time more reflective* way over the course of their studies. They abandon the attitude: *"The authority will already know what is right"* and adopt the attitude: *"I am responsible for what is right with my own conscience and knowledge "*. This new perspective means *empowerment*: The person no longer feels like a cog in the wheel, but as someone who is allowed to *think and make decisions* - makes a difference: is allowed to do and wants to do. This is particularly important for aspiring clergy: a priest who has learned to think critically will also encourage the congregation to be mature - and, like a deus ex machina, will *not be afraid of clever questions and answers*.

On the content level, a *more modern perspective* on tradition and authority emerges. Learners realize that tradition is not something rigid, but a living process in which they can participate. This can be very inspiring: Faith is experienced as something that *continues to be written today* - by everyone who honestly searches for truth. This creates a *dynamic* attitude instead of a merely static reception of tradition. If, for example, religious education teachers undergo this transformation, they will act less as dogmatic imparters of knowledge in the classroom and more as *facilitators of searching*. This is often motivating for students because they feel that *their own thinking is being taken seriously*.

The modern view of learners after such skills development is also characterized by *a sense of responsibility*: People have learned that freedom always goes hand in hand with responsibility. Those who make independent judgments are aware that they must also bear the consequences. This inner responsibility is ultimately the mature mind of a personality - no longer blind, but *reflected and affirmed*. Paradoxically, critical questioning often leads to *a deeper will to live* where it is really important: Namely in the basic values. If someone has considered all the arguments and comes to the conclusion that the Church is right in its option for the poor, for example, then they follow this magisterium with full conviction. Such a reflection "with head and heart and hand" is more sustainable than one that is merely forced. At the same time, learners have gained a new freedom to *say yes to an alternative consideration when in doubt, even* if something contradicts their well-formed conscience. This balance of loyal agreement and courageous reflection on an alternative is what *makes the judgment mature*.

The transformation can also be seen in the learners' *demeanor*: They become able to offer constructive criticism - no longer out of spite, but because it serves the cause. For example, a theology student could say in a discussion group after her training: *"I appreciate my church, but I see a need for reform in point XY and I justify this as follows..."* - Such a voice carries weight and shows that *critical love for transformation* is possible. Learners become multipliers: A religion teacher, for example, who has internalized these skills herself, will encourage her students to think independently. A young pastor will *allow questions* in the congregation and promote synodal discussions because she knows that a *strong, honest community of faith* will grow from this.

In the end, competence building leads to a *church of responsible Christians*. This is a modern image of the church: not just a pyramid from top to bottom, but a *network of leaders*. Each individual - whether layperson or cleric, teacher or student - contributes with their own voice, sharpened by education. This can start on a small scale (e.g. in a family discussion about a moral issue) and have an impact on a large scale (e.g. when committed lay people get involved in church councils and make qualified arguments there). The learners experience a kind of *emancipation in faith*, which does not end in arbitrariness, but in deep solidarity: they argue objectively, but for a common goal - to find the truth and the good in the light of faith: through joint questions and answers. That is the essence of dialog.

This communicative transformation is ultimately also *spiritually* significant. Many report that after a phase of critical questioning, they arrive at a *more mature understanding of faith*: God is rediscovered as someone who wants *free dialog*, not puppets. Trust in God can grow because people no longer bind themselves to Him out of fear or pressure of authority, but out of free conviction. That is perhaps the most beautiful fruit: Believers who stand *fearlessly and freely* before God, in the knowledge of their responsibility, but also in the knowledge of God's understanding of our honest questions - and answers in dialog.

Synodal processes: Learning through participation and critique of power

A special aspect of this competence building is learning from and through *synodal processes, democratic participation and the reflective handling of power in the church*. Current church developments - think of the *synodal path* in Germany or the world synod on synodality - offer a lively learning field for how joint consultation and decision-making can work. Here, many of the skills mentioned are tested on a large scale: believers from all walks of life come together, discuss openly and struggle for reform. For students (be they theology students or interested lay people), participating in or observing such processes is extremely instructive.

In synodal assemblies, for example, it becomes clear what *critical self-reflection* by authorities looks like. The church in Germany has publicly recognized that a *"conscientious and self-critical look at internal power structures"* is necessary in order to remain credible.

When bishops and laypeople debate the abuse of power and reform together, everyone involved learns that **authority must be justified**. Nothing is simply accepted any more, but the question is asked: *What is power used for? Does it serve people and the Gospel?* Such a process models for all believers how to reverently but firmly put authority to the test. Teachers can take up such real-life examples: for example, have students read minutes or reports from the Synodal Path in class and have them analyze which values and arguments clash there. This makes it possible to experience *the church as a learning community*.

Synodal processes also promote *democratic participation in* a space that was traditionally hierarchical. In terms of capacity building, this means that believers experience in practice what it is like to *have* a *voice*. Young theologians who take part in a synod as listeners often report how empowering it is to *have their voices heard*. An important learning objective becomes tangible here: *every* baptized person shares responsibility. Synodality is reminiscent of the biblical image of the "people of God", in which every sensus fidei (sense of faith) is taken seriously. In these processes, learners see that *participation* does not mean chaos, but can lead to better decisions. Modern synodal formats

- such as working in small groups, systematic *listening phases* for the grassroots and even online participation - show that the church can learn from secular participatory methods without losing its essence.

On the contrary: "Synodality, walking together, has been part of the church's self-image since the early church".

When learners understand this statement, they realize that critical participation, raising one's voice, is not a new kind of rebellion, but actually a *return* to Christian origins.

Figure13 : Conscience between good and evil .

A pensive young man stands in the center of the picture, visibly torn between two inner voices. A small angel with a halo and wings sits on his left shoulder, trying to speak to him in a calm and friendly manner. On the right shoulder, on the other hand, sits a red devil with horns, a trident and a pointed tail, grinning and trying to influence him. The scene symbolizes the struggle of the human conscience between good and evil, between moral insight and temptation. The background is neutral in order to emphasize the emotional tension of the inner conflict.

Didactically, synodality can also be practiced on a small scale. *Synodal elements* can be incorporated into church education courses - for example, voting together on improvements at the end of a course or allowing all participants to vote equally on decision-making issues. This allows prospective church employees to experience what it means to work in flat hierarchies. They learn that *leadership also involves listening* and that good ideas can come from anywhere. In terms of power relations, synodal processes sensitize learners to the importance of *transparency and the separation of powers*. For example, the synodal path formulated the demand to reorganize power in the church, to give women and lay people more rights in order to prevent abuse.

When students read such texts, they automatically reflect critically on the existing hierarchical system. They are provided with criteria: *How do I recognize abuse of power? Which structures promote participation?* - This knowledge flows back into their own actions in the community and classroom.

Synodal experiences can be personally very formative: Anyone who has experienced how a wide variety of people search for the truth at eye level in a synodal group will no longer want to do without *the ideal of participation*. It changes the attitude towards the church: away from *"those up there decide"* to *"we are all the church"*. It is precisely this transformation that the formation of competence is intended to bring about. Synodality on both a small and large scale teaches us to combine *humility and courage:* Humility on the part of the office bearers to listen and allow themselves to be corrected; courage on the part of the laity to speak up and take responsibility. The result is a church in which *critical thinking and spiritual life go hand in hand.*

For learners, this means that the topics of *power and participation* become an integral part of their ethical judgment. They not only learn to make personal moral decisions, but also to evaluate *structures* morally. For example, after a synodal training course, a religion teacher could deal with the topic of "power in the church" in class and work out with the students why democratic co-determination is also relevant in the church - for example, to prevent abuses and train the *conscience of the community*. In this way, individual competence is combined with *institutional learning.*

Synodal processes therefore act as a laboratory for the skills described here. This is where the learning objectives become tangible:

Independent judgments (when synodal representatives contribute their conscience), critical questioning of authority (when old and young together ask bishops questions) and conscience formation (when everyone prays and discusses what God's will might be today). For the target group - whether generally interested or future theologians - active engagement with synodality is an opportunity to experience *the changing church* and to learn how a living, mature community of faith can function.

A rewarding path: via the personal contribution of opinion to mature faith

The ability to *make self-determined ethical judgments and critically reflect on religious authorities* is not a luxury, but an indispensable competence for responsible Christians of our time. The previous explanations have shown the educational goals behind this - namely freedom and responsibility in faith - and the specific skills required for this. It has become clear that these skills can be practiced personally (through reflective practice and continuous learning) as well as taught in a targeted manner (through didactic methods that promote critical thinking and participation).

Getting there may be challenging, but the *practical examples* and methods show: It is feasible and already a reality in many places. As a result, learners experience a transformation towards a *new perspective on faith*: they see themselves as active co-creators, understand authority as a service and not as coercion, and realize that the church as a whole is also capable of learning. Modern synodal developments confirm this impressively by promoting *participation and criticism of power* in the church and thus also encouraging the faithful to make their voices heard.

For the target groups - believers, those with a general interest in religion, students of theology, religious education teachers and prospective clergy - this is a *great opportunity*. Those who follow this path of competence building not only grow professionally, but also personally and spiritually. Such a mature faith is deeply rooted and yet open, critically scrutinizing and yet humble. It enables us to find our bearings in the complex moral questions of our time - not because we have ready-made answers, but because we have learned *to ask the right questions and make conscientious decisions*. And it enables us to be an *authentic voice* in the community of believers that can help ensure that the Church remains credible, just and sustainable.

The end result is the ideal of the *"mature Christian"*: people who walk their path in the light of faith with *an alert mind and an educated conscience*. Such a person can respect authorities without becoming uncritical; they can think independently without acting egotistically. He knows that God's spirit blows not only through hierarchs, but through *all* believers - and does his part to ensure that this spirit is heard. Promoting this is the aim of any good theological and ethical education. It requires commitment from teachers and learners alike, but it is worth it: because a church in which members can make independent judgments and have a courageous and critical say is vibrant and credible. The path to this begins with every single step of questioning, thinking and making decisions of conscience - a path that this text would like to encourage: democracy and voting are practiced in the church community.

Exercise 6:
Living sexuality responsibly, pleasurably and reflectively: Developing skills

The exercise deals with developing the skills to live sexuality responsibly, pleasurably and in a socially reflective manner. The aim is to promote a sexual-ethical attitude that is characterized by respect, freedom and a sense of responsibility. Sexuality is understood positively as an expression of communication and identity. Teaching objectives include self-determination, relationship skills, empathy and justice as well as the prevention of abuse and discrimination.

Key skills include comprehensive sexual education (knowledge about the body, sexuality and diversity), relationship skills (communication, empathy, respect), reflection on sexual ethics (ethical judgment), self-reflection (coming to terms with one's own sexuality and identity) and power awareness (sensitivity to power relations and consensuality). The goal is sexual maturity, which enables independent and responsible decisions.

Ways to develop skills include self-study, self-reflection and biography work, practical exercises in everyday life and support from trusted discussion partners. Other didactic methods include dialog rounds, values discussions, role plays, project-based forms of learning and the involvement of external experts.

A modern perspective recognizes sexuality as a valuable gift from God, affirms sexual diversity and calls for a responsible approach to lust and physicality. The church and education are responding with structural changes such as wedding ceremonies for same-sex couples and inclusive language in teaching materials.

- ***Learning and development objective:*** *The most important competence is sexual maturity. The learning objective is to enable learners to deal with their sexuality in a responsible,* reflective and self-determined way, with respect for themselves and others.

- **Good practice example:** *Role-playing to practice consensus and boundaries in relationships. Learners simulate situations and then reflect on boundaries, consensus and respectful interaction in order to train relationship skills and awareness of power.*

- **Church support through:** *Clergy can provide support through pastoral care, open and respectful communication and the promotion of a positive attitude towards the body and sexuality. They help to convey sexuality as a positive element of human identity and divine creation.*

- **Local budget use:** *Community funds could be used for sex education workshops, fees for external experts, materials for sex education and events to prevent sexualized violence and discrimination.*

- **Adaptation of the school curriculum:** *The curriculum should be expanded to include sex education content that teaches reflective, responsible and pleasurable sexuality. Content includes body knowledge, consent, respect for diversity, ethical reflection on sexuality as well as practical exercises on communication and relationship skills.*

The ability to live sexuality in a responsible, pleasurable and socially reflective way is a **skill** that can - and must - be consciously developed. Today, sexuality is no longer considered a taboo subject, but a positive component of human identity and relationships. Even in church debates, it is recognized that sexuality has an independent value and can be understood as an expression of communication that must be *"learned like a language"*.

Meaning and teaching objectives of a new sexual ethics

Accordingly, the *educational goal* of modern sexual ethics is to enable people to deal with their sexuality in an enlightened, self-determined way. In educational processes, both adolescents and adults are offered *learning opportunities* to gradually develop the skills that form the basis of a mature, responsible sexuality. This is about far more than biological facts - it is about personality development, value orientation and social skills.

Social and ethical issues come to the fore: How do we treat different sexual identities with respect? What language do we use in church and teaching so as *not to exclude anyone*? How do we combine pleasure and responsibility? Such questions guide the development of skills. The aim is to promote an attitude towards sexual ethics that is characterized by *respect, freedom and a sense of responsibility*. After such an educational process, learners should neither repress sexuality nor live it out thoughtlessly, but be able to shape it in *a pleasurable and responsible* way - in accordance with personal values and with respect for others. At the same time, they should be able to reflect critically on social norms and, if necessary, take a stand for those who are marginalized. In short, the teaching objectives include self-determination, relationship skills, empathy and justice. This forms a basis for preventing sexual abuse and discrimination and instead promoting a *positive sexual culture* in which dignity and pleasure are not contradictory.

Central competencies: Knowledge, reflection and relationship

When developing skills in the area of sexuality, various *sub-skills* are specifically trained. Important skills to be developed include

- **Sexual education (knowledge):** A sound *knowledge of sexuality* is the basis for responsible behavior. This includes knowledge about one's own body, sexual health, reproduction and contraception, but also about emotional and psychosocial aspects of sexuality. Only those who are well informed can make informed decisions and overcome myths or false shame. This knowledge includes understanding *sexual diversity* - from different orientations to different lifestyles. Such knowledge conveys self-confidence in dealing with sexuality.
- **Relationship skills:** Sexuality is deeply relational - it unfolds in relationships with ourselves and with others. The ability to form *sustainable relationships* is therefore key. This competence includes communication, empathy and respect. Learners should recognize that *desire and lust* can be embedded *in a context of love, friendship, fidelity and responsibility*. A church orientation guide, for example, emphasizes that *relationship skills* should be the central theme of all sex education: only in respectful relationships do concepts such as *diversity, self-determination, pleasure and fun take* on a constructive dimension. It is about responding to others, respecting boundaries and finding joy in sexuality together, without power imbalances or coercion simply by talking about it.
- **Reflection on sexual ethics:** This refers to the ability to make well-considered judgments on ethical issues relating to sexuality. Learners develop the ability to *critically reflect on values and norms in the area of sexuality* - both their own and those of society or religion. For example, they discuss what responsibility one bears in a sexual relationship, or how lust and love are in harmony with respect and justice. Insights from theology *and* the humanities are incorporated here. Cardinal Marx emphasizes that the church's sexual morality has long ignored the realities of life and must incorporate new

162

theological and human scientific findings. Sexual ethical reflection competence therefore means not accepting dogmas unquestioningly, but bringing them into dialog with conscience, reason and lived experience. Those who have this competence can, for example, justify why discriminatory attitudes should be rejected or why mutual *consent* is an indispensable criterion for morally good sexual behavior.

- **Self-reflection:** In addition to the ability to make ethical judgments in general, *self-reflection* is a core competence in its own right. It refers to the ability to examine *one's own* sexuality, identity and biography openly and honestly. Learners should ask themselves: *What values and images have I internalized about sexuality? Where do I feel shame or insecurity, and why? What experiences have I had and how have they shaped me?* Through such reflection, you develop an awareness of your own needs and boundaries. Church representatives note that many people have developed feelings of guilt and shame in their socialization due to church guidelines. This is where self-reflection comes in, as it helps to recognize and transform *internalized negative messages*. The result is a *consolidated sexual identity*: you accept yourself as a sexual being with dignity and learn to see your own lust as a positive value instead of something "sinful". This inner work is a prerequisite for dealing with sexuality freely and responsibly.

- **Awareness of power:** An often neglected but crucial skill is awareness of *power relations* in the context of sexuality. This means recognizing power and dependency structures - whether between adults and adolescents, teachers and students, clergy and believers, or even between partners. Those who are power-conscious understand the importance of *consensus* and know the risks of abuse. This includes being able to *set and respect boundaries* and being sensitive to situational imbalances. Studies show that young people with egalitarian role models are less likely to live in violent relationships. Educational programs that address *gender equality and power issues* have been shown to reduce intimate partner violence. The church has learned painfully from its sexual abuse cases against young people, starting with male priests, that a lack of sexual maturity and education is a risk factor for boundary violations. Therefore, responsible sexual competence also includes critically reflecting on power: for example, being aware of one's own role of authority (in the case of teachers or clergy) or actively reducing imbalances. Power-conscious people promote encounters at eye level - the basis of any ethically acceptable sexual interaction.

- **Sexual maturity:** The ultimate goal of all these sub-competencies is *sexual maturity* - i.e. *autonomy and maturity* in sexual matters. A mature person can *make self-determined* decisions about their sexual life and takes responsibility for them. They have built up sufficient knowledge, empathic understanding and the ability to reflect in order to evaluate situations ethically on their own. This also includes *language skills* - being able to talk openly about sexuality - and *the ability to make decisions*, e.g. in matters of family planning, the organization of a partner relationship or dealing with one's own needs. Sexual maturity is demonstrated by the fact that someone neither blindly follows social expectations nor allows themselves to be guided by unfounded fears or feelings of guilt, but instead lives consciously *and* with pleasure according to their own values. This competence reflects the highest level of personality development in the area of sexuality: one is *morally capable of acting*, reflective and yet authentic. Ultimately, this also means respecting the maturity of others - in other words, not imposing one's own morals on anyone, but respecting the diversity of lifestyles.

Together, these skills form a *whole* that enables people to live sexuality in a fulfilling and responsible way . The aspects mentioned - from *knowledge* to *empathy* and *reflection* to *autonomy* - are interlinked. For example, *empathy for the needs of others* is consciously practised alongside factual knowledge, and the *responsibility* to make decisions in the light of dignity and love is emphasized alongside personal freedom. This interplay is what makes for a competent approach to sexuality.

Ways to develop individual skills

So how can you *personally learn* this comprehensive skill? - It is crucial to accept sexuality as a *field of learning*: as something that continues to develop throughout one's life. Individual learning in this area means above all combining *experience and reflection*. Some practical approaches on how to train yourself are:

- **Self-study and searching for information:** First of all, everyone can start with themselves by actively building up their knowledge. Literature on sex education, guides on relationships and sexuality, but also current theological articles (e.g. the letter Amoris laetitia by Pope Francis) can help to broaden your horizons. Anyone who gets to know the variety of perspectives - medical, psychological, ethical, spiritual - will develop a more holistic understanding. For prospective theologians or religious education teachers, for example, it is advisable to study both church doctrinal documents and *sexual science findings in* order to integrate both worlds. It is important to be open-minded and willing to question any dogmas that may have been handed down. In this way, you learn step by step to form your own informed opinion.

- **Self-reflection and biography work:** Knowledge alone is not enough - a personal examination of your own history and attitudes is key. For example, you can keep *a diary* in which you record your experiences, feelings and questions about sexuality. Or you can remember the sexual morals you were taught at home or in church and critically examine what still holds true today. *Biography work exercises* can help: For example, the task of writing a letter to your younger self about what you wish you had known about sexuality in the past. Such methods promote self-awareness. Talking to trusted people - friends, partners or mentors - is also valuable: by talking about your thoughts and possible insecurities, the topic becomes normalized and you gain new feedback. The more you reflect on yourself, the more an authentic, internally convinced foundation of values grows.

Figure14: Be yourself!

A cheerful young man smiles as he holds a handwritten poster with the words 'BE YOURSELF' up to the camera. The sign is lovingly decorated with colorful hearts in rainbow colors. In the background is a large rainbow flag, symbolizing diversity, acceptance and LGBTQIA+ pride. The image conveys positivity, self-love and a strong statement for individuality and tolerance.

- **Practical exercise in everyday life:** Sexual competence is also learned *by doing*. This means consciously looking for or accepting situations in everyday life in which you can try out the skills mentioned. For example, *communicative competence* can be practiced by talking openly with your partner about your desires and boundaries - even if it takes some effort at first. Or you can take part in a workshop or course that offers role-playing, e.g. to practise saying "no" in unpleasant situations. It is also important to *learn and set boundaries*: This can mean taking a clear stance in the event of harassment or not silently accepting abusive jokes in a circle of friends. Every successfully mastered situation strengthens confidence in your own ability to act. For prospective religious educators, practical practice can mean designing and implementing teaching units on the topics of love, friendship and sexuality during their training - learning by doing. Encounters with people outside your own "bubble" are also part of this: Those who consciously seek out conversations with LGBTQIA+ Christians during training, for example, or take part in inclusive youth clubs, learn through encounters and empathy. These *changes in perspective* often have a more lasting impact than theory.

- **Support and feedback:** Individual learning does not mean doing everything on your own. *Support* is particularly helpful with such sensitive topics. This can be a trusted discussion partner, pastor, therapist or supervisor. Personal questions and perhaps also difficulties or fears can be discussed in a protected environment. For aspiring clergy, for example, it is valuable to have spaces in their training where they can talk about their own sexuality - be it in confession, in self-awareness groups or in mentoring meetings. Feedback from outside enables blind spots to be recognized: perhaps unconscious prejudices or insecurities that can still be worked on. Positive confirmation is also motivating - for example, if a coach gives you feedback that you have gained charisma and clarity, this encourages further development.

To summarize: Through a combination of *knowledge acquisition, self-reflection, practical application and support*, everyone can continuously work on their own sexual ethical competence. It is a process that begins with small steps but leads to fundamental personal maturation.

Didactic methods and practical examples

How can the aforementioned skills development be promoted *pedagogically*? - In educational work (schools, universities, church adult education), a variety of *didactic methods* and content have proven to be effective in making sexuality a fun and reflective topic at . A mix of methods that *imparts knowledge, encourages reflection and enables experience* is key. Here are a few examples:

- **Dialogue rounds and values discussions:** Open group discussions create trust and provide space to ask questions. Teachers or course leaders can initiate moderated *discussion rounds* in which, for example, statements such as *"Sexual orientation is a private matter for the church or for people"* or *"Pornography harms every relationship or can also revitalize it"* are discussed controversially. Through such discussions, participants learn to formulate their own positions and understand other points of view. It is important to create an *appreciative atmosphere* in which no one is exposed - possibly supported by discussion rules. *Dilemma discussions* are also helpful: an ethical case is posed (e.g. *"A religious student comes out as heterosexual by introducing his first girlfriend - how should the youth group react?"*) and the group discusses possible options for dialog. In this way, reflection on sexual ethics is practiced in a very practical way.
- **Biography work and self-reflection methods:** As mentioned above, methods of *self-reflection* also promote competence building in groups. Writing exercises, for example, can be used in school or university contexts: Participants anonymously write thoughts on *"My first approach to the topic of sexuality"* or note down associations with terms such as "lust", "purity", "queer". These outputs can be collected and discussed in order to show just how diverse the influences are. Another method is the *"letter to my younger self"* exercise, which can also be carried out in class and shared (on a voluntary basis). Such didactic approaches encourage personal confrontation, which increases self-awareness and empathy.

Letter to my younger self

Dear younger me,

I remember well that moment when you, as a believing teenager, publicly introduced your girlfriend for the first time and outed yourself as heterosexual - even if we didn't call it that at the time, of course. It seemed completely normal, but deep down you had the feeling that you were suddenly revealing something that was very private and sensitive. How would the youth group react? Would they see you differently?

Today, with a little distance and much more knowledge about sexuality as a wonderful, God-given part of our humanity, I know that your courage was important and right. Looking back, I wish that the youth group had reacted with a more open, relaxed and appreciative attitude. That sexuality would not be met with silence or embarrassment, but would be recognized as a matter of course and discussed openly - also and especially in the context of faith.

At the time, you felt a little insecure, as if you had broken an unwritten rule, even though you were just being honest and authentic. Today I know that it is precisely this openness that is needed to develop a healthy attitude towards sexuality and faith: sexuality is not a threat to faith, but an enrichment, an expression of our humanity and our God-given ability to love and live relationships responsibly and with joy.

And I remember something else very clearly: in addition to the initial uncertainty you felt, there was also a certain admiration, but also a touch of envy among your friends. I can still see the looks of amazement and almost a little disbelief on their faces when you introduced your first girlfriend. They perhaps didn't want to admit it to themselves at the time, but they would have liked to have had the experience themselves. This unspoken envy showed you at the time how significant and special this moment actually was. Today I understand that this envy was not meant in a negative way, but rather an expression of the longing for closeness, acceptance and belonging - exactly what we were all so desperately looking for as teenagers back then.

I would say to you today: be proud of your courage to show your faith and your love openly. Because sexuality belongs to you - and therefore also to your life of faith. I hope you can continue on this path and encourage others to be honest and respectful about their sexuality - no matter what it looks like.

In deep solidarity,

The you of today

- **Role plays and scenic learning:** Practical exercises bring theoretical knowledge to life. For example, a **role play** can be designed on the topic of *consensus*: Two learners simulate a party situation in which one person seeks physical advances and the other hesitates - they then analyze together how to recognize and respect boundaries. Or different roles are assigned (e.g. parent, young person, priest, teacher) and a fictitious conversation about the introduction of gender issues in confirmation classes is improvised. Such **scenic methods** make it possible to put oneself in other perspectives and train communication skills. Through the subsequent feedback discussion, everyone involved learns what worked well and where misunderstandings arose. Prospective religious education teachers in particular benefit from having played through conflicting topics before they encounter them in real life.
- **Project work and case studies:** *Projects* and *case analyses* are effective in longer-term learning units. For example, a project group can work on the topic of *"Language in sexual ethics"* - the learners examine biblical passages, church texts and current media reports to determine how sexuality is spoken about (e.g. more conservatively or openly). The project could lead to guidelines for *inclusive language* in church and school, which are then presented. Another possibility is to work on real *case studies* from educational practice: e.g. how a school deals with trans pupils or how a pastor has provided pastoral care to a same-sex couple. Such case studies combine theory and practice and provide *examples of good practice* from which we can learn.
- **External experts and media:** The *involvement of external experts* - such as sex educators, psychologists or theologians specializing in sexual ethics - also has a didactically enriching effect. A guest lecture or a joint Q&A session with a queer person from the church can open up horizons and reduce fears of contact. Films, documentaries or digital media can also serve as an impetus: A sensitive documentary about adolescent love or a YouTube clip on the topic of consensuality often speak

directly to young people and provide material for discussion. The key is to select material that both portrays *lust in* a positive light and addresses *responsibility* - in order to convey the desired balance.

In addition to methods, the *content and framework conditions* also play a role. Modern sexual ethics education focuses on *diversity and inclusion*. For example, teaching materials and examples should be deliberately chosen to be diverse: they should not only show traditional marriage between a man and a woman, but also unmarried couples, rainbow families, people with disabilities in romantic relationships, etc. Attention should also be paid to *language* - gender-sensitive and inclusive formulations signal that *everyone is* really meant. Appreciative language rejects derogatory or generalizing terms and instead speaks of "partners", "loving relationships" instead of just "marriage", "people of all orientations", etc. In this way, the addressees learn a linguistic approach that does not exclude anyone.

Good practice: Various educational initiatives in the church and society already provide role models that can be used as a guide. For example, the diocese of Limburg published ten guidelines in 2022 to promote sexual education skills in pastoral work. These guidelines set out specific content - from "Strengthening body awareness and personal identity" to "Accepting sexual orientation, gender diversity and lifestyles" and "Learning to understand child and adolescent sexuality".

Such guidelines help teachers to *systematically* cover all relevant topics in the classroom: body awareness, acceptance of diversity, developmental psychology, teaching values, protection against assault. Another example: In Austria, a church orientation guide entitled *"Committed to life and love"* was published, which focuses less on methods and more on *basic attitudes*. It focuses on love, self-respect and the ability to build relationships and invites people to engage in an *appreciative discussion* about sex education. Experts particularly praise the *"body-friendly attitude"* it expresses - in other words, the encouragement to positively accept one's own body and pleasure.

These explanations make it clear that the church is increasingly concerned *not to exclude pleasure*, but to embed it responsibly. In the area of youth work, the *Protestant Youth* in Germany is setting an example of how to integrate queer realities: for example, the Association of Protestant Youth (aej) decided in 2022 that all youth facilities would become *safe spaces* for LGBTQIA+ young people. Staff and volunteers are trained to create a welcoming culture and conscious attention is paid to *sensitive language* in order to avoid stereotypes and discrimination. Such concrete measures - from guidelines and orientation aids to action plans - are examples of good practice that show how the skills mentioned can be promoted in educational and community practice. They encourage people to approach the topic of sexuality *openly, creatively and responsibly.*

Role play

Here is a suggestion for a *role play* that specifically trains the competence *"living sexuality responsibly, with pleasure and reflection"* and can be excellently integrated into both school and extracurricular contexts (e.. youth work, youth groups, school ethics or religious education lessons):

🎲 Role-playing game title: "Between closeness, desire and respect - recognizing, communicating and maintaining boundaries"

◎ Aim of the role play: Participants should learn to reflect on their own needs and boundaries in (fictitious) relationship situations and at the same time respond empathetically to those of others. This trains *relationship skills, the ability to reach consensus, self-reflection and awareness of power.*

💭 Competence goals:

- Being able to perceive and express your own limits
- Recognize, formulate and respect consensus
- Reading and interpreting emotional and physical signals
- Practicing communication in intimate contexts
- Respectful treatment of sexual diversity and identity

👥 Roles (examples):

- **Person A:** curious, but insecure in the relationship
- **Person B:** very open and physically interested
- **Person C:** Friend who observes and gives feedback

- **Person D:** Person of trust (e.. pastor or social worker) *(Roles can be gender-neutral or individually identifiable)*

📄 Situation scenario (example): Person A and person B have been friends for some time and realize that they are attracted to each other. One evening they spend time together. The mood is familiar. Person B makes tender hints - Person A feels flattered, but also insecure. Both have to formulate their boundaries and sensitively classify the reaction of the other. Person C observes the conversation as an outsider and then gives feedback on communication, respect and perception of signals.

👤 Implementation (30-45 minutes):

1. **Introduction (5-10 min):** Brief input on consensus, boundaries, consensus (e.g. traffic light principle: green - yellow - red).
2. **Role play (15-20 min):** Groups of 3-4 people (example: A, B, C, possibly D). The scene is acted out.
3. **Reflection (10-15 min):** Reflection questions in the group:
   o How did you feel in your role?
   o How did you recognize agreement or uncertainty?
   o What non-verbal signals were there?
   o What would you have wished for from the other person?
   o What worked well? What was difficult?

📚 Supplementary didactic notes:

- Clarify *rules of conduct* in advance: respectful interaction, no evaluation of real experiences, voluntary participation.
- Moderate sensitively, especially with young people who may have had stressful experiences.
- Follow-up with materials on consent, communication, sexual diversity and body knowledge.

✝ Optional church connection:

- Debriefing in the light of the Christian view of humanity: Sexuality as an expression of love, communication and dignity.
- Invitation to a spiritual impulse (e.g. *"You are wonderfully created"* - Psalm 139).
- Discussion with a pastor about desire, responsibility and faith.

Modern perspectives: Impulses for church and education

Recognition of sexual diversity: The development of these skills leads to a much *more modern view of sexuality* among learners. Instead of prohibitions and taboos, the focus is *on values such as dignity, love and diversity.* The church itself is undergoing a change here: sexuality is increasingly being recognized as a *"positive life force"* and a valuable gift from God to mankind.

Instead of reducing it to procreation alone, a renewed sexual ethic emphasizes the *personal significance* of sexuality - as an expression of love, intimacy and communication. Pope Francis, for example, writes that sexuality is "a wonderful gift" from God.

This positive view frees lust and physicality from the stigma of sinfulness. Learners who gain this modern perspective can understand sexuality as an *enrichment* of their lives, not as a threat to morality.

A key aspect of the new view is the *recognition of sexual diversity.* Modern sexual ethical competence explicitly includes valuing *queer identities.* Initiated by the Synodal Path, the Catholic Church in Germany first stated that every person is created by God with their sexuality and has an inviolable dignity*, regardless of their sexual orientation.*

Homosexual orientations are not self-chosen and not disordered, but are just as wanted by God as heterosexual orientations. Accordingly, there are calls to actively combat any discrimination based on sexual identity. Such statements mark an epochal change: opposite-sex love is placed on *an ethically equal footing* with same-sex love. In a groundbreaking text, it was said that responsible sexuality is based on dignity, self-determination, love, fidelity, mutual responsibility and, if necessary, fertility - *regardless* of the orientation of the partners. The decisive factors are exclusivity and reliability in the relationship, not the sex of the lovers.

This clearly states: Living homosexuality *is not a sin.* This new theological insight is likely to have a lasting impact on the attitudes of many students. Those who internalize this message will question anti-queer statements in church or school and advocate *inclusion* instead.

There are also concrete changes with regard to the *language* and presentation of sexuality. In church announcements and religious instruction, more attention is being paid to *inclusive language* - away from a one-sided male-heteronormative approach and towards formulations in which *everyone can* find themselves reflected. For example, current educational plans state that pupils should learn about "different lifestyles and sexual orientations without prejudice".

Church texts, such as the above-mentioned orientation guide, invite us to work on a *"body-friendly attitude"*, including in sermons and the liturgy. This means, for example, that terms are used in prayers and hymns that emphasize *the goodness of the creation of the body*, or that words such as "disordered" are avoided in pastoral care in connection with consensual sexuality. Learners are aware of such changes - whether through the media or through their own church teachers - and develop a sense of how language and attitude are connected. An inclusive, appreciative language creates realities: it enables, for example, a non-binary young person to feel accepted in a church youth group, or an unmarried couple to know that they are not judged by the church, but supported.

In addition, the modern perspective leads to *structural changes* in the church and education. When desire and diversity are recognized, old rules and regulations have to be adapted. In some German dioceses, blessing ceremonies for homosexual couples are already being practiced, and the official church is openly discussing changing its teachings on marriage, contraception and remarriage. Educational institutions are revising their curricula: topics such as *sexual self-determination, gender equality and the prevention of sexualized violence* are being given more space. Religious education teachers, who are trained in sexual ethics, are now introducing the topic across all subjects - for example, by talking about *love and responsibility* in religious education lessons and, of course, also affirming *same-sex love* as accepted by God. This enables young people to credibly experience that faith and sexuality are not opposites, but that faith can provide a framework for living sexuality meaningfully and joyfully.

In church practice, the modernized view is reflected, for example, in official apologies to the LGBTQIA+ community. In 2021, for example, the Protestant Church in Hesse-Nassau explicitly asked queer people for forgiveness for the exclusion and suffering inflicted on them by the church. Such gestures underpin the cultural change. The learners recognize: *The church can learn* and revise its stance when knowledge and rethinking require it. This knowledge also strengthens their own willingness to learn and remain open throughout their lives.

Figure15: Church as a learning organization.

Ultimately, a modern view of sexual ethics *means reconciling pleasure and responsibility*. Dealing responsibly with lust means *accepting* lust as something created by God, but at the same time consciously enjoying it without hurting oneself or others. Learners develop an understanding of sexuality that does not distinguish between "pious" and "pleasurable", but combines both. For the church, this could mean in future that issues such as masturbation or non-marital sexuality are viewed in a more relaxed way - less as a violation and more in terms of: *is it done in a loving, responsible and good way?* Such a view was discussed in the Synodal Path. The impact on educational work would be considerable: young people could speak honestly about such topics without having to fear moral devaluation, and teachers would have guidelines to give answers that resonate with the lifeworld of young people.

The ability to live sexuality in a responsible, pleasurable and reflective way is therefore not innate - it is learned, between the poles of personal development, education and social discourse. Our society - and the churches in particular - have recognized that open and value-based sex education is essential in order to enable individual fulfillment as well as to offer protection against abuse and discrimination. Those who develop the skills described above gain a mature attitude: they can *be themselves* in their sexuality and at the same time respect the dignity of others. This ideal image of a sexually mature personality radiates into institutions. The church and education system will change as a result of such people - towards places where *sexual diversity is seen as an enrichment*, where people can laugh and love with a sense of responsibility, and where faith and life come together in a liberated, respectful coexistence. The challenge is to continue along this path consistently - *committed to life and love*, as the saying goes. Then sexuality will no longer be a source of conflict, but a source of *joy, meaning and community* that has its rightful place in the church and in society.

Exercise 7:
Talking about sexuality in religious education without fear - developing skills in practice

The exercise deals in depth with the need to talk openly and without fear about sexuality in religious education. The aim is to reduce fears and feelings of shame, establish a culture of open discussion and impart knowledge about sexual diversity, health and ethical issues. Teachers and pupils should learn to reflect on their own values in the context of their faith, listen empathetically and respectfully acknowledge diversity.

Essential skills include communication and education skills (clear, age-appropriate language, technical knowledge), shame-free communication (positive use of language, open discussion atmosphere), an anti-discriminatory attitude (appreciation of sexual diversity) and diversity awareness (positive perception of differences). In addition, spiritual competence, i.e. empathetic listening and mindful speaking, plays a central role. The teachers' personal learning path includes self-reflection, further training, peer-to-peer exchange and practical exercises, supported by spirituality and self-care.

Didactic approaches for religious education include the creation of a protected discussion framework, transparent lesson design with learner participation, low-threshold entry methods, interactive exercises (e.g. role plays), the use of media and creative methods as well as the involvement of external experts.

- ***Learning and development objective:*** *The most important competence is shame-free communication. Learners should be able to talk openly about sexuality without fear in order to promote an atmosphere of appreciation and acceptance.*
- ***Good practice example:*** *The method of the anonymous question box, in which churchgoers and schoolchildren can submit questions about sexuality anonymously. These are then*

dealt with respectfully and competently in church services or lessons, which reduces fears and promotes openness.

- **Church support through:** The faithful, clergy, priests or bishops can contribute to issues of sexual diversity and ethical sexuality through open sermons, discussion opportunities and a supportive attitude. In doing so, they create role models and spaces for fear-free communication.
- **Local budget use:** Financial resources could be used for further training for teachers on sex education, external workshops with specialists, creative teaching materials and events that support an open culture of discussion.
- **Adaptation of the school curriculum:** The religious education curriculum should explicitly include a fearless, respectful and open approach to sexuality. Content includes sexual health, diversity and ethics, practice-oriented communication exercises and reflection on one's own attitudes and beliefs.

An open culture of discussion in religious education promotes a fear-free exchange on sensitive topics: Talking about sexuality in religious education is often a challenge for many teachers in their first years of teaching and for young learners. There are often fears, feelings of shame or insecurities when it comes to intimate issues. At the same time, most young people think about this very thing: "Church, Christian religion and sexuality - it's such an unknown thing...".

You know that church institutions have long shaped sexual-normative moral concepts and that, unfortunately, problems such as sexual abuse of young altar boys by male priests have existed and continue to exist in religious contexts.

A modern approach to religious education takes these reservations seriously and creates a space at school in which sexuality can be discussed without fear, shame and respect. This requires targeted *skills development* - for both teachers and students - so that communication on this sensitive topic can be successful.

Teaching objectives: What should be achieved?

Clear teaching objectives should be formulated so that discussions about sexuality in the context of faith are successful. *Teaching objectives* are the desired outcomes of the learning process - i.e. what learners should know, be able to do and have developed in terms of attitude at the end. The focus here is particularly on

- **Reducing fear and openness:** Learners should reduce fear and shame when dealing with the topic of sexuality and gain confidence in an open culture of discussion. The aim is for no one to blush or fall silent as soon as sexuality is brought up.
- **Knowledge transfer and education:** Another teaching objective is to impart basic knowledge about sexual health, ethics and diversity. This is done in religious education from a value-oriented perspective that is linked to the theological view. Pupils should recognize that sexuality is *not* a taboo, but a natural part of being human and of creation.
- **Reflection and value formation:** Learners should be enabled to reflect on their own values and attitudes towards sexuality in the light of their faith. This also includes getting to know biblical

or church positions, questioning them and relating them to the reality of life.

- **Respect and empathy:** A central goal is to develop respect for other perspectives, lifestyles and identities. In discussions about sexuality, students should learn to listen to each other, to tolerate different opinions and to react compassionately - an approach that is in line with Christian charity.

These teaching objectives make it clear that religious education can become a "place of practiced shame sensitivity" where students experience recognition and appreciation and can open up without fear. By exemplifying *freedom from fear and openness* themselves, teachers create the basis for achieving these teaching objectives.

Competencies to be developed

In order to achieve these teaching goals, various *competencies* must be developed - for teachers as well as for students. The most important areas of competence are listed below:

- **Communication and education skills:** This includes the ability to provide factually correct and age-appropriate information about sexuality (education skills) using clear, inviting language. Teachers need specialist knowledge about sexual development, diversity and ethical issues in order to respond competently to questions. At the same time, this area includes conversational skills, i.e. actively addressing topics, moderating questions and not avoiding sensitive aspects. Those who have this competence can, for example, calmly explain what the church says about love or make terms such as "LGBTQIA+" understandable.
- **Shame-free communication:** This is about the *personal attitude and atmosphere of the conversation*. Shame-free communication means that neither the speaker nor the listener is embarrassed. Teachers should learn to use neutral or positive terminology instead of derogatory or embarrassing language. They need to convey non-verbally and verbally: *"It's okay to talk about it."* Students should also practise speaking openly, without swearing or giggling, and respecting boundaries. This

skill is closely linked to self-reflection - you have to understand your own shame in order to overcome it.

- **Anti-discriminatory attitude:** An appreciative, anti-discriminatory attitude is essential. This means strictly rejecting *any form of degradation* based on gender, sexual orientation or family background. Teachers need knowledge about the diversity of sexual identities and lifestyles in order to avoid conveying unintentional prejudices. Students should develop the competence to respect different perspectives and lifestyles as equal. This attitude can be seen, for example, in the fact that sexuality or homosexuality is not concealed or problematized in class, but is treated as part of diversity as a matter of course.
- **Diversity awareness:** It is also important to promote an awareness of diversity. Diversity competence means not only tolerating differences, but perceiving them positively. In terms of sexuality, this includes, for example, dealing with different sexual orientations, gender identities (e.g. trans* people) or cultural imprints of shame and shame boundaries. Religious education teachers should familiarize themselves with inclusive theology and pedagogy of diversity in order to consider the perspectives of all students in the classroom. For learners, diversity awareness means that they recognize that Sexuality can look different for every person, and this is enriching and intended by God.
- **Spiritual discipline - empathic listening and mindful speaking:** In the context of faith and teaching, the inner attitude also plays a role. Empathic listening means *listening with the heart*, as is practiced in pastoral care. Teachers should really *listen to* their students, without rushing to judgment, and perceive between the lines what moves them. Mindful speaking means choosing words carefully, combining truth with love and enduring silence when necessary. These skills have a spiritual dimension: they are rooted in respect for the other person as an image of God. Those who communicate mindfully and empathetically live a form of spiritual practice in everyday school life.

These skills are interlinked. Together, they make it possible to talk about sexuality without fear - *informed, respectfully and sensitively*. For teachers, they also mean professional and personal development, as their own attitude is questioned and trained.

Individual learning: personal paths to competence

The development of these skills begins with each teacher and each individual. *How can you personally learn* to talk about sexuality in the context of faith without fear and with competence? Some practical steps:

1. **Self-reflection and further training:** First of all, you need to be honest with yourself. What are my own preconceptions or taboos regarding sexuality and faith? What situations in the classroom frighten me? You can explore your own boundaries of shame by writing in a diary or talking to friends. At the same time, teachers should stay on the ball professionally: read current literature on sex education and theology, attend further training courses or take part in workshops. For example, church educational institutions offer seminars where you can practise communication about love and sexuality. A look at materials such as *"Inclusive Religious Education of Diversity"* or current study books on *queer theology* and *queer Christology* will also broaden your own knowledge and sensitize you to diversity.

2. **Exchange and mentoring**: It helps immensely to exchange ideas with colleagues and fellow students. By talking to others (e.g. in revision groups at university or in the teachers' college), experiences can be shared and tips passed on. For example, you could find out how colleague X mastered a discussion about contraception in religious education, or which methods worked well with the topic of sexual orientation. In this kind of collegial exchange, fears are put into perspective (*"We are both confident about this topic"*) and solutions are developed together. Prospective clergy can look for a mentor - such as a pastor who is known as an expert coach - and learn from their experience in dealing with topics that require dialog.

3. **Practical exercise in a protected environment:** Nothing replaces doing. Before you go into a full classroom discussion,

you can practise on a smaller scale. Role plays are ideal for this: with a trusted colleague or in a seminar, try answering tricky questions or moderating a parents' meeting on the topic of sex and faith. *Microteaching approaches* (presenting small teaching excerpts in front of friends) also make it possible to get feedback on your own impact. It is important that this takes place in *a safe space where* feedback is allowed. In this way, you gradually gain confidence in your choice of words and charisma.

4. **Spirituality and self-care**: Last but not least, personal spirituality should be used as a resource. Those who are rooted in faith can draw strength and serenity from it to tackle difficult conversations. Before a lesson on sexuality, a moment of silence or prayer can help you to center yourself and adopt a loving attitude. Self-care is also important: if anxiety arises, breathe consciously, possibly meditate. And if emotions come up after an intense discussion, you can also allow yourself to relax or "release" what is bothering you in prayer.

These individual learning steps gradually turn an insecure teacher into someone who can say with conviction*: "Yes, we can talk openly about sexuality in religious education - and it's good for everyone."* Although the process is personal, it does not have to be lonely; it is accompanied by literature, community and faith.

Didactic approaches: Teaching and practicing skills

In addition to individual preparation, the question arises *as to how these skills can be taught and practiced in the classroom.* Religious education teachers have a dual responsibility: they must act confidently themselves and at the same time enable their students to communicate courageously and in detail. The following didactic methods and teaching principles have proven their worth:

- **Create a protected framework:** At the very beginning of every series of lessons on sensitive topics, there should be an agreement for a protected space. A trusting classroom atmosphere is the basis for all further activities. The teacher and class can work out rules together: for example, a confidentiality rule (*"What is discussed here can also be discussed in the* school playground - but responsibly, objectively and without names"), respectful language (no laughing, no derogatory terms) and the right not to have to answer a question. The teacher consistently ensures that these rules are adhered to. Through such agreements, the young people feel: I can open up here without being persecuted outside.

- **Transparency and participation:** It takes away a lot of anxiety when pupils know exactly what to expect in class. It is therefore advisable to make the course of the lesson transparent. For example, you can give an overview at the beginning of the unit: *"Today we are talking about love and the body, next week about media and sexuality..."*. The class can also be involved - for example, by prioritizing topics or contributing their own questions. One tried-and-tested method is the *anonymous question box*: Pupils post notes with questions or concerns about sexuality - anonymously if they wish. The teacher takes up these questions as they progress and answers them objectively and without judgment. In this way, what really moves the young people is included, but the teacher still has control over when and how it is discussed. Incidentally, this is an exercise that priests can also implement in Sunday services: Informational counseling instead of a sermon.
- **Low-threshold introduction:** The first real round of talks on sexuality in particular needs an initial introduction. *Indirect methods* can be used here. For example, a short film clip or a song (possibly from the charts) that deals with love and physicality can be played - this serves as a conversation starter without anyone having to reveal anything personal. Alternatively, a literary text or a biblical verse can serve as an icebreaker. For example, show a picture of Genesis 2:18 (*"It is not good for man to be alone"*) and let the students associate what closeness and being alone mean to them. This gets them talking about *relationships and intimacy* before explicitly saying "sexuality". Such indirect approaches reduce shame and enable the first open words.
- **Interactive exercises and role plays:** Practical exercises in the classroom are essential for practicing communication skills.

Role plays can deal with situations such as: *A friend comes out as gay - how do I react?* or a *discussion between parents and teenagers about sexual morality*. Through playful experimentation, young people learn to put into words what they are thinking and at the same time learn through observation which conversation strategies are well received. Exercises from theater pedagogy, such as *placing people on a scale of opinions* (e.g. from *"I think intense kissing before marriage is okay"* to "I only think it's okay with the mouth" along a line), also bring movement to the topic and show the diversity of positions. It is important that such activities are always followed by an evaluation: How did we feel? What did we learn? This turns the game into a conscious learning loop.

- **Use of media and creative methods:** Young people live in a media-influenced world, which is why media should also be used and critically reflected upon in religious education on the topic of sexuality. For example, positive content could be used, such as the *"Make Love"* video series or sex education websites from a church perspective to show that sexuality can also be discussed *in an appreciative manner*. Creative methods also loosen up the atmosphere: designing collages about "dream relationships", a poetry slam about shame, or groups developing pro/con arguments from the perspective of biblical figures (e.g. *"What would Ruth say about online dating?"* - humorous but profound). Such methodical approaches enable learning with head, heart and hand.

- **Involve external expertise:** A teacher does not have to do everything alone. It can be very effective to invite guests or external projects. Many churches or initiatives offer workshops, for example on love, friendship and sexuality from a Christian perspective. There are also special offers on LGBTQIA+ topics: Projects such as *diversity@school* send queer teamers into schools to break down fears of contact and impart knowledge in interactive workshops. Such external input takes the pressure off the teacher, brings a breath of fresh air and often also authenticity into the classroom - for example, when a young homosexual Christian talks about their own life, the young people learn directly from an example of lived diversity in faith. It is important to follow up on the experience so that it does not remain a one-off event.

These didactic approaches are all aimed at *practising communication* and making it possible to experience that openness neither hurts nor destroys one's own values. On the contrary: in the protected learning space, young people can gain positive experiences that enable them to speak confidently and respectfully about sexuality outside of school. Many of these methods can be adapted for future clergy - whether in confirmation work, youth work or adult education in the church.

Good practice examples from religious education

Theory is important, but nothing is as convincing as successful examples from practice. So let's take a look at some *good practice experiences* in which fear-free communication about sexuality in religious education has been successful:

Example 1: Lesson series "Sexuality and intimacy" (Year 8/9) - At a secondary school, a religion teacher planned a unit lasting several weeks in order to approach the topic carefully and comprehensively at the same time. As an introduction, he chose the creation text Gen 2:18 (*"It is not good that man should be alone"*). The pupils looked at a suitable picture and wrote diary entries about their longing for closeness and friendship. The following lessons focused on sexual diversity: the class watched a short video clip showing various couples in love (straight, gay, lesbian, with and without disabilities) and noted down their impressions. This led to a discussion about prejudices and the question "Can love be colorful?". The teacher introduced *the positions of different religions on the topic of homosexuality* (collection of materials), so that the young people discussed how faith and sexual diversity go together.

Finally, each learner formulated a sentence on a card that has become important to him or her in dealing with love and sexuality (e.g. *"I respect my own boundaries", "God loves me as I am"*). These cards were hung up on a class poster as a tree of values. The unit showed impressively that religious education can be a place where knowledge, self-reflection and faith come together: In reflection, many young people stated that they had never felt taken so seriously with this topic. The teacher reported that the mixture of biblical impulse, creative tasks and open discussion created a *trusting dynamic* in which even previously silent pupils openly joined in the discussion.

Example 2: Project "Let's Talk about Sex - Youth Work Meets School" - In another setting, a pastor cooperated with a school to offer an afternoon workshop. A *sex-positive discussion space* was created under the title *"Let's talk about sex: between shame and blessing"*. Interested parents were also invited along with pupils from the upper school. As an introduction, the pastor read out a short text by a young Christian who reconciled his *homosexuality and his faith* - he spoke honestly about his own experiences and how he was ultimately known in the church community. Afterwards, the religious education teacher and church representative jointly moderated small groups in which open questions could be asked: *"What does the Bible really say about sex before marriage?"*, *"How do you deal with pornography?"*, *"What are the church's new guidelines on LGBTQIA+ people and the solemnization of their marriages?"*. The mixture of professional input and personal exchange led to a lively dialog. At the end, the young people formulated wishes for the church in a plenary session, including: *more honesty* in dealing with sexuality, *no discrimination* against LGBTQIA+ members and offers such as sacramental marriage ceremonies for loving relationships.

It is good practice on two levels: Firstly, the young people experience church in a different way - ready for dialog and close to their life issues. Secondly, they learn in a protected environment that you can talk about anything if everyone involved remains *honest and empathetic*. Such examples are encouraging. They prove that it is possible to break out of the usual silence or blushing. Of course, not every classroom discussion is ideal, but every positive experience helps to change the culture at school and church. Once it becomes known that Class 9b talks about love, body and faith in *a "completely normal" way*, then perhaps other classes or congregations will also dare to tackle the topic. Good practice radiates - and can be built on.

Übüng: Microteaching

Microteaching exercise that can be used specifically in religious education lessons to *develop skills in speaking about sexuality without fear*. It not only trains linguistic and content-related skills, but also self-awareness, presentation confidence and feedback culture.

🎓 Microteaching exercise: "My 3-minute unit - talking about sexuality without fear"

🕐 Aim: Students practise presenting short lesson excerpts (mini-inputs or guided discussion situations) in front of a small group. They reflect on their linguistic impact, body language, clarity of content and how to deal with shame or taboo boundaries.

☁ Competencies that are promoted:

- Shameless and clear communication about sexual topics
- Empathic speaking in a protected environment
- Dealing with insecurities and linguistic self-control
- Perception of non-verbal signals and reactions
- Feedback skills - giving and accepting constructive feedback

📌 Procedure of the exercise (approx. 45-60 minutes):

1. preparation (10-15 min): The students choose one of several prepared tasks (or design their own). Possible topics:

- Explain what "consensus" means - in an age-appropriate, open and appreciative way.
- Give a short impulse on the topic of "physicality and creation".
- Initiate a conversation situation in which sexual diversity is discussed.
- Tell why you think respect is important in sexual relationships.

The students prepare in *small groups of 3-4 people for 3 minutes speaking time* each - alone or with a short group discussion.

2. implementation (20-25 min): Each person in the group gives his/her short input to the others. The group listens attentively. Each contribution is followed by a structured feedback dialog.

3rd feedback phase (approx. 5 minutes per person): The group gives feedback using the *"I see - I feel - I wish"* method:

- **"I have seen ..."** (body language, flow of speech, presence)
- **"I have felt ..."** (understanding, trust, irritation, connection)
- **"I wish for ..."** (Tips for further development)

♀ Optional: The presenters keep a parallel **self-observation checklist** (e.g. "Was my language clear and appreciative?", "Did I maintain eye contact?").

▢ Reflection impulse (in plenary or in writing):

- What have I learned about myself and my impact?
- Which sentences or words did I consciously choose - or avoid?
- Where do I still feel insecure? Where did I feel safe?
- What does it mean for me as a religious person to talk about sexuality?

✖ Method tips:

- Prepared sentence starters help with the introduction: "Sexuality is for me ...", "It is important that we ...", "What encourages me about the topic ..."
- Provide cards with terms such as "consensus", "respect", "pleasure", "diversity", "faith", "body" as impulse generators
- Music, sitting circle or tea light as framing elements for a trusting atmosphere

✝ Spiritual connection (optional): At the end, a short blessing or an impulse can be given, e.g: *"God has created us as feeling, thinking, loving people. May our language be open, our hearts mindful and our bodies at home."*

Reflection: Modern perspectives and necessary change - key competence for religious education in the 21st century

Finally, it is worth taking a look at the big picture: what more modern view of sexuality and language in the context of faith can learners gain from all this? And what should change in the church and religious education as a result?

First of all, the learners gain a *perspective that is free of taboos*. Whereas in the past sexuality was often associated with shame and silence in a church environment, young people now learn that it can and should be talked about - *openly, honestly and without fear*. This experience can be almost liberating. Learners recognize sexuality as a natural part of their personality that they do not have to hide from God. The Bible contains life-affirming voices on physicality (*"And they were naked and not ashamed"*, Gen 2:25), and such impulses can also be rediscovered in the classroom. As pupils learn to find language for the previously unspeakable, their self-esteem grows: they do not have to be ashamed of their questions and feelings. On the contrary, they experience recognition and appreciation - a culture of recognition that prevents shame.

This more modern view no longer links faith and sexuality as opposites (à la *"one to God, the other to the devil"* - a tragic mistake of the past), but as aspects of being a holistic human being.

In addition, learners develop a *sense of diversity and justice* in the church context. They see that an anti-discriminatory attitude is not optional, but is part of the core of Christian charity. If, for example, it is discussed in religious education that all people - whether hetero, homo, bi, trans or inter - are images of God, then this shapes the young generation: God is then also an image of them. Young people will be less inclined to accept exclusionary statements from the pulpit. Instead, these young people already bring the desire for equality with them to church. A modern view of sexuality in the context of faith also means moving away from pure rhetoric towards an ethic of responsibility and love. Learners understand that sexual relationships are to be judged in the light of values such as *respect, voluntariness, fidelity and attentiveness* - and not on the basis of outdated norms or claims to power. This creates a critical awareness: One may respect traditions, but must also ask where tradition has become oppression. It is this critical love of the church - loyal but honest - that can initiate change.

This new culture of conversation should lead to a number of changes in *religious education and the church*. On the one hand, religious education teachers and theologians need more training in the aforementioned communication skills. Seminars on sex education, diversity and shame-sensitive teaching should become a natural part of the curriculum. Only then will future teachers feel equipped instead of avoiding the topic. On the other hand, the church in a broader sense should also adopt this openness. Priests, pastors and youth workers - they all need to *find a language* that speaks about sexuality without offending. It would be desirable if, for example, sermons occasionally celebrated the beauty of human love or addressed responsible sexual ethics instead of leaving it to the secular media. The church can regain a great deal of trust here if it shows that *We have understood that God accepts the whole person - soul and body.*

Another change concerns the question of power: in the history of the church, the treatment of sexuality was often also an instrument of control and power (for example through strict moral teachings or the concealment of abuse). The new generation, strengthened by open religious education, will hopefully help to ensure that abuses of power are named and stopped. They will learn that a person's worth does not depend on whether they conform to church norms. This realization undermines the power imbalance that was based on fear and ignorance. In a church that is changing, the focus is instead on dialog and a willingness to learn together. Young people contribute their questions and perspectives and are listened to. This will make the church more sustainable - *more inclusive, more humble and closer to people.*

In summary, it can be said: If religious education today enables young people to talk about sexuality without fear, then a generation will grow up for whom faith and life issues belong together as a matter of course. These young people will go into their communities with an enlightened, free view and demand changes there - more openness, more equality, more truthful conversations. Model projects are already showing how beneficial it can be when the church no longer beats around the bush, but *speaks plainly*: about love, lust, boundaries and responsibility. Such a church has the potential to slowly restore damaged trust (especially after abuse scandals) because it no longer sweeps anything under the carpet.

The ability to talk about sexuality in religious education (and beyond) without fear is a *key competence for religious education in the 21st century*. It combines pedagogical skill, professional knowledge and a value-driven attitude. For teachers and prospective clergy, this means continuing their own education, overcoming their own shame and courageously breaking new ground in communication. For students, it opens up a protected space in which they *can be who they are*, ask any questions and learn to accept others in the same way. In the long term, this development will change schools and churches: Away from fear and taboos, towards honesty, diversity and charity in the language that is lived. It is an inspiring vision - and it begins with every classroom discussion that is already being conducted openly and lovingly today. With this in mind: *Let's talk about it - God is in the middle of the conversation.*

Exercise 8:
Shaping the world with head, heart and hand - self-acceptance and ethical action: Acquiring skills for conscience and compassion

The exercise focuses on the development of self-acceptance and a sense of ethical responsibility. The aim is to teach learners to accept themselves with their strengths and weaknesses, to process mistakes constructively and to act responsibly and compassionately on the basis of an educated conscience. Learners learn that they are accepted unconditionally - by themselves, by others and, in a religious context, by God - which promotes a deep basic trust. The aim is also to raise awareness of social injustice and the willingness to actively take responsibility for themselves and society.

Essential competencies include self-reflection and self-acceptance, dealing with guilt and forming a conscience, empathy and charity as well as social-ethical judgment and commitment. These skills enable learners to make ethical judgments, act with empathy and critically question social structures.

Didactic approaches to promote these skills include dialogical forms of discussion, biographical reflection, role-playing games on ethical dilemmas, exercises of conscience, project-based forms of learning and meditative and spiritual exercises. Such methods create a safe space for individual and collaborative learning and thus sustainably promote the development of personal and social skills.

- ***Learning and development objective:*** *The most important personal skill is the ability to accept oneself, as this forms the basis for dealing with oneself and others in an empathetic and responsible manner. The learning objective is to accept one's* own strengths and weaknesses and to act ethically and compassionately on this basis.

- **Good practice example:** A "reconciliation walk" in the community or school, where participants symbolically lay down burdens, write letters of forgiveness to themselves and light candles for others. This method enables a tangible connection between self-acceptance, coming to terms with guilt and a new beginning.

- **Church support through:** Supporting believers, clergy, priests or bishops by speaking openly and authentically about self-acceptance, guilt and forgiveness, offering pastoral care and initiating projects that make reconciliation and social responsibility visible.

- **Local budget utilization:** Community funds could be invested in workshops, seminars and materials for ethical education, such as fees for external experts, the implementation of projects on civil courage and social responsibility as well as spiritual exercises and meditation offers.

- **Adaptation of the school curriculum:** The curriculum should integrate topics such as self-acceptance, conscience formation and ethical behavior more strongly. Specifically, modules on empathy training, reflection exercises on ethical dilemmas and social projects to test ethical skills in practice would be necessary. The aim is to enable students to act responsibly and compassionately in society.

The development of *self-acceptance* and a sense of ethical *responsibility* should help learners to lead a reflective and compassionate life. The central goal is to learn to accept oneself in one's own strengths and weaknesses and to act on the basis of an educated conscience. Learners should recognize that they are *unconditionally accepted* - by themselves, by others and, in a religious context, also by God - and draw a basic trust from this. Building on this, they should be able to admit personal guilt and accept forgiveness in order to *make new beginnings* possible. Further aims are to raise awareness of social injustice and the willingness to take responsibility for themselves and others in society and the church. Learners should therefore develop a sense of what constitutes a *"good and just life"* for all and be motivated to actively stand up for *charity, justice and human dignity*.

Competencies to be developed

In order to achieve these teaching objectives, a wide range of **skills** are promoted:

- **Self-reflection and self-acceptance:** The ability to honestly recognize one's own strengths and limitations and to value oneself. This includes admitting mistakes and learning from them without falling into self-deprecation. Studies emphasize that true humility does not consist of excessive self-deprecation - because this would be to misjudge the fact that every person is created by their Creator as *lovable and multi-talented*. Rather, it is important to see oneself realistically and accept one's own limitations. This self-acceptance is a prerequisite for successful interpersonal relationships, as only those who accept themselves can also accept others.
- **Dealing with guilt and forming a conscience:** The competence to deal constructively with one's own misconduct and guilt. This includes *neither denying nor suppressing guilt,* but recognizing it and taking responsibility - in contrast to the "delusion of innocence" of many modern people who do not admit their own mistakes. Learners should develop an *educated conscience* that serves as an inner authority for moral decisions. This conscience needs to be sharpened through ethical reflection:

what does my inner compass tell me in difficult decisions? In this way, *ethical judgment* is practiced, i.e. the ability to make well-founded decisions in complex situations according to moral standards. Such competence of conscience is expressed, for example, in resisting temptations to look the other way or the *scapegoat mechanism* (blaming others) and instead acting honestly and responsibly.

- **Empathy and charity:** the ability to put oneself in the shoes of others and act compassionately. Those who accept themselves are also more likely to approach others openly and respect their dignity. This competence includes *compassion for those who suffer*, the ability to forgive and to act in solidarity. For example, Christian ethics require us to treat others as we would like to be treated ourselves (Golden Rule; see Mt 7:12). This includes working for the well-being of others and not accepting injustice. Empathy forms the basis for social responsibility - be it in a small interpersonal context or in the larger social context.

- **Social-ethical judgment and commitment:** The ability to critically question social structures and to stand up for *social justice*. Learners should understand that ethical action is not only required in private life, but also in politics and society. They recognize that biblical and ethical values such as justice and human dignity are benchmarks against which social conditions must also be measured. In this way, they acquire the ability to understand phenomena such as poverty, racism or environmental destruction as *ethical challenges*. This is about understanding *structural guilt:* in other words, the complicity that we bear when we are part of unjust systems or benefit from them. Structural sin refers to sin that *is anchored in the system* - e.. unjust ideas, laws or practices that keep injustice going. This insight enables us not only to act morally as individuals, but also to recognize injustice in our own environment or in institutions and to have the courage to change.

- **Ethical action competence:** Finally, learners should develop the ability to *put their conscience into action* - in other words, to act responsibly and pro-socially. This includes moral courage (standing up for values in everyday life, even if it takes courage), consistency in a sustainable lifestyle, mindful treatment of fellow human beings and creation as well as a willingness for reconciliation. Skills development aims to develop an attitude of *taking responsibility*: Students learn to take responsibility for the consequences of their actions and to actively contribute to the good instead of remaining passive. This competence to act combines the aforementioned skills - self-awareness, conscience, empathy - into concrete action in everyday life.

Individual learning: paths to self-acceptance and conscience formation

Everyone can work on developing these skills in their personal life. *Self-acceptance* begins with self-reflection: Regular reflection or journaling about your own experiences, feelings and decisions can help you to recognize patterns. For example, ask yourself: *Where did I show my strengths? Where did I experience my limits?* It is important to adopt a benevolent attitude towards yourself - to make *friends with yourself*, as it were. Practical exercises from mindfulness or spirituality support this. A short self-compassion exercise can be to pause in moments of stress, consciously perceive your own unpleasant feelings and say to yourself in a comforting way: *"This is a difficult moment. May I be kind to myself and accept myself as I am."*

Such simple sentences strengthen the feeling: I am imperfect, but valuable - and I can give myself just as much *kindness and forgiveness* as others.

Dealing *with feelings of guilt* also needs to be learned. Anyone who has made a mistake can take individual steps towards reconciliation: first honestly admit to yourself what went wrong and learn from it. Then - if possible - ask for an apology or make amends. It is equally important to be able to *forgive yourself*. From a religious perspective, trusting that God forgives and frees people from entanglements can help here.

This trust opens up a new beginning and takes away the weight of destructive feelings of guilt. From a secular perspective, one can realize that mistakes are human and do not have to mean lifelong judgment.

Exercises such as writing a letter to your *future* self (in which you promise yourself forgiveness and give advice) can be healing.

The formation of conscience can be promoted individually by consciously exposing oneself to ethical questions. For example, you can pause when making difficult decisions and mentally consider the possible consequences and principles: *"What do I feel is right? Would I be able to justify my decision to my own conscience?"* It helps to familiarize yourself with ethical guidelines - such as the Ten Commandments, the Golden Rule or modern ethical principles such as justice, human rights and sustainability.

The *Golden Rule* is a fundamental ethical principle that appears in a similar form in various religions, cultures and philosophical traditions. It is formulated in general terms:

> *"Treat others as you would like them to treat you."*

In the Christian tradition, Jesus formulates it as follows in the Sermon on the Mount (Matthew 7:12):

> *"Whatever you want people to do to you, do it to them!"*

The Golden Rule summarizes in a simple and understandable way what moral behavior can look like in everyday life. It calls on people to empathize with others and to act with respect, fairness and compassion.

The Golden Rule is universally applicable: it helps to avoid conflicts, promotes peaceful and respectful coexistence and serves as a guide for ethical and responsible behavior.

The *Golden Rule* and *Kant's Categorical Imperative* appear similar at first glance, but differ significantly in their ethical derivation and application:

Golden rule:

"Treat others as you would like to be treated yourself."

- The Golden Rule is based on empathy and reciprocity.
- It is based on your own wishes and needs, which you transfer to others.

- The problem with this is that it is subjective: Not everyone wants to be treated equally. One's own preferences could be transferred to others without taking their perspective adequately into account.

Kant's Categorical Imperative:

"Act only according to that maxim by which you can at the same time wish it to become a general law."

- Kant's imperative demands that we act according to *universalizable principles*, i.e. principles that could apply to everyone.

- It is not based on individual desires, but on *reason*. It requires us to question ourselves critically: "Would it work if everyone behaved exactly like me?"

- It is *not subjective but objective* and demands strict universality and rationality of ethical action.

The Golden Rule appeals to our empathy and humanity, while Kant's Categorical Imperative is based on a strictly rational and universal justification of ethics. For every action, Kant demands that we ask ourselves whether the maxim behind it could also function as a general law - regardless of personal desires.

Figure 16: The Golden Rule and Kant's Categorical Imperative.

Criterion	Golden rule	Categorical imperative
Orientation	Subjective wishes, empathy	Reason, universality
Universality	Limited universality; could transfer individual preferences	Strictly universal, objective, generalizable
Basis	Empathy, reciprocity	Reason and logical consistency
Example	*"I help because I want help myself."*	*"I help because a world in which no one helps could not possibly function sensibly."*

In addition to the *Golden Rule* and Kant's *Categorical Imperative*, there are other rules and ethical principles that everyone can use to guide their own conscience:

Principle of responsibility (Hans Jonas)

"Act in such a way that the effects of your actions are compatible with the permanence of real human life on earth."

- This principle calls on us to consider the long-term consequences for future generations and the environment when making decisions.
- It emphasizes ecological and social sustainability.

Principle of the lesser evil

"If you have to choose between two negative options, choose the one that causes less harm or suffering."

- Particularly helpful in moral dilemmas where no ideal decision is possible.
- Promotes pragmatic, responsible decisions.

Principle of human dignity / principle of human rights

"Always act in a way that respects and protects the dignity of all people." - *"Act in such a way that people receive their universal rights and these are safeguarded."*

- Is based on the conviction that every human being has an inalienable dignity, regardless of origin, status or deeds.
- Fundamental human rights are universal and apply everywhere and at all times - they should also apply to canon law.
- Committed to respectful interaction and recognition of the rights of others.

Utilitarian principle (Jeremy Bentham, John Stuart Mill)

"Act in such a way that you promote the greatest possible happiness for the greatest possible number of people."

- The aim is to maximize benefits (happiness, joy, well-being) and minimize suffering for as many people as possible.

- Can be helpful to check decisions for their practical consequences.

Principle of charity (Christian)

"Love your neighbor as yourself." (Mt 22:39)

- Oriented towards the Christian commandment of love.

- Emphasizes empathy, care and solidarity.

Discourse ethics (Jürgen Habermas)

"Act according to standards that everyone could agree to in a reasonable, free discourse."

- Emphasizes communicative understanding and legitimization through joint agreement.

- Promotes dialog skills, plurality and consensus building.

Principle of empathy and compassion

"Always put yourself in the other person's shoes and act with compassion and mercy."

- Encourages you to perceive actions from the perspective of others.

- Promotes empathy, sensitivity and understanding.

Depending on the situation and their own ethical convictions, each person's conscience can be guided by different principles. The ideal is to combine several of these rules in order to act in a differentiated, responsible and humane manner.

When the Catholic Church denies queer people the sacrament of marriage, it violates several of the aforementioned ethical rules. In the following, I will explain in detail which rules are being violated and what a corresponding maxim for action could look like:

1. the Golden Rule (*"Treat others as you would like to be treated"*):
The Golden Rule calls for empathizing with other people and acting

according to how you would like to be treated. By refusing the sacrament of marriage to queer people, the church is treating them differently than it would like to be treated - namely with acceptance, dignity and appreciation. If the church itself were affected, it would presumably demand acceptance and recognition. A just maxim for action would therefore be: "We administer the sacrament of marriage to all people, just as we would wish to be treated in the same situation."

2. Kant's Categorical Imperative (*"Act only according to that maxim which you can at the same time will as a general law."*): Kant's principle requires that one's own conduct must be generalizable. Refusing the sacrament of marriage to queer couples is not generalizable, as it is based on discrimination that is not based on reasonable arguments. If this practice were to be applied universally, it would create a society that structurally excludes people on the basis of their sexual identity. The maxim according to Kant would therefore be: "We grant the sacrament of marriage to all people because only this would be reasonable and morally viable as a general law."

3rd principle of responsibility (Hans Jonas: *"Act in such a way that your actions are compatible with the permanence of human life on earth"*): Jonas calls for acting sustainably and responsibly towards future generations. By not recognizing queer partnerships as equal, the church creates a climate of discrimination and exclusion, which in the long term contradicts a solidary, sustainable society. It would be responsible to recognize partnerships that are based on love, responsibility and mutual respect on an equal footing. A responsible maxim would therefore be: "We recognize every loving and responsible partnership as sacramental, regardless of its gender composition, in order to ensure social sustainability and solidarity in the long term."

4th principle of the lesser evil (*"Choose the option that causes less harm"*): By withholding the sacrament from queer people, the Church causes pain, marginalization and psychological distress to those affected. The lesser evil would clearly be to grant queer couples the sacrament and thus avoid discrimination and suffering. A maxim for action based on this would be: "We choose the option that causes less harm and avoids suffering by also allowing same-sex couples to receive the sacrament of marriage."

5. principle of human dignity (*"Always act in such a way that you respect and protect the dignity of all people"*): The dignity of a person includes being accepted in their being and identity without restriction. If queer people are denied the sacrament of marriage, the church violates their dignity by treating their relationships and their love as inferior. In contrast, a humane maxim for action would be: "We respect and protect the dignity of every person by making the sacrament of marriage accessible to all couples without distinction."

6th Utilitarian principle (*"Act in such a way that you promote the greatest possible happiness of the greatest possible number of people"*): The goal of this principle is to promote happiness and well-being for as many people as possible. Denying marriage to queer couples reduces the happiness and well-being of those affected without benefiting anyone. The better maxim for action would therefore be utilitarian: *"We also grant the sacrament of marriage to same-sex couples in order to promote happiness, social participation and well-being for as many people as possible."*

7th principle of love of neighbor (*"Love your neighbor as yourself."*): This Christian principle demands unconditional acceptance and love. If the church denies queer people the sacrament, it is not acting in love, but in rejection. A maxim based on love of neighbor would be: "We treat queer couples with the same loving acceptance and support as we ourselves want to be loved and supported, and administer the sacrament to them."

8. discourse ethics (Habermas: *"Act according to norms that everyone could agree to in a free discourse"*): Discourse ethics calls for understanding, consensus and dialog. A decision against marriage for queer couples is not a consensus-oriented decision, but a dogmatic-hierarchical one. In a free discourse, the majority would probably speak out in favor of an inclusive practice that does not discriminate against anyone. The discursive ethical maxim would therefore be: "We decide in open dialog for a norm that is fair to everyone and therefore also allow sacramental marriage for same-sex couples."

9. principle of empathy and compassion (*"Act with empathy and compassion and put yourself in the other person's shoes"*): This principle calls for empathically putting oneself in the shoes of those affected. By denying queer couples the sacrament of marriage, the church is failing in precisely this respect: it is showing a lack of empathy and sensitivity. It would be empathic to recognize the happiness and value of these relationships and to act accordingly . The empathic maxim for action would be: "We put ourselves in the shoes of queer couples, understand their desire for acceptance and dignity and act compassionately by also granting them the sacrament of marriage."

In summary, it can be said that the Church's current practice of denying queer couples the sacrament of marriage *violates all of* these important ethical principles. A reflective, ethically responsible attitude would therefore necessarily mean no longer excluding queer couples, but allowing them the sacrament of marriage on an equal footing.

That the Catholic Church fails in all nine of the ethical principles outlined above - the Golden Rule, Kant's Categorical Imperative, responsibility, lesser evil, human dignity, utilitarianism, charity, discourse ethics and empathy - in relation to queer couples and the sacrament of marriage is a clear sign that there is a profound ethical and theological malaise here. Such a fundamental and comprehensive deviation from recognized basic ethical principles shows that the Catholic Church is currently unable or unwilling to meet the ethical standards that it itself publicly represents and preaches.

The urgent need for action for Rome and the head of the Church - if it still wants to be taken seriously as such - lies on various levels:

First: Theological re-evaluation: The Vatican urgently needs to carry out a thorough theological re-evaluation of the doctrine of marriage. A differentiated, serious and transparent reflection on what love, relationship and sacrament really mean is unavoidable. Rome should make it clear that the quality of a relationship does not depend on the gender constellation, but on fidelity, responsibility and mutual commitment. To this end, it is necessary to consult theological expertise from academia and pastoral practice. Within one to two years at the most, comprehensive expert commissions should formulate results that contain concrete proposals on how to theologically substantiate an inclusive sacramental marriage for queer couples.

Secondly, take dialog and plurality seriously: The Catholic Church should immediately initiate a transparent and open dialog process in which queer people and their families are directly involved. This is not about symbolic alibi events, but about a serious culture of discussion. Open forums, talks with those affected and discussions at local, regional and global level must take place within the next few months in order to reach a consensus-oriented solution. Rome should create binding guidelines and supporting structures within a year to enable and promote this dialog worldwide.

Third, an official statement and apology: Since the Church has caused significant suffering, marginalization and discrimination, Rome should officially release a clear statement within a year publicly acknowledging and taking responsibility for wrong decisions regarding queer people. There needs to be a clear acknowledgement that past practices have been discriminatory and wrong, coupled with a sincere apology to those affected. This would be a decisive step towards regaining credibility and restoring lost trust.

Fourthly: Immediate pastoral measures: Parallel to the theological and dialogical reappraisal, immediate practical steps are needed to reduce discrimination and provide pastoral support to queer people and couples. This includes immediate instructions from Rome that queer couples are explicitly and openly welcomed in church communities and that their relationships are explicitly valued and recognized. Marriage ceremonies for queer couples should be made officially possible in the short term (within a year) in order to make it clear that queer partnerships are respected and supported by the church.

Fifth: Adaptation of church law: The church must make fundamental adjustments to church law within a maximum time frame of three years. The canon law provisions that currently discriminate against same-sex couples and exclude them from the sacrament of marriage must be revised. This adjustment should be made by means of a papal decision or at a synod specifically convened to make binding decisions on issues of equality, gender justice and queer inclusion - if the head of the church does not consider himself strategically capable of making such decisions.

Sixth: Sustainable education and awareness-raising work: Parallel to the theological and legal changes, a broad educational initiative is needed, to be established within the next two to four years. Church employees, priests, bishops and especially teachers and pastoral staff must be intensively trained and sensitized to act in a non-discriminatory and inclusive manner. Rome should develop, fund and implement binding educational programs worldwide as soon as possible.

Seventh: Long-term cultural change: In order to ensure that the Catholic Church acts in an ethically responsible and humane manner in the future, a comprehensive change in church culture is required in the medium term. Overcoming patriarchal, discriminatory and authoritarian structures is imperative. Within the next few years, the Church should establish a new culture that is characterized by transparency, openness and responsibility - from the parish level to the highest management levels of the Vatican institutions.

The failure of the Catholic Church to adhere to the nine ethical maxims means that the Pope in Rome must act urgently and comprehensively. In the short term, the official apology, allowing marriages and a clear public statement are on the agenda. In the medium term (two to five years), the dialog process, theological reassessment and adjustments to canon law must take place. In the long term (up to five years), a sustainable change in church culture is required so that the church is actually in line with its own ethical principles in the future and queer people are finally given justice and recognition - through the sacrament of marriage when marrying queer couples.

In order for individuals to change their attitude and act in an ethically responsible, open and respectful way when dealing with homosexual and queer couples, and ultimately gain a better and clearer ability to judge love, they can implement and internalize the following concrete steps:

A) Conscious self-reflection: First of all, people should honestly question their own inner attitudes. This includes identifying prejudices and stereotypical assumptions about queer couples and recognizing where they come from. Am I open to diversity, or am I shaped by fears and prejudices? By realizing that our attitudes are often culturally shaped and not rational, we have the opportunity to change them.

B) Practicing empathy and perspective-taking: An important step is to consciously put yourself in the shoes of queer people: How would I feel if I were denied recognition of my love? Empathy strengthens the understanding that every form of love based on mutual respect, loyalty and responsibility is valuable - regardless of gender or sexual orientation.

C) Seek encounters and dialog: An effective way to change attitudes is to seek direct exchange with queer people and get to know the reality of their lives. Personal encounters make it possible to break down prejudices and authentically recognize how similar we are in our desires for love, recognition and happiness. This makes abstract ethical principles comprehensible and practicable in everyday life.

D) Informing and expanding knowledge: Better judgment grows through solid knowledge about queer identities and relationships. This includes engaging with scientific, theological and ethical positions. Anyone who knows that homosexuality and queer identities have long been scientifically recognized as natural variants of human sexuality loses the basis for prejudice and recognizes that, ethically speaking, all people and relationships have equal dignity.

E) Applying the "Golden Rule" and Kant's imperative in everyday life: A crucial step is to consciously apply the "Golden Rule" *("How would I feel if my relationship were rejected?")* and Kant's imperative *("Is my attitude universally justifiable?")* in everyday life. This means actively thinking about how you would like to be treated in situations and acting accordingly: Treating every love as respectfully as you would want your own to be treated.

F) Take responsibility (Hans Jonas): Individuals should recognize that they bear responsibility - not only for themselves, but for society as a whole. An ethically responsible attitude means making a conscious contribution to creating an inclusive, humane environment. This includes taking a public stance against discrimination and actively standing up for the rights of queer couples.

G) Take human dignity as a yardstick: Every ethical decision in dealing with other people should be consistently based on human dignity. In relation to queer couples, this means remembering that dignity belongs equally to every person - regardless of their sexual orientation. This requires continuous self-examination: Am I acting in a way that respects and preserves the dignity of others?

H) Living mercy and appreciation: A respectful approach to queer people and their relationships automatically follows from an inner attitude of mercy and appreciation. It means not excluding people, but actively recognizing that their love is just as valuable and legitimate as our own. Compassion also means expressing loving care and acceptance in conversations, gestures and encounters.

I) Developing resilience and courage: Ultimately, it is necessary to be self-confident and resilient in order to remain true to one's own ethical convictions - even if the environment is not yet ready. It means taking a courageous stance, openly supporting queer couples and speaking out against existing prejudices and discrimination, even if this can be uncomfortable. In the long term, resilience strengthens the ability to act consistently and ethically.

By putting these nine steps into practice and making them part of their everyday life, people will gain a clear ethical judgment in the long term that is characterized by openness, empathy, a sense of responsibility and respect for the dignity of every human being. They will no longer have unanswered ethical questions when they meet a loving couple - regardless of whether this couple is heterosexual, homosexual or queer in any other way. Instead, they will automatically react with understanding, respect and appreciation because they will have realized that love in all its forms is equally valuable, equally worthy and equally valid.

Literature and films can inspire: For example, reading the story of a person who followed their conscience despite resistance can encourage you to examine your own attitude. Spiritual practices such as meditation or prayer can train the inner voice by providing space for *self-exploration* and clarifying the image of God. In this way, a reliable conscience grows step by step, which you can fall back on in moral dilemmas.

Last but not least, individual skills development also includes *self-care* and balance: if you want to take care of others, you also have to take good care of yourself. This includes taking your own needs seriously (rest, healthy boundaries, physical and mental well-being) so that you don't burn out. Here you can ask yourself: *Where do I have to say "no" in order not to give up on myself?* - in line with the insight that you don't have to be a *superhuman*. A Christian view emphasizes that we should *not* be *heroes, but people.* Accepting our own limits and seeking help when necessary is part of a mature self-acceptance. Those who practise this remain capable of acting in the long term and retain the strength to remain true to their values.

Didactic methods: teaching in the classroom and community

In order to pass on these skills to others - whether at school, university or in church educational work - *holistic and practical methods* are needed. Didactically, the first priority is to create a safe space for reflection and dialog. Teachers can, example, initiate discussions on questions such as *"Can you accept yourself, even when you are taking your first steps?"* or *"Where do you encounter injustice and a lack of human rights in your environment and in your community?".* Through such discussions, participants learn to *exchange perspectives* and justify moral judgments. *Lifeworld orientation* is important: cases and examples from the real world of experience of the learners are most likely to hit home.

Concrete exercises and teaching units could look like this:

- **Scenic play and role reversal:** In a unit on conscience, a teacher could have the students act out a moral dilemma situation - such as a case of theft, bullying or civil courage. Through role-playing, the participants experience first-hand the inner conflicts that arise when you have to choose between looking away or intervening. In the follow-up discussion, they reflect on what the *"inner voice"* was in the situation and how it felt to do the right thing (or not to do it). Such methods promote empathy and *ethical decision-making skills* because they appeal to both head and heart.

- **Biography and case work:** Stories of real people who have stood up for their convictions can serve as *case studies*. For example, the story of a whistleblower who could no longer tolerate abuses in her company and therefore risked her job - what does this tell us about conscience and courage? Or a story from the Bible such as that of the Good Samaritan, which becomes an impetus for discussion: *Who are the "overlooked" today, and how can we act?* The learners work in groups to work out what they learn from such stories about guilt, responsibility and charity. It is important to draw parallels with their own lives: *"Where could I be the Samaritan? Have I perhaps also been the priest who passed by? Where did I not pass by? Where did I support my network with a queer person?"*.

- **Exercises of conscience:** One methodological building block can be the *formation of conscience on a small scale*. For example, students could be asked to anonymously write down a situation in which they felt guilty (without naming names). These notes are collected and read aloud (without exposing them). Together, there is a gentle discussion about which feelings occur (shame, remorse, fear) and how they can be dealt with constructively. Alternatively, moral decision questions can be asked: *"Imagine your friend has done something wrong. Do you cover up or do you report it?"* - and let them discuss what their conscience advises. Such conversations make abstract concepts tangible and show that *everyone struggles with moral conflicts* and that no one is alone.

- **Project work and service learning:** Projects in which learners become active are particularly suitable for socio-ethical topics. For example, a *project against discrimination* at school: the class works together to develop an action (such as an exhibition or a workshop day) on racism and exclusion. They go through the tried and tested three-step *process of seeing - judging - acting*: First, they look closely at where exclusion happens in everyday school life; then they *judge* why this is wrong against the background of human rights and Christian charity; finally, they *act* by developing measures to show courage and promote a climate of appreciation. This action-oriented approach, based on the *"See-Judge-Act"* method, for example, not only trains learners' minds, but also their energy. A *social internship* can have a similar effect: students or pupils spend a few days in a social institution (homeless charity, sheltered workshop etc.) with a questionnaire for interviews, for , and then reflect on what they have learned about justice, compassion and the limits of individual performance. Such experiences shape their conscience and sensitize them to *structural problems* (such as poverty or exclusion) that they might not have noticed from a distance.

- **Rituals and reflection:** In a church context or in university chaplaincy, rituals can be included that make dealing with guilt and forgiveness tangible. One example is a *reconciliation path*: during Lent, teachers or pastoral care workers design several stations where participants can lay down stones (as a symbol of burdens), write a letter of forgiveness to themselves, light a candle for someone else, etc. Such exercises combine spiritual dimensions with personal reflection. Such exercises combine spiritual dimensions with personal reflection. *Meditation exercises* in class - such as a dream journey in which one encounters one's own conscience as a person and enters into conversation - can also be used creatively to stimulate inner processes.

An *inspiring and appreciative tone* is crucial in all of these methods. Teachers themselves should deal with the topic authentically and also be allowed to indicate their own limitations or previous learning processes. This creates a climate in which learning takes place at eye level. First steps can be seen as learning opportunities. Didactically, this means *starting with first steps before perfectionism*. After all, developing skills in this area is a lifelong process that cannot be completed after one unit - but you can plant important seeds and take the first steps.

Good practice examples

Good practice shows how theoretical concepts come to life. Here are some *examples* from different contexts:

Example 1: Class without exclusion - a school project on charity. At a secondary school, a religion teacher initiated the *"Class without exclusion"* project. The starting point was an incident of bullying in the classroom. Instead of just sanctioning , the teacher used the moment as a learning opportunity: together with the pupils, she worked on the topics of *empathy* and *responsibility* in workshops. In a role play, some took on the role of the bullied, others the role of the perpetrator or the one looking the other way - which left a lasting impression on many. The class then drew up a *class charter* in which they set out how they want to treat each other. Everyone signed the pledge to stand by those who are weaker and to state their own boundaries before frustration turns into aggression. This project is an example of how social and emotional competence can be increased through experience-based learning. The students developed more self-confidence (some later spoke openly about their own insecurities instead of hiding them behind aggression) and a sharper conscience towards injustice in everyday school life. The project received a lot of recognition from parents and school management and was repeated in subsequent years with new classes.

Example 2: "Steps into the open" - seminar for prospective clergy. A voluntary seminar was offered at a theological college that dealt explicitly with personal guilt and liberation. The course called *"Schritte ins Freie"* was aimed at students of theology and prospective clergy who wanted to look at their own biography in the light of *grace and responsibility*. In this seminar, there were units on *conscience formation* (with texts by theologians such as Dietrich Bonhoeffer on the "cost of discipleship" and from the psychological side on feelings of guilt), but also very practical exercises. In one session, each participant wrote a letter to a person they had wronged - without the intention of sending it, but to confront their own guilt. Another session focused on *self-care*: the students were asked to draw up a weekly schedule that included time for their own spirituality, relaxation and friends as well as service to others. The seminar was accompanied by counseling sessions in which self-doubt and vocation issues were discussed openly. Many participants reported that they emerged stronger from this course: They had learned that *admitting their own weaknesses* does not contradict being a good pastor - on the contrary, it makes them more human and credible. This good practice example shows how spaces can be created in the training of religious education teachers and clergy to combine personal maturation and professional ethics.

Example 3: "School without racism - school with courage" as a practiced responsibility. Many schools across Germany have joined the *"School without Racism - School with Courage"* network. This is more than just a title - it is a *commitment by* the whole school to actively combat discrimination and promote respectful coexistence. At one participating school, for , a student working group was formed that regularly plans activities: From workshops on everyday racism, to project days on the topic of *social justice*, to pat:inships with refugees in the community. In lessons and school life, the topic of *acting fairly* is made visible time and again - for example through posters with positive messages or the joint celebration of diversity festivals. Teachers report that this initiative has led to a noticeable **cultural change:** Students are more likely to intervene if someone is being discriminated against, and they also dare to address social grievances in class. This case study illustrates how competence-oriented value formation (empathy, civil courage, sense of responsibility) can be implemented at school level. The school practises on a small scale what applies to society at large: *everyone bears responsibility for ensuring that dignity and justice are practised.*

Example 4: Parish project "Sharing guilt - easing burdens". In one parish, the pastoral team recognized that many people were dealing with unresolved feelings of guilt and life burdens - whether it was a single mother who felt guilty about not having enough time for her children, or a business owner who had to make tough staff cuts and was now plagued by remorse. A community project called *"Sharing guilt - easing burdens"* was therefore launched. The core was a *series of talks* on four evenings. Each evening began with a short impulse: one evening a therapist spoke about the difference between *guilt* and *shame*, another time an older member of the congregation talked about the experience of confession and the liberating effect of absolution. Afterwards, there were moderated discussions in small groups in which the participants could - voluntarily - share their own experiences. This was accompanied by a prayer circle where intercession was made for personal conversion and renewal. The project created a space in which *conscience formation and pastoral care* went hand in hand: Some participants found the courage to address long-repressed conflicts and ask for forgiveness; others learned to judge themselves more graciously and truly accept God's forgiveness. At the end, there was a service of repentance in which symbolic slips of paper with transgressions written on them were burned - a sign of a new beginning. This example of good practice shows how the congregation and church can make a practical contribution to people experiencing both *personal healing* in relation to guilt and developing a stronger sense of ethical behavior (as many resolved to change certain behaviors in the future, e.. to treat employees more fairly). Such initiatives can serve as a model for other communities to remove the taboos surrounding guilt and forgiveness while promoting responsible action.

Exercise on biography and case work

Exercise on biography and case work entitled *"Priests who passed by - and those who stopped"*. The exercise combines biblical storytelling, modern case studies and biographical reflection. It is ideal for religious education lessons (Sek I/II), for Konfi work or workshops on ethics, conscience and responsibility.

🕐 Exercise objective: The students deal with real and fictional stories in which people have acted courageously or indifferently. They analyze the motives, draw parallels to the biblical story of the Good Samaritan and reflect on their own role in everyday life between looking the other way and moral courage.

📌 Title of the exercise: "Priests who passed by - and those who stopped"

⧗ Time frame: approx. 60 minutes

☐ Introduction (10 min): The teacher reads (or shows via video/comic) the story of the *Good Samaritan (Luke 10:25-37)*.

Impulse question for the class: "Who acts courageously in the story - who acts fearfully or indifferently? And why?"

🗄 Work phase - group work (25 min): The learners are given two case histories with different outcomes:

😊💼 Case 1 - Marie, the whistleblower: Marie works in the HR department of a church organization. She learns that reports of sexual assault within the organization are systematically ignored. After several failed internal discussions, she turns to a national counseling center. As a result, she loses her job. She does not talk about it publicly - but she knows that she acted according to her conscience.

Questions about case work:

- Why was it so difficult for Marie to act?
- What makes her move courageous?
- Who is the "injured party" in this story - and who is the "priest who passed by"?

🏠 Case 2 - Jakob, the parish priest: Jakob leads a rural parish. A gay confirmand confides in him that he is being bullied because of his sexuality. Jakob is deeply affected - but he remains silent for fear of causing tension within the church council and the congregation. He later learns that the boy has left the congregation. Jakob begins to question his silence.

Questions about case work:

- What role does Jacob play in the story?
- What prevents him from acting?
- What would it take for him to become a "Samaritan"?

✏ Reflection and transfer (15 min): The students answer the central reflection question in individual work or in their group:

"Where have I myself ever been like the Good Samaritan - or like the priest who passed by?"

They either write short personal scenes ("I remember ...") or talk about them in small groups (voluntary).

👤 Closing round (10 min): In the plenary session, volunteers can report on what they have learned. It is possible to conclude with a quote or spiritual impulse: *"Not everyone can do everything. But everyone can do something - and sometimes that's exactly what counts"* or *"Charity doesn't start with heroic deeds - but often with simple ones: Don't pass by."*

💭 Competencies that are promoted:

- Ethical judgment
- Reflection of conscience
- Empathy and perspective-taking
- Reference to one's own living environment
- Biblical-ethical interpretation of everyday experiences

Figure17: Marie, the whistleblower.

Reflection and outlook: Modern perspectives on guilt, ethics and responsibility

Nowadays, there is a change in the way we think about responsibility, human rights and ethical behavior - and this change should be actively embraced by the church and education. On the one hand, *today's perspectives* emphasize the individual psychological aspect: guilt is no longer seen solely as a legal and moral transgression that entails punishment, but as an *experience* that must be processed. Psychology and education point out that too much unresolved guilt can lead to self-rejection and illness, while dealing with it in a reflective way contributes to maturation. Accordingly, education should be based on the *ability to take the first steps towards moving on.* In a modern educational environment, learners gain the understanding that *making mistakes is human; what matters is what I make of them.* This attitude promotes *self-responsibility instead of external control.* Instead of merely fearing external norms, young people learn to trust their conscience and develop inner convictions. The statement *"Man has a conscience; the formation of conscience is necessary"* is explicitly emphasized in modern religious curricula - i.e. individuals are trusted to become capable of judgement and insight themselves instead of being controlled by dogmatic pressure.

At the same time, modern perspectives are broadening the focus from the individual to the *social structure.* Traditionally, guilt was often understood in terms of individual morality in church preaching (keyword "personal sins"). Today, the *structural dimension of guilt and sin* is increasingly being recognized: Social sin mechanisms - racism, non-existent human rights, environmental destruction, unjust distribution of goods - involve the individual, even if they have not subjectively carried out any "evil" actions. This insight stems from liberation theology, among other things, and has found its way into the church's consciousness

For the church, this means that it must critically question its own structures. In the course of current reform processes (e.. the synodal path in Germany), there has been talk of *"structural sin" within the church* - for example, where abuse of power and discrimination have been systemically encouraged. An adequate view here requires transparency, reappraisal and change. In reflecting on our topic, this means that learners should understand that guilt is not just something that *they* can have *personally* before God or fellow human beings, but that we are all involved in larger contexts. However, this does not lead to fatalism, but to a *shared responsibility* to make these structures more humane and just.

What needs to change or deepen in *the church and educational practice* if these modern insights are taken seriously? First of all, *guilt* should be de-tabooed - moving away from a purely guilt-based, fear-driven approach towards a healing approach. In the church, it was long said that in order to be forgiven, you had to repent and confess your sins - which makes sense in terms of content, but was often done in an atmosphere of fear and shame . In future, the moment of *healing and reconciliation* should be emphasized more strongly. When someone recognizes their guilt, the church should act less as a judge and more as a *supportive community that helps them* take the next step and make amends where possible. This paradigm shift - *from the moral pulpit to guidance* - makes the church more accessible to people today who are looking for meaning and ethical orientation but do not need dogmatic finger-wagging, but rather *encouragement and a sense of purpose*. It is fitting that many church initiatives today focus on pastoral discussions, life counseling and social projects instead of preaching dogmas.

A corresponding change should take place in education: Religious education and ethics classes can be places where *conscience formation and social awareness* go hand in hand. A modern curriculum integrates topics such as human rights, sustainability, diversity and mental health. For example, the topic of *dealing with failure* could be explicitly addressed so that students learn to deal with feelings of guilt or missing first steps without condemning themselves. Or *examples of moral courage could be* dealt with in order to show what ethical action in society can look like in concrete terms - in the first steps. This type of content expands the classic canon, which in the past mainly consisted of church commandments or purely biblical stories, to include *current issues*: This also includes addressing how a priest can find his same-sex love *by taking first steps*. After all, only failing to take the first steps can be a sin in love - just as it is for civil courage.

Figure18: World-Shaper with head, heart and hand.

Head, Heart and Hand

The picture entitled "Weltgestalter:in mit Kopf, Herz und Hand" is a colourful, stylized illustration that visualizes the concept of holistic education - inspired by the reform pedagogical guiding principle of promoting people who take responsibility for the world with intellect, emotion and energy. At the center of the illustration are three young people in front of a large globe, which symbolizes the world and our shared responsibility: on the left, a young man with dark skin is reading a book while formulating a thought with a raised index finger. He symbolizes the head, i.e. knowledge, education, reflection and insight. A girl with red hair stands in the middle at , holding a large heart in front of her chest. She embodies the heart, i.e. compassion, empathy, love and an ethical sense of responsibility. On the right is a young man with tools (hammer and wood) and an easel. He represents the hand, i.e. practical action, design, implementation and the ability to act in everyday life and in society. In the background is a harmonious, green landscape with trees, houses, a wind turbine and a rising sun - symbols of sustainability, the future and hope. The picture title "Head, heart and hand" is placed centrally at the bottom and clearly summarizes the picture's message: Education is not just about imparting knowledge, but about strengthening the whole person - in thought, feeling and action - and thus becoming a shaper of a better, fairer and sustainable world.

In addition, the distribution of roles is changing: teachers are becoming more like *moderators and initiators*, while learners participate more actively and help shape projects (as shown above in the good practice examples). Competence orientation means not only transferring knowledge, but also practicing skills. This concept, which has long been standard in general education, should also apply to theological education. For example, it calls for religious education to contribute to the *ability to judge, empathy and the ability to engage in dialog*, instead of just asking for catechism knowledge.

A *more modern view of ethical and religious or Christian and universal action* also involves looking beyond one's own tradition. Church and school should promote interreligious and intercultural dialog in order to enable shared ethical learning. Many values - justice, compassion, human dignity - are not Christian monopolies, but universal. When learners understand this, an *inclusive* conscience grows: one that thinks beyond group and denominational boundaries for the good of all. This is essential in a pluralistic society.

In conclusion, it can be said that the ability to accept oneself and act on an ethical basis is a core competence for a successful personal life and responsible coexistence. At a time when individualism and global crises are equally present, we need people who have both *a compassionate heart* for themselves and others, as well as *an alert mind* that recognizes injustice and courageously stands up to it *with their hands and actions*. Education and the church have a joint responsibility to promote this development of skills - in an inspiring, clear and practical way. If more and more people succeed in combining a healthy self-esteem with a trained conscience, a lot could change: guilt would no longer be concealed as a paralyzing burden, but used as an impetus for reconciliation and improvement. Ethical action would not be misunderstood as the duty of "saints", but as *everyone's contribution* to a more humane world. In the church, such an attitude would mean that mercy and justice would remain the highest principles - structural sins would be tackled and service to others would be placed above the preservation of power. In education, it would mean training young people to become *encouraged world shapers* who know how to use their heads, hearts and hands. In short: a modern conscience, coupled with self-acceptance, is forward-looking - for each individual and for the community. The task of teaching and learning this remains a worthwhile challenge for us all.

Exercise 9:
Designing images of God creatively - opening up new spiritual spaces

This exercise deals with the creative design of images of God in order to open up new spiritual spaces and enable diversity in faith. The aim is to make learners aware that all concepts of God are limited and changeable. Teaching objectives include understanding the imagery of God, becoming aware of the diversity and changeability of images of God, deepening the personal relationship with God, getting to know diverse biblical images of God and promoting respect and openness towards different ideas.

Competencies to be developed include spiritual imagination (the ability to grasp God in a variety of images), creative visualization (the ability to creatively represent inner ideas), the ability to tolerate and allow diversity, the ability to reflect on one's own image of God, the ability to engage in dialogue and communication, and the ability to criticize and judge one-dimensional or problematic images of God.

Personal learning paths promote daily reflection rituals, spiritual imagination exercises, creative design and sharing in the community. In religious education, methods such as creative imagination exercises, symbolic dialogs and physical forms of expression help to open up and critically reflect on biblical images.

- ***Learning and development objective:*** *The most essential personal ability is the spiritual power of imagination. The learning objective is to enable learners to creatively develop their inner images of God, to consciously reflect on them and to gain spiritual depth through a variety of images.*
- ***Good practice example:*** *A fantasy journey in which learners imagine God visually and then creatively paint or design their inner images. This method enables individual and diverse forms*

of expression of the relationship with God and promotes creative and spiritual competence.

- **Church support through:** Believers, clergy, priests or bishops can support by being open to diverse images of God in sermons, liturgical texts and congregational activities. They promote spiritual imagination through creative worship services and pastoral conversations that recognize and integrate diverse concepts of God.
- **Local budget use:** Financial resources could be used for creative workshops to design diverse images of God, materials for artistic and meditative exercises as well as fees for external speakers who convey diverse theological perspectives on images of God.
- **Adaptation of the curriculum at school:** The curriculum in religious education should explicitly promote diversity and creativity in dealing with images of God. Specifically, modules on creative visualization, reflecting on one's own ideas of God and dealing with different theological traditions and biblical images of God would be necessary. In this way, students can learn to develop and express images of God independently and critically.

How do you imagine God? Perhaps you think of the old man with a long beard on a cloud - a familiar image, but one that no longer helps many people. In our modern world, more and more people feel that traditional images of God are losing their plausibility. This makes it all the more important to develop new and diverse images of God. If we learn to shape images of God creatively, we can *open up new spiritual spaces* in our personal faith. A broader image of God leaves room for personal experiences, questions and doubts, and enables different people to find access to God.

In the following, the focus is on *how this competence to form a creative image of God can be promoted* - individually and especially in religious education. *Teaching objectives*, *skills* to be developed, practical *learning paths*, *didactic methods, good practice examples* from schools and churches as well as a *reflection* on the modern view of images of God that has been gained are highlighted.

Teaching objectives: Why diverse images of God?

In religious education as well as in personal faith practice, there are several *teaching objectives* that are linked to the development of diverse images of God:

- **Understanding the imagery of God:** Learners should understand that we can only ever speak about God in images, signs and symbols. God is greater than all our ideas - every image can only ever show a small part of God. This also gives rise to the biblical reference to images: no image can fully capture God so as not to make a false claim to absoluteness. This awareness protects us from considering a single image of God to be absolute.
- **Awareness of diversity and changeability:** A central goal is to recognize that people have different ideas about God and that this diversity is normal and enriching. No image of God is simply "right" or "wrong" - rather, every idea reflects personal experiences and cultural influences. Even children learn in this way, , that *different images of God can exist side by side* and can change over the course of their lives.

- **Deepen personal relationship with God:** By expressing their own image of God (e.g. in words or pictures), learners can become more aware of their relationship with God and develop it further. *The aim* is to promote a trusting, living relationship with God that has room for growth and new experiences.
- **Getting to know biblical images of God:** A variety of biblical names and metaphors of God (such as *rock, mother, light, shepherd, castle, comforting bear*, etc.) should be discovered and understood. In this way, learners recognize how rich the tradition of images of God is, and they can interpret the meaning of these images. This broadens the horizon beyond just one familiar image of God.
- **Promote respect and openness:** An important aspect of teaching is the attitude of respecting one's own and other people's ideas about God. Pupils should experience that their questions, doubts or even the statement "I don't believe in God" are taken seriously and accepted. This openness creates a trusting learning environment and at the same time reflects the diversity of human experiences of faith.
- **Enable critical questioning:** Finally, this also includes discussing *critical objections to images of God*. Learners should understand why rigid or one-sided images of God can be problematic - for example, if God is only seen as a punishing judge or exclusively in female form. Through such reflections, they learn to question their own images and correct them if necessary, instead of clinging to the "traditional image of God", which no longer applies to their lifeworld.

In summary, these teaching objectives should lay the foundation for learners *to be able to speak about God* without being restricted by narrow ideas. They should discover the variety of ways to talk about God and thus find *new approaches to faith*.

Competencies to be developed

In order to achieve these teaching objectives, certain **skills** are developed. It is about skills and attitudes that relate to dealing with concepts of God - in one's own life of faith and in dialog with others:

- **Spiritual imagination:** The ability to visualize God with *our inner imagination* is central. This *power of imagination* makes it possible to go beyond familiar images and dare to try something new. For example, learners practise imagining God not only as a king, but perhaps as a warming light, a loving mother or a friendly presence. A strong spiritual imagination helps them to *sense* God's presence in different images and thus deepen their own image of God. The variety of biblical images (such as God as a "fortress in times of trouble" or as a caring "mother in childbirth") can serve as inspiration here.

- **Creative visualization:** Closely related to this is the ability to *creatively visualize* inner ideas. Whether through painting, drawing, collages, sculptures, poetry or music - creative visualization means giving your own idea of God a form of expression. This ability strengthens the awareness of *how* one actually imagines God. Anyone who paints a picture, for example, may first notice which symbols (colors, shapes, figures) are important for their own image of God. Creative design makes faith more tangible and also promotes exchange: others can see what you have drawn or made and understand what moves you.

- **Tolerating and allowing diversity:** *Tolerance towards different images of God* is a key competence. Learners should practise allowing different ideas to stand side by side - both within themselves (in the course of their lives) and in the community. This means that they can listen to how others talk about God without immediately judging. They learn that *their* image of God is not the only possible one. This openness is particularly important in religiously pluralistic classes: in dialog with other denominations or religions, for example, it is necessary to be able to understand several approaches to God. Those who develop this competence ultimately recognize that *God cannot be pinned down to a single image* - and this is precisely where faith is enriched.

- **Ability to reflect:** The competence profile also includes being able to *reflect on one's own image of God*. This includes considering the origins of one's own ideas (family, childhood, church tradition, personal experiences, ideas about one's own sexual orientation) and understanding how they have changed. Learners develop the ability to ask themselves: *How has my image of God changed when I compare past and present ideas?* (This reflection can take place, for example, in an exercise in which young people draw images of God that they had in different phases of their lives on a timeline). It is equally important to reflect on the *situationality* of an image of God: Does my image hold up in times of crisis (such as the coronavirus pandemic)? Does it fit my values? Does it fit my sexual experience or orientation? By asking such questions, we learn to distinguish between image and reality and to recognize that God is ultimately greater than any image.

- **Dialogue and communication skills:** Talking creatively about images of God requires the ability to express oneself and to listen. It is therefore a skill to *communicate about one's own idea of God* - whether in writing, orally or artistically - *and to* have the ideas of others explained to them. Pupils practise putting their images into words: *"For me, God is like..."* and can explain their thoughts in discussions or presentations. At the same time, they learn to ask questions about the presentation of others and to listen without judging. This ability to engage in dialog promotes empathy and mutual understanding within the group.

- **Critical and judgmental skills:** Although diversity is desired, young people must also learn to *critically question images of God.* This competence means, for example, recognizing when an image of God is exclusionary for other people. Lessons can address how a "one-dimensional, cis-male, white image of God" excludes many. Learners should practise recognizing such one-sidedness and dealing with it constructively - for example by adding complementary images (e.g. female, same-sex oriented or culturally different images of God). This also includes being able to respond to critical questions from outside: for example, the projection thesis (*"You only made God up"*) or the suffering argument (*"Can God exist in the face of suffering?"*). Competent students can argue why they nevertheless believe in a loving

God - perhaps precisely *because* they have a multifaceted image of God that also takes into account silence, doubt and the otherness of God.

Through these skills, learners become *spiritually mature* overall: They have the imagination and expressiveness to live and communicate their faith authentically. They learn not to be afraid of unfamiliar images, but to see them as an *opportunity* to come closer to the mystery of God - which everyone can and should know.

Individual learning: Paths to a diverse image of God

So how can these skills be developed *individually*, i.e. outside the classroom? Here are some practical suggestions on how everyone can personally promote their *spiritual and creative development of God:*

- **Daily reflection rituals**: A simple way to start is to regularly take time to think about your own image of God. For example, you can keep a faith diary and work on questions such as: *"How did I experience God today?"* or *"Which image fits my feeling of God today?"*. On some days, God may seem like a good friend, on others he may seem as distant and mysterious as the universe. This self-reflection sharpens the awareness that one's own image of God is not rigid, but resonates with one's experiences.
- **Spiritual imagination exercises:** *Spiritual imagination exercises* help to create inner images. A tried and tested method is *Ignatian reflection* or an imaginary journey during prayer time: for example, imagine meeting God in a specific place. *What does God look like? What does he, she or it say?* You can lead such meditations yourself (with soft music in the background) or there are guided meditation texts available. It is important to record what you have experienced afterwards - for example by drawing or writing it down - in order to *become aware of* the *imagined image of God and let it take effect.*

Ignatian meditation (also known as "Ignatian contemplation" or "Ignatian meditation") is a spiritual method of meditation and reflection that goes back to Ignatius of Loyola (1491-1556), the founder of the Jesuit order. It is particularly anchored in Ignatius' "Spiritual Exercises".

Characteristics of Ignatian Reflection:

1. **Imagination (power of imagination):** Empathizing with biblical scenes or situations in one's own life through vivid imagination plays a central role. The aim is to use your own senses (seeing, hearing, feeling) to immerse yourself as intensively as possible in a biblical story or spiritual scene.

2. **Personal encounter with God**: Ignatius is concerned with an inner encounter between God and the person contemplating. This personal experience should deepen faith and lead to closeness to God.

3. **Structured approach**: The analysis follows a clear structure, often consisting of:

   o Preparation (creating peace, awareness of God's presence)

   o Empathize with the specific scene (e.g. a Gospel text)

   o Reflection and inner contemplation

   o Closing prayer and reflection (review)

4. **Affective perception**: Particular attention is paid to feelings and inner movements such as consolation (spiritual joy, peace, confidence) and desolation (restlessness, fears, doubts). St. Ignatius recommends observing these inner movements attentively and using them to gain clues for your personal life path and decisions.

5. **Decision-making (discernment of spirits):** One goal of Ignatian contemplation is to gain clarity in decision-making processes by consciously engaging with God's guidance and learning to discern between helpful (comforting) and hindering (disconsolate) impulses.

Typical sequence of an Ignatian meditation (briefly summarized):

- **Preparation**: Find a quiet place, pray, become calm inside.

- **Introduction**: Realize that you are in the presence of God, ask for openness.

- **Meditation (imagination):** Putting yourself concretely into a biblical scene (e.g. Jesus' encounter with people), perceiving it with all your senses, empathizing with it yourself.

- **Linger inwardly:** Let the scene take effect, perceive feelings and thoughts, talk to God about it.

- **Conclusion:** Prayer or personal exchange with God about the experience; subsequent reflection.

Ignatian contemplation has proven itself over the centuries and is still a widespread method of spiritual guidance and in the everyday spirituality of many people.

Ignatian reflection exercise of a queer person:

First, I find a quiet, protected place, take a deep breath and feel my body, my sensations. I become aware that God is present - not abstract, but concrete, approachable, loving, as a God who knows, lives and understands queer love. I imagine how this God becomes human in Jesus, how he experiences human feelings, longings and touches. I imagine how Jesus meets other men and how this encounter creates a deep closeness, recognition and connection that is characterized by love, appreciation and tenderness.

In my mind's eye, I see scenes in which Jesus is together with his disciples and I wonder what it could mean if these relationships were not just friendly, but were based on a special, deeper, even romantic affection. I notice how Jesus looks at other men with a loving gaze, feel his heartbeat, the warmth of his hand as he lays it on the shoulder of a disciple. I hear his voice, soft and clear, and perceive how a natural and sacred expression of queer love manifests itself in his gaze, his closeness, his affection.

In my heart, I allow this queer God to speak lovingly to me and tell me: "I know you, I understand your longings, your dreams, your love. Your love is good, true and holy, just as my love is good, true and holy." In this encounter, I allow God to gently touch and heal my longing, my hope, my desire for physical closeness, as he accepts me exactly as I am.

At the end of this reflection, I have an inner conversation with God: I thank him that he has come so close to me as a queer God and perhaps ask how I can integrate this love more strongly into my life. Finally, I say goodbye, grateful and strengthened in the fact that God's same-sex concept of love is part of my spiritual reality and that I am loved, supported and blessed in this reality.

- **Creative design at home:** You can also become *artistically active* outside of the classroom in order to develop new images of God. You could decide to do a creative activity once a week: e.g. take a Bible passage or a psalm and paint a picture that expresses the image of God in it (e.g. Psalm 23: God as shepherd). Or create a collage of magazine pictures that symbolize something divine (rays of light, people hugging each other, natural phenomena, etc.). It's not about works of art for the gallery, but about the process: *while creating, you intuitively feel what appeals to you or disturbs* you - perhaps you notice that you prefer to use abstract colors rather than a figure, or that you suddenly insert a female element. This is how your imagination grows.
- **Reading and learning from a variety of sources:** One way to expand your own thinking about God is to engage *with different theological voices.* This can mean reading books or articles that *present new images of God* - e.g. writings of feminist theology that describe God in female images, or mystical texts that use poetic images. You can also find inspiration outside of Christianity: For example, how does Sufism (Islamic mysticism) understand God? What images of the divine are there in Far Eastern religions? Such impulses can enrich your own image of God *without you having to give up your own faith.* On the contrary, you often recognize similarities and can *look beyond your own nose,* which again leads to more tolerance.
- **Prayer with symbols and names:** In personal devotions, you can experiment with *addressing God with different names or symbols.* Instead of always starting with "Dear God" or "Lord", you could pray: "Gracious Mother in heaven..." or "You eternal light...". This may sound unfamiliar at first, but it opens up new

feelings. Those who address God as Mother, for example, may feel a more intense sense of security; those who call on God as Light will pay more attention to glimmers of hope in everyday life. The use of objects in prayer - a candle as a symbol of God's light, a stone for God as a rock - can also make *the idea of God tangible to the senses*. Such rituals expand the inner image of God step by step.

- **Exchange in the community:** After all, you also learn a lot individually when you *talk to others about beliefs*. In an intimate group (circle of friends, home group, youth group), you can have a targeted discussion: Everyone describes how they imagine God. Just listening often opens up new perspectives (*"I've never thought of it like that before!"*). The important thing here is to keep an open mind, ask questions (*"What does it mean to you that God is like...?"*) and not try to convince each other. The exchange can show *how differently and personally God is experienced* - and yet you may also be able to hear God's voice for your own life in the stories of others.

What all these individual learning paths have in common is that they are *active and experiential*. You *do* something - paint, write, meditate, talk - and this is precisely how you develop the ability to *perceive and represent God in a variety of ways*. It is not about theoretical definitions, but about a lively, playful approach to the content of faith. Over time, an inner *"toolbox"* of images and symbols grows from which one can draw in various situations in life. This personal enrichment then radiates back into church life and teaching when people share their experiences.

Support in religious education: methods and exercises

The development of skills can be systematically and creatively guided in religious education lessons at school. Teachers have the opportunity here to use suitable methods to awaken and encourage pupils' spiritual imagination. It is important to adopt a didactic approach that is exploratory, appreciative and varied . Below are some methods and specific exercises that religious education teachers have used successfully:

Introductory ritual: make people aware of existing images of God

At the beginning of a series of lessons on "images of God", it is a good idea to collect the *ideas that* the learners *already have*. This creates awareness and enhances the knowledge that the students bring with them. Two tried and tested examples:

- **Brainstorming with word cards:** The teacher asks the question: *"What words, images or comparisons can you think of about God?"* All the pupils' spontaneous associations (e.g. "father", "light", "protector", "question mark", "love", "old man", "everywhere and nowhere", etc.) are noted down on index cards. The cards are then arranged visibly together in the room - for example, sorted thematically or grouped around a central term. This exercise alone shows the *range in the class*. It can be very diverse, from familiar images to critical statements. Nothing is judged, everything is allowed to stand for the time being. This *transparency of ideas* serves as a starting point for the further learning process. (A variation: instead of words, prepared pictures or symbols can also be placed in the middle, from which everyone chooses one that corresponds to their own idea of God).

- **Working with drawn pictures:** A fascinating variation is to bring real *children's and young people's drawings of God* into the lessons. They can be drawn and defined by an AI. The pictures can be hung up in the classroom - deliberately *in very different ways*: some show God in human form (e.g. on a throne), others symbolically (e.g. as a light or heart), still others were thought-provoking or completely abstract. Then each student chooses the image that comes closest to their own idea (or that they want to explore). In small groups, the young people then discuss *why* they have chosen this particular image, what they like about it or what is strange about it. This method immediately creates a personal involvement: everyone sees themselves reflected in a picture and starts talking about it. This makes it possible to experience *how differently God can be seen - and* that some motifs recur. At the end, all the pictures were looked at in plenary and the groups explained what they had discussed. The class recorded important results and open questions on posters. This created a *common learning basis* that could be referred to again and again later in class.

Both forms of introduction aim to *make the diversity of concepts of God visible* and to involve the pupils directly. They also signalize this: Here, you can be honest about what you think - doubts and unusual ideas explicitly included.

Creative imagination exercises in the classroom

Once the topic has been introduced, specific *exercises* can be carried out *to expand the images of God. Creative and holistic methods* in particular help students to develop new ideas:

- **Imaginary journey with design:** A proven method to stimulate the spiritual power of imagination is the *imaginary journey*. Teachers read out a calming, visual story that sends the young people on an inner journey. In one lesson (class 6), for example, the following impulse was used: *"Imagine you discover a precious book with pictures of God in a special place. You leaf through it - which pictures do you see? Finally you come across the one picture that shows God as you imagine him to be. Take it out and look at it carefully...".* After this meditative journey, the pupils were given the task: *"Create the picture you discovered in the book"* - in other words, they painted or drew the picture they had seen inwardly. It was deliberately emphasized that there was no right or wrong and that everyone was free to put their own ideas on paper. The young people hung the results at the front of the board at and then looked at them together. In the discussion, everyone was allowed to explain **why the picture turned out the way it did** and what it means. The class was amazed: for example, there were pictures of God as a helping hand, as a colorful rainbow, as an eye in a storm or as a loving embrace - all very different! It quickly became clear *that no two images are the same and yet each one has its justification*, because no one has ever seen God in the flesh!
- **Symbolic dialog and body language:** Images of God do not always have to be drawn; they can also be developed through *symbolic actions*. One possible exercise is the *"God statue"*

dialog: Various everyday objects or images (e.g. a stone, a candle, a mirror, a cross, an empty bowl) are distributed. The pupils choose an object and think about it: *How could this show my image of God?* Then everyone presents their object and explains their association (e.g. *"I chose the stone because God is very firm and reliable for me - like a rock."* Or: *"I take the mirror: although it shows my face, it reminds me that there is something of God in everyone."*). Such performative elements make concepts of God *tangible* and appeal to the head, heart and hand at the same time.

- **Open up biblical images:** Of course, this also includes working with biblical texts in order to get to know *classic images of God* and to develop new ones based on them. Group work is a good way to do this: Each group is given a biblical passage in which a particular image of God appears - for example a psalm (God as shepherd, Psalm 23 or God as protective fortress, Psalm 18), a prophecy (God as mother, Isaiah 66:13 or as loving bear, Hos 13:8), a parable (the father in the parable of the prodigal son, Luke 15) or a theophany narrative (God in the burning bush, Exodus 3). The groups read the text and answer key questions: *How is God described here? What comparisons or characteristics are there? What does this image mean for the people in the story?* They then creatively present what they have found out - for example with a small poster with symbols and key words.

All presentations and interpretations of God together result in a **panorama of biblical images of God** that shows the diversity in the Bible itself. The learners see: Even the biblical authors had different experiences - God is comforting like a mother *and* powerful like a king *and* caring like a shepherd etc. In the discussion, you can then ask: *Which of these biblical images speaks to you personally?* Is there one that has surprised you in a new way? This builds a bridge from the texts to your own ideas.

Figure 19 : Fish is Fish .

- **Critical examination (Feuerbach, "Fish is Fish"):** In addition to creative activity, a *critical view* is also part of comprehensive competence. This can initially be approached in an age-appropriate way - e.g. with the well-known picture book *"Fish is Fish"* (Leo Lionni) in elementary school. This story was used in a Year 2 class to help children understand that every living creature imagines the unknown according to its own experiences. The fish imagines all animals as fish - and the children realized: *"We humans often imagine God as human, just as the fish imagines everything in fish form."*

This "aha" experience helped them to understand that our image of God is shaped by our limited experiences, and it made them open to *unfamiliar concepts of God*. In higher grades, you can go further philosophically: for example with Ludwig Feuerbach's criticism (*"Man created God in his own image"*) or Sigmund Freud's view (*belief in God as a wishful image of father protection*).

Ludwig Feuerbach formulated the central thesis critical of religion: *"It was not God who created man in his own image, but man who created*

God in his own image." By this, Feuerbach meant that religion was ultimately a projection of human wishes, desires and ideals. In his imagination, God embodies everything that appears desirable to man - goodness, love, justice, perfection - but only as a reflection of his own hopes. Thus, God was not a real existing being outside the human world, but an expression of human needs, a being created to provide comfort, orientation and meaning. Feuerbach's criticism aimed to expose religion as self-alienation and to lead people back to themselves: Instead of projecting their own positive powers onto God, people should recognize them as part of themselves and thereby gain autonomy.

Sigmund Freud viewed belief in God as a psychological projection of a deeply rooted human desire for a strong, protective father. In his perspective, religion arises from childhood needs for protection, security and authority, which people transfer from their early relationship with their father and project onto an imaginary, heavenly father figure. In this interpretation, God is an idealized image of a father who offers comfort, reduces anxiety and provides support. However, Freud also saw this as an immature form of coping with human fears and insecurities, a kind of collective illusion that ultimately had to be overcome in order to achieve emotional maturity and self-responsibility.

There are also psychological and religious studies approaches that interpret images of God not only as a projection of a father figure, but also as an expression of a deeply rooted human need for a protective mother figure. The psychoanalyst **Erich Fromm** in particular argued that God could also be seen as a symbol of maternal love and security. Fromm described the "mother religion" as a religious attitude in which God is primarily understood as an unconditionally loving, caring and protective entity, similar to a mother who offers her child security and protection.

Feminist theologies and approaches to the psychology of religion have also increasingly focused on the fact that people are just as likely to imagine God as a maternal figure and draw spiritual strength from this. **Luisa Muraro**, for example, refers to the need of many people for a spiritual representation of motherly love, which is reflected in the veneration of Mary or in ideas of the divine Sophia . Carl Gustav Jung also picked up on archetypal images of God in which maternal elements are present and emphasized that these representations are deeply rooted in the human psyche.

The projection of God as a protective, loving mother was certainly reflected upon and represents a recognized addition to Freud's classical, paternal view.

The idea of a queer God comes primarily from queer theology, which does not define God as unambiguously male, female or heteronormative, but as a figure who consciously transcends the rigid boundaries of gender, sexuality and identity.

Queer theological approaches argue that God is in itself an expression of diversity and ambiguity - a deity that cannot be clearly assigned, but remains fluid and open. God is conceived here not only as transcendent, but also as transgressive: he/she/it transcends social norms, gender roles and sexual boundaries, which means that people who place themselves outside of mainstream society feel particularly at home in this image of God.

Some queer theologians, such as **Patrick Cheng, Marcella Althaus-Reid** and **Linn Marie Tonstad**, emphasize that this idea is not simply an arbitrary projection, but actually draws on the biblical and theological tradition: the diversity and ambivalence in God's nature (such as his diverse, sometimes gender ambiguous representations in the Bible) allows and even supports a queer concept of God.

A queer God is therefore by no means just a theoretical gimmick, but a powerful and meaningful theological symbol: There are people who feel recognized and confirmed in this image of God with their identity, their longings and their spirituality. In this way, a queer concept of God simultaneously represents a challenge to traditional images of God and enables a liberating religious experience for all believers.

Such theses can be discussed in Secondary II to challenge the students: *Is God just a product of our desires?* Instead of stifling the discussion, you can use it to get back to the personal level of faith: Many young people realize in such discussions that their personal image of God *can partially invalidate* this criticism because it is *not* a rigid, wishful image, but something that also includes doubt, otherness and the unavailability of God. In this way, they learn to argue for their image of God and, if necessary, to correct it - an important skill for a reflective, mature understanding of faith.

This range of methods - from artistic design and meditative exercises to theological discourse - shows how *varied lessons on God's image competence can be*. It is crucial that the pupils are actively involved and have an experiential connection. Then they can understand intellectually *and* emotionally what it means: *"God is bigger than our images - but our images help us to imagine something of God."*

Good practice examples from schools and churches

There are already successful projects both in schools and in church education work that show how the ability to have diverse images of God is promoted in practice. Here are two inspiring examples - one from the classroom, one from church youth work - that illustrate what constitutes *good practice* in this area:

Primary school example: "We have different ideas about God"

In a Catholic elementary school (Year 2), a religion teacher carried out a teaching unit *entitled "The question of God"*, which exemplifies how children can be gently introduced to diverse images of God. The unit started with the children being given the task: *"Draw God as you imagine him."* In this way, each child was allowed to *draw their own picture* of God on paper - there is no right or wrong. Afterwards, all the pictures were hung up in the classroom like a small exhibition. The teacher created a *"museum tour"* with soft meditative music: the children walked around and silently looked at the pictures of their classmates. This phase was very impressive, as the children realized *that no two pictures were the same*. In the subsequent discussion round (sitting circle), anyone who wanted to was allowed to place their picture in the middle and say: *"This is how I imagine God, because..."*. Some described a friendly old man, others drew symbols such as a big heart or the sun. The class was amazed at the *diversity of ideas about God -* which was exactly what the teacher had intended. She made it clear to the children that all our ideas can only show parts of God, no one has ever seen God exactly. Therefore, different images are *okay and even important* to express something about God.

In the next lesson, the teacher used the story *"Fish is fish"* by Leo Lionni. With this fabulous story, the children were able to playfully understand that the unknown is always imagined from the familiar. When the fish in the book imagines a bird, it thinks of a fish with wings - because it knows nothing else. The children transferred this insight to the question of God: *we humans often imagine God as a person because we don't know him directly!*

At the end, the conclusion on the board was: *"We have different ideas about God."* Such experiences form a foundation on which children can develop an *open, curious image of God* that "grows" with them.

Youth and community example: "My image of God" campaign and creative exhibitions

There are also inspiring projects in the church's educational work. The Rottenburg-Stuttgart diocese provided an outstanding example with its *"My image of God"* campaign. Students of all ages across the diocese were invited to submit pictures expressing their idea of God. The response was enormous: almost 3,000 children and young people from 163 schools took part. A jury selected particularly impressive works, which were then exhibited publicly - e.g. at the Katholikentag in Ulm.

This project showed several things at once: firstly, the *development of images of God across the age groups.* From childlike, concrete depictions to philosophical, abstract paintings, everything was included. The head teacher emphasized the importance of religious education in not only allowing such *differentiated images of God* to develop, but also accompanying them in terms of content. Because it is not enough for the pictures to be painted - you also have to talk about what they mean

Such projects in schools and communities are encouraging: they show that faith and creativity belong together and that young people are very willing to engage with God in depth *if* they are allowed to do so in a contemporary and participatory way.

Figure20: Collage of God (I).

🎨 Exercise: "Collage of God - Who is God for us today?"

🌀 Aim of the exercise: The students work together to create a *visually expressive collage* in which they express different images and ideas of God. In doing so, they creatively and critically examine traditional and modern images of God and reflect on their own ideas, longings and experiences in the context of faith, life and society.

🏹 Topic: *"What images do we have of God? What statements, feelings, questions, symbols or hopes do we associate with God - as individuals and as a society? And what skills do people need to discover God in the world today?"*

🌀 Learning objectives and skills:

- Reflection on own and others' images of God
- Perception of the diversity of biblical, social and individual concepts of God
- Creative expression of religious interpretation skills
- Development of spiritual creative power
- Promoting religious communication in the team

✂ Materials:

- Old newspapers, magazines, journals (brought by students and collected in a common "pool")
- Scissors, glue, large sheets of drawing paper or poster board
- Colored pencils, felt-tip pens, watercolors, etc.
- Optional: Bibles, books of poetry, quotation cards or small impulse cards on images of God

📚 Procedure:

1st introduction (10-15 min)

Short input on different biblical and theological images of God:

- God as father/mother
- God as light, wind, fire
- God as justice, love, power
- God as mystery, companion, source, creator, shepherd ...

Key question: *"If we wanted to describe God with words, colors and images - what would that look like?"*

2nd collection phase (15-20 min): All students search the newspaper and magazine pool for images, headlines, symbols or words that they associate with their idea of God or with questions about God. They cut out what appeals to them - contradictory, emotional, provocative things are also allowed.

3rd design phase (30-40 min): Working individually or in small groups (2-3 students), they create a *God collage* on a large sheet of paper or poster:

- Design parts graphically (colors, symbols, personal words)
- Supplement parts with cut-out graphics and terms
- A colorful, broken, polyphonic expression of the question: *"Who or how is God for me / for us today?"*

4th presentation & gallery walk (15 min): The finished collages are hung up. The class walks around the "gallery aisle", quietly looking at the works of the others and leaving small sticky notes with thoughts or questions.

Volunteers present their picture. Guiding questions:

- What did I want to express?
- Where did I have doubts, breaks or new ideas?
- Which words and images particularly appeal to me - and why?

☐ Variant / continuation:

- Digital version as Canva or PowerPoint collage
- Integrate biblical images of God as a basis for quotations

Figure21: A collage of God (II).

Reflection: Modern perspectives and changes in church and practice

Through targeted skills development in the area of shaping the image of God, learners gain a *more modern view of images of God* - and thus often also a changed view of faith and the church. Finally, we will reflect on *the new insights* that arise here and *what consequences* this should have for the church, religious education and spiritual practice:

- **God beyond narrow categories:** Modern learners recognize that God cannot be pinned down to a specific image - neither to a gender, nor to a human form, skin color or role. This awareness is central in today's world, where traditional one-sided images of God (such as the exclusively male, white "Lord") are being questioned. Young people and students of theology are learning that *God eludes human categories.* At the same time, there is a growing realization that *every person* is valuable *as an image of God* - regardless of gender, sexuality or origin. If everyone is an image of God, then the diversity of people also reflects something of the diversity of God. This view leads to more inclusion: people feel more addressed by the question of God if they do not have the feeling that God is only a matter for men, for example. As the Federation of German Catholic Youth (BDKJ) has put it: *"In the official church, we often encounter a one-dimensional, cis-male, white image of God. ... God cannot be assigned to any gender or other human category".* Accordingly, it has a liberating effect when we are allowed to think of God in a more diverse way: *diverse images of God have a liberating effect on obstacles, constraints and impairments and allow freedom for self-determination.* Learners feel this freedom in small ways - for example, when they discover that they can also call God *"mom"* or see both strength and tenderness in God. This freedom can give rise to new spiritual spaces in which people can breathe a sigh of relief: God can be different, I myself can be different before God.
- **Changes in the church:** The church as a whole can benefit enormously from this developed competence. If believers internalize more diverse images of God, *liturgical and parish*

practice will also become richer. Developments are already becoming apparent: In many congregations, there is a growing sensitivity to an inclusive, diverse approach to God. For example, different biblical images are being used more frequently in prayers and songs - God is not only addressed as "Lord", but also as "mother", "friend", "source of life", for example. Here the church will (have to) continue to move forward in order to lift up the treasure of its own tradition: For the Bible knows numerous images of God that have long been neglected in preaching (e.g. God as comforting mother, as light, as rock, as mother eagle and much more).

Inspired, competent believers - like those we train in religious education and theology studies - can become ambassadors of this diversity. They will be the ones who introduce new linguistic images into congregations in the future, establish inclusive formulations in prayers and introduce creative-artistic elements into spirituality.

- **Impulses for religious education:** In teaching itself, the *teaching of images of God* should be consistently developed in a competence-oriented and dialogical manner. This means moving away from lessons that impose a correct idea on the students towards lessons that ask questions, stimulate and accompany them. The methods described show what religious education can look like today: process-oriented, student-centered, creative. Teachers act more as moderators and initiators than as lecturers. This approach should become the standard, as it has proven to be motivating and sustainable. If learners feel that their own relationship with God is allowed to take center stage - and not the memorization of dogmas - they are more willing to actively participate.

Today's religious education therefore attaches importance to making competence goals transparent*). In concrete terms, this means that* pupils work on their image of God again and again over the years, at different levels - sometimes narrating in elementary school, sometimes comparing in secondary school, sometimes critically questioning in upper secondary school. This *cumulative learning* enables a *growing image of God*. In addition, further training for religious education teachers should focus more on how to use creative methods). *The religious education of the future* should continue to work on such concepts in order to help young people develop a faith that is personally sustainable and open to growth.

- **Spiritual practice and personal life of faith:** Finally, today's view of images of God also shows each individual new ways for their own *spiritual practice*. If I have understood that God can meet me in different images, then I can look out for such encounters more consciously. Faith thus becomes a kind of *adventure of discovery*. Perhaps I will visit other churches or religious celebrations to see how God is spoken of there - that can broaden my horizons. These *new spiritual spaces* - whether created in the church or visited privately - lead to a more lively relationship with God. People with a diverse image of God can often get through crises better because they have more "leeway" to think of God differently, even in suffering (not just as punishing or absent, but perhaps as compassionate or still there in secret). This undogmatic view therefore gives rise to a faith that is *both critical and trusting*: critical of the flat answers of relevant doctrine, but trusting that God can always be found anew.

The ability to shape images of God creatively and in a variety of ways thus proves to be a key competence for a living faith in today's world. Those who have learned to allow God's diversity will find that this actually opens up new spiritual spaces - in their own hearts, in the classroom and in the congregation. The church becomes more pluralistic, more open to dialogue and closer to people when it recognizes the many faces of God. Religious education teachers and theologians are at the forefront of accompanying this process: By encouraging people to search for images for the unspeakable, they perform a service to the *freedom and depth of faith*. Ultimately, it means constantly trying to track down the infinite God anew. This may be challenging, but it is also immensely enriching - because *discovering God is an adventure for life.*

Exercise 10:
Promote the ability to engage in dialog in faith: Recognizing common ground in diversity

This exercise deals with the promotion of the ability to engage in dialog in faith in the context of religious and cultural diversity. The aim is to encourage young people to deal openly, respectfully and constructively with different beliefs. Teaching objectives include learning respectful communication and cooperation, discovering shared values despite existing differences and developing critical tolerance and reflective judgment. Learners should be enabled to perceive diversity as an opportunity and contribute to peaceful coexistence as active bridge builders.

Sub-competencies of dialog skills include interreligious competence (knowledge of other religions, appreciative attitude), intercultural competence (understanding of cultural contexts and empathy), linguistic expression (clear communication of religious concepts and ideas), dialogic communication skills (active conversation, ability to deal with conflict, change of perspective) and competence in dealing with rituals and liturgy (respectful participation and understanding of religious practices).

Individual learning of dialog competence takes place through encounters, reflection on one's own position, the use of diverse media and literature as well as the practical practice of clear communication. Methodologically dialog-oriented and creative approaches such as role plays, exercises in changing perspectives and direct encounters with different religions are central to religious education in schools.

The effect of such a learning process leads to a modern view of religious diversity, in which differences are perceived as enrichment, common values are emphasized and conflicts are dealt with constructively. Learners develop a critical attitude towards extremism and relativism and at the same time strengthen their own religious identity and openness.

- **Learning and development objective:** *The most important competence is the ability to communicate through dialog. The learning objective is to enable learners to communicate constructively, respectfully and empathetically with people of other faiths and to shape diversity in a positive way.*
- **Good-practice example:** *Role-playing games and scenic representations of typical interreligious dialog situations in which learners actively adopt perspectives, resolve conflicts and work out common values. This method promotes direct empathy and communication skills.*
- **Church support through:** *Believers, clergy, priests or bishops can actively initiate dialog forums, promote interreligious encounters and promote a dialogical attitude through their role model function. They support the development of this competence by accompanying and promoting dialogical projects in communities and schools.*
- **Local budget utilization:** *Financial resources could be used for dialog events, excursions to religious sites, interfaith workshops, materials for religious education and fees for external dialog experts.*
- **Adaptation of the curriculum at school:** *The curriculum in religious education should explicitly include dialog-oriented modules. Contents include interreligious competence, conflict resolution methods, practical communication exercises, as well as excursions and encounters with representatives of other faiths. The aim is to train pupils effectively and sustainably to become individuals capable of dialog.*

We live in a pluralistic society in which different religions and world views come together. Diversity is seen as an opportunity and a challenge. For schools - and religious education in particular - this means an important task: young people should learn to deal with this diversity openly and respectfully. Religious education not only aims to impart knowledge about one's own faith, but also to *promote identity and the ability to engage in dialog*. This means that pupils should grow in their own convictions and at the same time develop the *ability to engage in dialog with other religious and ideological positions*. This ability to engage in dialogue in faith is a central educational goal today, as it enables people to recognize *common values* across religious boundaries and contribute constructively to peaceful coexistence.

Teaching objectives of the competence Ability to engage in dialog in faith

What exactly should learners achieve through this competence? Essentially, it's about being able to *consolidate existing knowledge and build bridges in an exchange with people who think differently*. In concrete terms, this means, for example:

- **Communicating and cooperating respectfully with people of other faiths:** Curricula require that pupils learn to *engage thoroughly* with other beliefs and to *communicate and cooperate respectfully* with members of other religions and worldviews. This includes active listening, asking questions and making themselves understood without prejudice.
- **Discovering common values:** The ability to dialogue in faith does not mean ignoring differences, but rather talking *about* differences and at the same time recognizing what connects us. Your own knowledge of faith helps you to find points of contact - *where do we share values?* What basic ethical convictions (e.g. reverence for life, justice, humanity) do we have in common? One aim is to strengthen *trust in what unites us* and to see differences as an enrichment rather than a threat. In this way, learners develop an understanding that diversity does not mean arbitrariness, but can be an opportunity for mutual enrichment.

- **Critical tolerance and judgment:** Another teaching objective is the ability to make informed and fair judgments about religious issues - in other words, to practice *"critical tolerance"*. Pupils should learn to formulate their own convictions, but also to approach criticism of religion (both their own and that of others) objectively. This includes developing well-founded opinions and allowing others to believe differently. This enables them to appreciate shared values as well as tolerate differences.

These teaching objectives ultimately aim to make young people *capable of plurality* - in other words, to deal constructively with diversity. Those who are capable of dialog in faith can be bridge builders in later life: in school, at work and in society, they can help people of different convictions *to understand each other and act together*.

Required sub-competencies: Interreligious, intercultural, linguistic and ritual-related

In order to develop the ability to engage in dialog in faith, several **sub-competencies** must be addressed. These interlock and complement each other:

- **Interreligious competence:** The ability to put oneself in the shoes of other religions, to know their basic features and to be able to assess differences and similarities. This includes a solid *basic knowledge of different religions* (beliefs, customs, festivals) and an open, appreciative attitude towards their members. Only those who understand the *language* and *symbols* of the other religion, at least to some extent, can engage in genuine dialog. Interreligious competence also means being able to explain one's own position in a discussion and being curious about the perspectives of others.
- **Intercultural competence:** Religion is always embedded in culture. Learners must therefore understand cultural differences in the expression of faith - e.g. different understandings of roles, clothing, food, social norms. Intercultural competence helps to avoid misunderstandings: It trains empathy and an eye for the context in which religious beliefs are situated. Those who are interculturally competent

recognize *why* someone acts or speaks differently and can adapt to this. This competence also promotes the sensitivity to recognize *shared human values* (such as hospitality or justice) in different cultural guises.

- **Linguistic expressiveness:** Dialogue takes place in language. Pupils therefore need the ability to *express their own beliefs clearly* - in words that outsiders can also understand. This includes learning understandable *religious language*: being able to explain important terms (e.g. "love of neighbor", "salvation", "karma") and bearing witness to one's own faith without overwhelming others. Equally important is the ability to listen actively and to paraphrase the other person's statements in one's own words. In religious education, this language skill is practiced by encouraging students to *ask questions, clarify terms and talk about their faith*. Language is the key to building bridges between different worldviews.

- **Dialogue skills in the narrower sense:** This is about practical communication skills. These include **conversation skills**, the ability to deal with conflict and empathy. Pupils learn to actively shape a conversation: e.g. by using *"I" messages* instead of accusations, by asking questions when things are unclear, by naming similarities and differences in a respectful tone. It is also important to be able to *take on each other's perspective* - in other words, to put yourself in the other person's shoes on a trial basis in order to better understand their point of view. This ability to switch between an internal perspective (one's own faith) and external perspectives (an external view of one's own faith and the faith of others) is crucial for genuine dialog. It also requires the *ability to reflect*: to be able to consider what you have learned after a conversation and where there may have been misunderstandings. All of this is what makes a person capable of dialog.

- **Competence in dealing with rituals and liturgy:** Since religion consists not only of *content,* but also of lived practice, the ability to engage in dialog should also include dealing with religious *rituals, prayers and festivals*. Those who are capable of dialog can, for example, take part in a religious celebration as a guest without fear of the unknown - and respectfully perceive the meaning behind the actions. In religious education lessons, pupils learn about their own religious rituals (such as Christian festivals, prayers, forms of worship) and become aware of their significance. At the same time, they learn about the rituals of other religions. This *liturgical competence* makes it possible to appreciate similarities (e.g. light rituals, prayers, chants) and to understand differences (e.g. dietary rules or prayer times). Practical experience is central to this: *religion should not only be discussed in theory, but also experienced first-hand* in order to really discover the spirituality of others. In this way, young people learn to *deal competently and respectfully* with religious customs that are initially unfamiliar - and also to be able to explain their own rituals to outsiders.

Taken together, these various sub-competencies form the *ability to engage in dialog in faith*. They show that it is not just about knowledge, but also about *attitudes and skills* that need to be practiced. The good news is that all of these facets can be developed in a targeted manner - both individually and in the classroom.

Individual learning of dialog skills

So how can you learn these skills personally? *Theory alone is not enough* - experience is crucial. One key lies in real *encounters*: If you want to learn about interfaith dialog, you have to engage in dialog *yourself*. This means that outside of the classroom, each individual can actively seek opportunities to enter into conversation with people of other worldviews.

Practical tips for individual learning:

- **Seek personal encounters:** Whether with friends, in the neighborhood or in local communities - direct contact reduces fear of contact. A conversation with a Muslim neighbor about Ramadan, a visit to a public Hindu temple festival or participation in a peace prayer event offer direct learning experiences. Such *dialog experiences* shape far more than just book knowledge, because you get to know people, not just abstract teachings.

- **Reflect on your own position:** The ability to engage in dialog also grows by coming to terms with *one's own* convictions. *Who am I, what do I believe and why?* Journaling, faith courses or conversations with mentors can help to clarify your own world view. This self-reflection makes you more confident in revealing something about yourself in dialog - and remaining open without feeling threatened. The more stable and at the same time more reflective your own identity is, the easier it is to have an exchange on an equal footing.
- **Read and use media:** In addition to personal contacts, you can learn a lot from literature, films and online resources. There are inspiring biographies of people who build bridges between religions, or documentaries about interfaith initiatives. Such content imparts knowledge about other faiths and shows *model situations* of dialog. It is important to inform yourself in a variety of ways - for example, listen to a podcast by a Jewish student, read a blog by an atheist or follow an interfaith youth council online. In this way, you can expand your understanding of diversity step by step.
- **Practicing language skills:** In practical terms, you can try to put complex religious ideas into simple words - e.g. explaining to a friend without a religious background what faith means to you. Or vice versa: ask others to explain their world view and ask about unfamiliar terms. This translation between different "language games" significantly improves the ability to engage in dialog. Learning foreign languages can also help indirectly because it opens up new cultural areas and ways of thinking - those who know a few words of Arabic or Hebrew, for example, often understand religious terms from these traditions better.
- **Develop patience and empathy:** Last but not least, individual learning of dialog skills is a process that requires patience. It also involves putting up with uncertainty or making mistakes in a conversation. It is important to remain *empathetic* - in other words, to keep reminding yourself that there is a person with feelings and dignity on the "other side" who is also seeking their truth. You can strengthen this empathic attitude through

meditation, prayer or simple reflection. It is like a muscle that grows with practice.

All these personal paths have one thing in common: *learning by doing*. Every genuine encounter, every open conversation and every reflected experience makes you a little more capable of dialog. You learn to see *differences not as a threat, but as a learning opportunity*. And you realize how enriching it can be when bridges are built between world views.

Teaching dialog competence: Didactics and Methods in Religious Education

The ability to engage in dialog can be specifically promoted in religious education at school. Modern religious education concepts emphasize *dialogical and action-oriented* teaching in which students are not passive consumers, but *active co-creators* of the learning process. Specifically, teachers can use the following didactic approaches and methods:

- **Creating a respectful climate:** The first step is to jointly agree on *rules for dialog*. For example, the class works out how to treat each other respectfully: let people finish speaking, no derogatory comments about other people's beliefs, confidentiality when making personal contributions, etc. These *basic rules* give everyone a sense of security. At the same time, the teacher should encourage a climate in which *questions* are *expressly encouraged from* the outset - even critical ones. Everyone is allowed to address ambiguities (*"Why do Muslims actually pray five times a day?"*) and show curiosity without being ridiculed. Such an appreciative framework is the basis for all other methods.

Figure22: Method for improving dialog skills: Think-Pair-Share.

- **Use diversity in the classroom:** There are often already pupils from different backgrounds in a religion class (Christian of different persuasions, Muslim, non-denominational, etc.). This heterogeneous learning group is not an obstacle, but a *resource*. Teachers can make targeted use of multi-perspective methods: For example, for a topic (such as *"What does fasting mean?"*), learners are given the task of first collecting answers from their own perspective in small groups. Mixed groups are then formed to share their results - this allows students to hear different perspectives first-hand. Another method is the *"think-pair-share"*: First, everyone thinks for themselves (think), then they exchange ideas in pairs (pair) - preferably with someone who has a different background - and then the results are discussed in plenary (share). Such methods make it possible for everyone to have their say and learn from each other.
- **Creative and dialogical exercises:** To train empathy and perspective-taking, *role plays* and scenic performances are suitable. For example, two students could act out a scene: a fictitious argument between a strict believer and a skeptic. The

class then observes and discusses what went well and where misunderstandings arose. *Change of perspective exercises* are also effective: students write a letter or diary entry *from the perspective of a person* with a different religion (e.g. *"A day in the life of a Buddhist monk"*). This allows them to imagine themselves in a different world. *Creative media projects* - such as designing a collage together on the topic of *"Common values of religions"* or creating a short video clip about an AI in which different students explain what faith means to them - promote teamwork and express different voices. Evaluation is important in all of this: the teacher should always provide space to talk about the experiences (*"How did you feel in the role? What did you learn?"*) in order to encourage reflection.

- **Enable encounters:** Nothing can replace real encounters - which is why religious education should incorporate *extracurricular places of learning* and encounter situations wherever possible. Excursions to places of worship of different religions, discussions with representatives of other faith communities or joint projects with groups of pupils from other schools are worth their weight in gold. For example, a mosque, a synagogue and a temple could be visited as part of a project day. On site, members of the community explain their religious practices and answer questions from the pupils. This direct experience - entering a different sacred space, experiencing silence in the mosque or chanting in the temple - *leaves a lasting impression.* The students may be surprised to discover similarities on site: *"They also light candles there, just like we do"* or *"The silence during prayer reminded me of our meditation."* Such impressions broaden the horizon. Studies and practical reports show that initial strangeness can be overcome through local encounters and genuine understanding can develop. If real visits are not possible, virtual encounters (e.g. video conferences with young people of another religion from a partner school) or visits to multi-religious events (such as the *"Open Mosque Day"*) can also be integrated.
- **Moderating dialogic classroom discussions:** A lot can also be learned in everyday classroom discussions if they are

deliberately designed to be dialogic. The teacher acts as a *moderator* here, bringing different positions in the class into discussion. Example: For a topic such as "Who is God for me?", voluntary pupils could start by describing their personal views. This is then discussed in plenary - the teacher makes sure that differences are not evaluated but explored. It is also important here: Record the results - e.g. make a whiteboard together with a column "Different ideas" and a column "Common values/questions". In this way, the pupils can visually see what unites them despite all their differences.

- **Practicing methods of conflict resolution:** Since dialog is not always without tension, teachers should also demonstrate how to deal with conflicts constructively. This can be done through *simulated conflicts* (role play in which two religions debate a controversial topic and the class works out solutions) or by *discussing real conflicts* in the world and how dialog can help to overcome them. This makes it clear that the ability to engage in dialog does not mean always agreeing, but rather remaining respectful despite differences and using common ground to live together.

All of these methods make religious education lively, *practical and dialogical*. The pupils practise *how* dialog works in a protected space. What is important here is that the teacher themselves should exemplify an *open, appreciative attitude*, as children and young people are strongly oriented towards the model. If they see that the teacher acts in a friendly and curious manner towards a guest of a different faith, for example , or mediates fairly in discussions, they will adopt this behavior.

Through these didactic approaches, religious education is shifting away from a pure teacher lecture to a *learning laboratory for dialog*. This is where the first steps can be taken and discussed, where understanding grows. Pupils experience this: Comparing religions is not just dry learning *about* something foreign, but a dialog *with* living people. In this way, the class itself becomes a place of encounter.

Figure23: A lesbian couple of women who can endure arguments and still come together.

A lesbian couple of women who can put up with arguments and still come together" - the emotional scene shows two women on a sofa. One of them, with her arms crossed and a tense expression on her face, looks hurt and angry. The other turns to her lovingly and with concern, places a reassuring hand on her arm and speaks with gentle facial expressions. The surroundings are calm and intimate, which emphasizes the emotional closeness and vulnerability. The picture stands for the ability to deal with conflict in relationships, for the art of listening to each other, enduring tensions - and yet remaining connected.

Good practice: examples of successful dialog promotion

Numerous schools and initiatives have already impressively demonstrated how interreligious dialog skills can be promoted in practice. Some inspiring examples:

- **Drei-Religionen-Schule Osnabrück:** There is an elementary school in Osnabrück that is run jointly by three religious communities - the Catholic, Protestant and Muslim communities (as well as cooperation with the Jewish community). Religious education initially takes place separately according to religion, but the children come together constantly in everyday school life. *Religious festivals* are deliberately organized together: Sometimes a festival is celebrated in the form of *"liturgical hospitality"* - i.e. the members of one religion prepare the festival according to their tradition and children of other religions are invited as guests. At other times, a *multi-religious festival* is celebrated, with all groups contributing to the success of the event with their respective prayers and songs.

For example, the children have not only learned about Christmas, Ramadan and Hanukkah from books, but have also experienced them in *practice*. Teachers and pupils also solve questions of coexistence in everyday life through dialog: *for example, how lunch is organized so that Muslim and Jewish children can observe their dietary rules - which dishes are acceptable for everyone, do you need separate dishes for halal and kosher?* Such organizational questions become a learning field: *the children join in the discussion and learn to find compromises* that do justice to each faith. Of course, this is not always conflict-free, but this is precisely where the learning effect lies - the pupils experience dialog as a lively process that sometimes requires debate, but produces solutions. This school model shows impressively *how being at home in one's own religion* and *being open to others* can go hand in hand.

- **Project "Pupils encounter the Abrahamic religions" (Year 10):** A six-month project was introduced at a secondary school in Hesse in which all tenth graders - whether Protestant, Catholic, Muslim or non-denominational - learn about *the three Abrahamic religions together*. The project begins with a kick-off event in which the importance of dialogue is emphasized. This is followed by various *modules*: The pupils acquire basic knowledge about Judaism, Christianity and Islam, they formulate their own questions (*"What have I always wanted to ask a rabbi, priest or imam?"*). There is an *excursion day* on which all three places of worship are visited, with a guided tour by members of the congregation and the opportunity for discussion. Particularly important: Before the face-to-face meeting, "dialogue rules" are drawn up together to ensure that every encounter is characterized by respect and genuine curiosity. After the excursion, the young people reflect: What impressed me? What prejudices may have been dispelled? At the end of the day, the young people see dialog not as dry theory, but as a *key to peace* and coexistence.

- **Cross-school interfaith workshops:** In some cities, schools from different sponsors cooperate to facilitate encounters. For example, there are project weeks in which pupils from a church grammar school and a state school with a high proportion of immigrants attend *joint workshops*. They work in mixed teams on topics such as "Religion and the environment" or "Justice in my faith traditions". Supervised by religious education teachers and sometimes external moderators (e.g. from interfaith youth networks), the young people use these topics to discuss their faith. *Creative methods* are often used in such workshops - for example, the teams paint a poster together, design a short play or create a prayer corner with symbols from different religions. At the end, the groups present their results to everyone, often in a festive setting to which parents are also invited. Such eye-to-eye encounter projects help to break down fears of contact. Aha experiences create a feeling of *solidarity across religious boundaries* without denying the differences.

- **Interreligious youth meetings and dialog forums:** Outside of school, there are offers such as youth meetings between religious communities (e.g. Christian-Islamic youth forums, interfaith summer camps, etc.). Teachers can integrate such events into lessons by reporting on them or inviting participants to describe their experiences. Such events make schools a lively place of learning and understanding.

These good practice examples show: *There are many ways* to make dialog skills a practical experience. Whether on a small scale (a class exercise) or in a large project - the decisive factor is that pupils *become active themselves, have real encounters and can reflect on* what this means for them. The examples given at are inspiring and encourage students to implement such approaches in their own lessons.

Sermon: "Blessed are those who seek peace - learning to resolve conflicts in the spirit of Jesus"

Dear sisters and brothers,

We all know the feeling when opinions clash, when injustice is felt, when words hurt - and the conversation comes to a standstill. Whether in the family, at school, in the community or in the worldwide coexistence of religions: Conflicts are part of life. But we can learn how to deal with them - and as believers, we are called to do so.

In the Sermon on the Mount, Jesus says: "Blessed are the peacemakers, for they will be called children of God." (Mt 5:9) This is not meant naively - but with profound courage. Making peace does not mean smoothing everything over or remaining silent. It means taking the conflict seriously - and still treating the other person with dignity.

Today I would like to show you a method that we can use in religious education, but also in the community: "conflict resolution through structured dialog". Imagine two people, two religions, two world views discussing a topic that moves them deeply - such as faith and science, sexuality, equality. They represent different positions. The aim is not to persuade each other, but to understand, respect and find ways of working together.

How does this happen? In a role play, for example, you can take one of the positions and speak with arguments - without being attacked personally. The others listen. Afterwards, we collect together: What did we understand? What was difficult to bear? And above all: What do we have in common despite our differences?

This exercise is more than just an educational game. It reflects what Jesus lived: He spoke with Pharisees and tax collectors, with Romans and fishermen, with women and children - not because they all had the same opinion, but because he saw them as human beings. The ability to engage in dialog is not a luxury, but a path that leads us to a credible testimony.

Because today in particular, our world does not need further division, but spaces in which we can endure conflict and still come together. Perhaps we won't succeed immediately. Perhaps it takes courage to let go of our own position without betraying ourselves. But God has given us a heart and a mind to use both: Clarity and compassion.

Dear congregation, I invite you to do a little exercise today and in the coming week: When you find yourself in a conflict - internally or with others - ask yourself: What is the other person actually trying to say to me? And how can I respond in such a way that dignity remains? That is peace work. That is discipleship.

And the peace of God, which surpasses all understanding, keep our hearts and minds in Christ Jesus. Amen.

Impact: A modern view of religious diversity

When young people are systematically trained in dialog skills, this changes their view of religious diversity in the long term - towards a *modern, enlightened and at the same time appreciative perspective.*

Learners who have had such experiences typically develop the following attitudes and insights:

- **Religious diversity as enrichment:** instead of being unsettled or threatened by diversity, they see something positive in it. They recognize that every tradition can contribute to an understanding of meaning and values. Religions are no longer pigeonholed as "wrong" and "right", but are seen as *different paths* that are all taken by people in search of truth and meaning in life. This attitude leads to more serenity and curiosity: when a classmate tells you about the Diwali festival, you listen with interest - just as you share your own celebrations. Diversity becomes normal and exciting at the same time.
- **Focus on shared values and humanity:** Through dialog, young people learn that despite all dogmatic differences, there are often surprisingly similar core ethical messages. For example, almost all religions emphasize ethical rules and maxims for action, charity, hospitality and forgiveness. This realization leads to a kind of *core view*: When looking at a foreign religion, we first look at *what* unites us - such as the pursuit of peace or justice - instead of immediately focusing on what divides us.

This does not mean denying differences, but it does mean seeing them in relation to the common foundations. Learners develop a *value-oriented tolerance*: they respect the dignity of every person, regardless of their convictions, and find unifying values that make it possible to live together. This creates a *sense of togetherness within the human family* without everyone having to think the same way.

- **Less prejudice, more knowledge:** One key effect is the reduction of stereotypes. Anyone who knows a Muslim personally is more likely to reduce prejudices against Muslims in general; anyone who has been to a synagogue will no longer believe anti-Jewish clichés without reflection. Instead, these young people have *concrete knowledge*: they can distinguish between what a religion really teaches and what extremists make of it. Overall, they are *more critical of the media*: if the news reports negatively about "religion X" in general terms, they are more likely to question this and remember their own encounters, which were usually more nuanced. This reflected understanding protects against fear-mongering and polarization.

- **Identity and openness at the same time:** Interestingly, many people report that they have learned to better understand and appreciate their own faith through interfaith dialog . Through exchange, you realize what is special about your own tradition - and what you may have long taken for granted. At the same time, the learners are no longer afraid of "mixing" or losing their own identity. They know: Openness towards others does not mean betraying one's own faith. On the contrary, one's own faith often becomes *deeper* when it is reconsidered in the light of other convictions. This balance of rootedness and breadth is a characteristic of the modern perspective: you can be *self-confident and firm in your faith* and still remain *open to dialog and capable of learning*. The students have practiced this area of tension on a small scale - and can now do it on a large scale too.

- **Dealing constructively with conflicts:** Those who have learned dialog react differently to religious tensions. Instead of withdrawing or becoming aggressive, he/she tries to mediate. The young people have learned that differences of opinion can be discussed peacefully and that even sensitive issues (such as different ideas about truth or salvation) can be discussed *if* the right conditions are created. They take this know-how with them. At school, for example, it can be seen in the fact that such students can de-escalate conflicts between different groups - after all, they have experienced in projects how solutions can be found through joint discussions. *In* the church or community, they can act as *multipliers*, for example by initiating interfaith discussion groups or explaining to skeptical parishioners why dialogue with the new Hindu neighbor is not a threat, but an opportunity. Overall, they contribute to making *both the school climate and church community life more inclusive and dialogical.*

- **Distance from extremism and relativism**: A modern view of religious diversity, which has emerged through education, also immunizes against two traps: Firstly, against a *cheap relativism* that claims *"it doesn't matter, all religions are the same"* - this attitude is overcome because learners have just learned to *look* and take differences seriously (and learn to appreciate them). They know that every tradition is unique and has its own intrinsic value. Secondly, against *fundamentalist narrow-mindedness* that only accepts one's own view and devalues others.

Because the students have gotten to know real people of other religions, they can no longer fall back into a pattern of enemy stereotypes or absolute isolation. They have understood the *dignity of difference* - that diversity is wanted and valuable - and cannot help but be skeptical of narrow-mindedness. This is immensely valuable for society: the younger generation is inoculated against fanaticism, so to speak, because they have experienced that *dialog* is *possible and fruitful*.

Overall, the promotion of dialog competence in religious education leads to learners developing an *attitude of plurality*: they can work constructively with people from different backgrounds in later life, be it in international studies, at work or in their own neighborhood. For schools, this means better cooperation in concrete terms - less bullying based on religion, more joint activities across class boundaries, a school climate in which diversity is celebrated (e.g. with multi-faith celebrations or projects). For the churches, it means long-term members who have *open doors and hearts:* They will be more willing to organize a neighborhood festival with the local mosque community or participate in interfaith prayers for peace. Such believers transform the church into a community that bears witness to its faith through dialog and *at the same time respects the faith of others.*

Outlook: Towards a culture of dialog together

The development of the competence *"ability to engage in dialog in faith"* is therefore far more than just an educational trend - it is a key to how we will live together in the future. This ability can flourish in religious education in particular, where questions of meaning, values and identity are discussed. Inspired by sound theological insights and creative pedagogical methods, students learn to be bridge builders. They practice *becoming familiar with the unfamiliar without losing its foreign appeal,* and celebrating what unites without erasing differences.

In the end, there is a vision: young people who leave school and can say that *dialog* is not just a word for them, but a lived experience. They have experienced how enriching it is to *discover common values in others* and how problems that seemed insurmountable can be solved through discussion and encounter. Such experiences shape their attitude in school, church and society. They become ambassadors of understanding - and that is exactly what our multi-religious world needs.

If we succeed in broadly promoting the ability to engage in dialog in faith, generations will grow up for whom the coexistence of religions is a matter of course. Through these learning processes, schools and churches are increasingly being transformed into *places of hope,* where the words *"Peace be with you"* can be experienced by all people - regardless of their world view. This is an inspiring perspective that encourages us to continue on our chosen path. Because every successful dialogue encounter, however small it may be, is a step towards a culture of mutual respect and charity in a colorful, diverse world.

Exercise 11:
Shaping spirituality in a gender-equitable, queer-sensitive and true-to-life way

This exercise highlights the need for an inclusive spirituality that includes people of all genders and lifestyles. Traditionally, spirituality has often been heteronormative, but today it is crucial to create a practice of faith in which everyone feels authentically addressed. Gender competence, inclusive spirituality and ritual competence are central to this. Gender competence sensitizes people to social gender diversity and inequalities and enables them to critically reflect on and openly expand images of God. Inclusive spirituality recognizes the diversity of forms of life and love and searches for theological images that present God as comprehensively loving beyond clichés. Ritual competence enables the practice of worship that does not exclude anyone by using inclusive language and symbols.

Personal learning of these skills takes place through self-reflection, conscious examination of diverse images of God, queer theological literature and spiritual practice. Mindfulness exercises and prayers that address God in various forms (e.g. "eternal one", "loving mother") open up new spiritual experiences. Exchanges and encounters with people of different gender and sexual identities promote a deeper understanding and compassion.

The passing on and teaching of this competence should be anchored in theological educational institutions and religious education. Texts and approaches of feminist and queer theologies as well as queer Christology can sensitize students. Practical exercises, e.g. writing gender-appropriate prayer texts and sermons, strengthen linguistic sensitivity and awareness of inclusive preaching. Projects and role plays in schools promote concrete experience of what an inclusive church looks like in practice.

In parish work and pastoral care, workshops and specialist days in which full-time and voluntary workers learn how to conduct queer-sensitive pastoral discussions and liturgies, for example on Christopher Street Day, are helpful. In particular, the linguistic reflection of sermons and intercessions in teams raises awareness of inclusive formulations such as "God, Father and Mother".

Practical examples show how this is already succeeding: congregations consciously use gender-inclusive language in church services ("brothers and sisters in faith" instead of "brothers and sisters"), intercessions ("father and mother in heaven") or liturgies (such as the EKBO collection of gender-sensitive service modules). Such inclusive celebrations and sermons send clear invitations to all people, regardless of gender identity and sexual orientation.

In the long term, this competence positively changes the image of the church and faith by promoting an image of God that is people-friendly and diverse. This enables a church in which equality and diversity are not the exception, but the norm - inspired by the biblical message (Gal 3:28).

- ***Learning and development objective:*** *The central competence is gender and diversity sensitivity, which enables learners to appreciate gender and sexual diversity and actively integrate it into their spiritual practice. The learning objective is to develop differentiated images of God that reflect diversity and shape spirituality inclusively.*
- ***Good practice example:*** *A workshop in religious education in which students consciously reformulate psalms and prayer texts in a gender-appropriate and diversity-sensitive way, actively practise images of God such as "motherly-fatherly God" or "eternal spiritual power" and reflect on the effect this has on them personally and on an inclusive community.*
- ***Church support through:*** *Both believers and clergy can be supportive through authentic public speech, for example in sermons or prayers. By consciously using queer-sensitive and gender-appropriate language and accompanying events such as blessings for queer couples or theological discussion evenings, they actively contribute to an inclusive church culture.*

- **Local budget use:** *Community funds can be used for further training, queer-sensitive materials (e.g. prayer collections, brochures on inclusive pastoral care), as well as for projects or events that promote the visibility and acceptance of diverse identities, such as workshops, discussion groups or inclusive community projects.*

- **Adaptation of the school curriculum:** *Religious education curricula must explicitly integrate topics of gender and sexual diversity. In concrete terms, this means making it mandatory in curricula that students critically examine traditional and modern images of God, use gender- and queer-sensitive language in practice and develop and reflect on inclusive spiritual forms. The training of religious education teachers should also be geared towards this content.*

There is an urgent need for an inclusive spirituality: in our pluralistic society, it is becoming increasingly clear how important it is to have a spirituality that takes *all* people into account. For a long time, traditional church language and practice ran the risk of only depicting a heteronormative two-gender world. Today, however, we understand this: *All people are equal before God*, regardless of gender, sexual orientation or lifestyle. The point is that all believers - women, men, non-binary and queer people - can live out their faith *without having to pretend or hide*. Building a gender-equitable and queer-sensitive spirituality is therefore a central learning objective for theology and the church. This *identity-appropriate competence* means proclaiming God's love in such a way that no one is excluded. It is *true to life* because it is based on the reality of people's lives and responds to current issues. In times when equality and diversity are highly valued in society, this kind of spirituality contributes to the *credibility* of the church and makes it a place of genuine encounter.

Develop essential sub-skills: Several interconnected skills are needed to make spirituality inclusive. Firstly, *gender competence* is necessary - i.e. knowledge about gender roles and identities and the ability to actively implement gender equality. Gender competence includes *understanding gender diversity as enriching*, recognizing social inequalities and counteracting them in one's own actions. Those who are gender competent reflect, for example, on how images of "female" and "male" shape their own image of God and learn to consciously expand these images. Secondly, an *inclusive spirituality* is required. This refers to a spiritual attitude that affirms different lifestyles and forms of love. Inclusive spirituality asks: *Where is God expressed in diverse experiences?* It ties in with feminist and queer theological approaches that discover images of God beyond narrow role clichés. For example, queer-feminist theology emphasizes that God is greater than our traditional ideas and unites both female and male aspects.

This *queer-feminist spirituality* teaches us to question old ways of thinking and to dare to create new, liberating images of faith. Thirdly, *ritual competence* is important: the ability to design worship celebrations and rituals in such a way that *everyone* feels addressed. Those with ritual competence can, for example, adapt language, symbols and prayers to reflect gender diversity. Finally, it involves developing *visions* for a more just church - in other words, imagining what a fully inclusive church could look like and taking steps towards it. This visionary power gives direction to competence and motivates change.

It is about individual learning - as personal development and practice: How can you personally acquire this comprehensive competence? Firstly, through *self-reflection* and a willingness to change. It helps to take a close look at your own spirituality: *What images of God do I carry within me? Do I unconsciously prefer a male image of God, and how does it feel to address God as a mother or as a mysterious reality?* Literature and testimonies can provide inspiration - for example, the *Bible in fair language* with diverse references to God, or biographies of queer Christians who talk about their journey of faith. Personal conversations and listening also play a major role. By interacting with people from different backgrounds - e.g. in queer faith groups or inclusive communities - you get to know other perspectives and experience the effects of exclusionary language and, conversely, how liberating inviting language can be. *Spiritual practice* can also be consciously designed to be inclusive. In prayer and meditation, we can practise addressing God in different images: sometimes as "loving God", sometimes as "Father and Mother", sometimes as "Eternal One(s)". Such prayers open the heart to new experiences. An example from an intercession shows this openness beautifully: *"Held by you, Eternal One, we recognize our dignity... Your radiance [is] in all who go their way beyond the norms of love, life and body."*. Through such words, one senses when praying: God envelops precisely those who live apart from rigid norms.

In addition, any form of mindfulness and charity practice promotes a basic attitude of respect. Anyone who learns to see every person as an image of God develops compassion and a keen eye for injustice - the best prerequisites for queer-sensitive pastoral care.

This must be passed on: Teach and promote the skill of respectfully dealing with diversity: Equally important is the question of how to teach this skill in education and church work. Diversity should not remain a niche topic in *theological teaching* - at universities and in the further training of pastors - but should become an integral part of it. This begins with seminar reading: texts from feminist and queer theology, such as the works of Marcella Althaus-Reid or Dorothee Sölle, train the eye for alternative perspectives. Discussion rounds on role models in the Bible and tradition help students to develop their own positions. *Practical exercises* are also essential. In preaching courses, prospective pastors can learn, for example, how to formulate blessing and prayer texts in a gender-appropriate way.

A possible task: Write an intercession in which God's motherly and fatherly love becomes clear - as in the prayer cry "God, our Father and our Mother!".

Such exercises sensitize them to language and ensure that future preachers have all believers in mind.

This competence can also be taught in *school practice and catechesis*. Religious education teachers can practise gender-inclusive language with their pupils, for example by consistently using female forms for God when reading out psalms or using gender-neutral terms. Role plays and project work on the topic of *"Church for all"* can allow young people to experience what inclusion looks like in concrete terms. It is important to create an open atmosphere in which questions about LGBTQIA+ and faith can be asked - this is how students learn that faith and diversity belong together.

Certain formats can also be used *in parish pastoral care*. Parishes could organize workshops or discussion evenings, e.g. *under the title "Spirituality for all genders"*. Parishioners could share their own experiences and new forms of prayer could be tried out together.

Some dioceses are setting a good example: for example, specialist days and training courses on *queer-sensitive pastoral care* are offered, where full-time and voluntary workers learn to value diverse lifestyles. Such training courses provide concrete practice in how to conduct pastoral conversations in an inclusive manner or how liturgies can be designed for Christopher Street Day, for example. *Public speaking -* whether sermons, devotions or speeches - is a central field of action: here, the choice of words determines inclusion or exclusion. Training sessions in which pastors analyze their language are therefore useful from a didactic point of view. They think about it together: *Where do I perhaps only address men ("Dear brothers")? How does it sound to choose neutral forms of address such as "Dear congregation" or "Brothers and sisters in faith" instead?* Such reflection in the team or with mentors anchors the competence in everyday preaching.

Inspiring practical examples are needed: nothing is more convincing than successful practical examples. In the area of *gender-appropriate intercessions and prayers*, there are already many templates that are encouraging. In some congregations, for example, it has become customary to address God in the intercessions with an ambiguous parental address: *"God, our Father and our Mother, all people are your beloved children..."*. This formula opens the horizon - it reminds us that God is there for us as both a mother and a father. Other prayer texts deliberately use female names for God such as *"Eternal"* or *"Holy Spirit"* in order to break up the one-sidedness of male language. Something is also happening in the language about the congregation: instead of brothers and sisters, people simply speak of *brothers and sisters*, and *"the Lord bless you"* sometimes becomes *"God bless us"*. In 2020, the Evangelical Church of Berlin-Brandenburg (EKBO) published a whole collection of worship building blocks for *celebrating worship in a gender-sensitive way*. These include formulations for *opening speeches, sermons and blessings* that do not exclude anyone. One suggestion is to sing not only *"peace to men of his good pleasure"* in the *Gloria*, but *"peace to all men"* in order to include everyone. Experts also recommend two linguistic strategies: either *make* all genders *visible* - for example, *"Dear Father in heaven, dear Mother in heaven"* - or use gender-neutral wording to also reflect the third, diverse gender: *"Dear gender-neutral God in heaven"*. Both ways lead to a language in which more people can find themselves.

Gender-appropriate intercessions & prayers

Formulated in inclusive, appreciative language - suitable for church services, school services, devotions or liturgical educational formats.

🙏 Intercessions (gender-appropriate):

1 Good God, we pray for all people who are searching for their identity
- whether they see themselves as women, men, neither or both.
Give them the courage to affirm themselves and give us the openness

to treat them with love and respect.
- *God, we ask you: Strengthen our compassion.*

2 God of peace, we pray for people in relationships - regardless of the constellation - who grow together, fail, forgive each other or start anew.
Bless all lovers with patience, clarity and mutual trust.
- *God, we ask you: Bless our diversity in love.*

❄ Prayers (gender-appropriate):

1. **prayer for identity and recognition:** God, source of all life, you have created us wonderfully - so different, so unique, so loved. You know our names, our hopes, our doubts. Help us to see each other without prejudice. Give us the courage to accept our identity - in dignity, with you at our side.
Amen.

2. **prayer for relationships in diversity**: God, who is love, you bless all those who sincerely seek each other, find each other, lose each other and return . In friendships, partnerships, families - in all their diversity - you are present with your blessing.
Teach us to love with open hands, trust with wide hearts and to live in mutual respect.
Amen.

In addition to the liturgy, there *are examples of sermons* that are designed to be queer-sensitive. When interpreting biblical texts, a *queer-friendly sermon* will perhaps emphasize that Jesus spoke remarkably often to people on the margins of society - which encourages us to actively include LGBTQIA+ people today. Some preachers tell the story of the centurion of Capernaum (Mt 8:5-13) in such a way that it becomes clear: The sick servant could also have been a same-sex partner - Jesus looks at *faith*, not convention. Such changes of perspective in sermons bring queer people into the center of the biblical message. Wedding ceremonies for all lovers (instead of just for straight couples) or youth devotions for Christopher Street Day are also examples of how spirituality can become true-to-life and queer-inclusive practice. All these examples send out an invitation: *You and your whole identity are welcome here.* Anyone who hears them immediately senses what is meant when we talk about gender-equitable, queer-sensitive spirituality.

Sermon: "God is bigger than our drawers - an invitation to love without exclusion"

Dear community,

Today I would like to talk to you about a topic that moves many people - some quietly, some loudly: queer identities and our church. It's not easy to talk about because there is so much pain, hope, longing and fear involved. And yet it is necessary. Because faith must never work against people - but always for them.

I believe in a God who is bigger than our categories. Bigger than male or female. Bigger than our ideas of "normal" or "right". I believe in a God who created every human being - with a unique identity, a living body, a story that matters.

Psalm 139 says: "You have made me wonderful. I thank you that I am amazingly and wonderfully made." This applies to everyone. For heterosexual people as well as queer people, for cisgender and transgender people, for people who cannot - or do not want to - be categorized. God's yes is valid. Without conditions.

But we know: Many queer people have not felt God's yes in the church, but rejection. They have been told: "The way you love is wrong." Or: "You can stay - but only if you keep quiet." Or: "You're welcome, but your relationship isn't." And I ask: How can a church that proclaims the God of love make people small in their love?

Jesus never excluded. He saw people that no one else went to. He ate with those who shunned others. He didn't say: "Change, then you are welcome", but: "You are welcome - and this love changes everything." That is still true today.

I dream of a church where queer people are not only accepted, but celebrated. Where their stories are heard. Where their partnerships are blessed - not as an exception, but out of conviction. Where their faith has space, is allowed to grow and inspires us.

And I believe that this dream is not a contradiction to the gospel. On the contrary. It is a consequence of it. Because the gospel calls us to think bigger and bigger. To love more radically. To act more courageously. To become more visible to those who are often overlooked.

Dear congregation, let us create spaces in which people do not have to bend in order to belong. Let us find language that heals, not hurts. And let us never forget: Whoever loves has already recognized God - because God is love (1 John 4:7).

Amen.

This includes a promoted, modern perspective with a long-term effect: the expertise developed here not only changes individual prayers, but also promotes a more modern view of faith and the church as a whole. At its core is a *human-friendly image of God*: God is no longer perceived as a distant patriarchal authority, but as a loving presence that *affirms diversity*. This attitude shapes the community in the long term.

Figure24 : Everyone finds a place at God's table.

The picture shows a warm, inclusive scene with the title "ALL ARE WELCOME AT GOD'S TABLE": In the center sits a figure of Jesus with an open, friendly expression on his face, he wears a red heart symbol on his chest - a sign of love and affection. Around him sit and stand people of different origins, age groups, gender identities and roles: a Black youth, an older woman, a woman with a priest's inner garment, a man wearing glasses, a Black woman with a rainbow heart earring (symbol of queer inclusion), a male priest and a girl. A golden cross is visible behind them, embedded in a bright, friendly backdrop with soft clouds - a reference to God's presence and hope. Everyone is facing each other, relaxed and peaceful - a vision of community that unites rather than divides differences. The picture expresses in modern imagery: God's table is open to all. No one is excluded. Everyone is allowed to be who they are.

A church that acts in a gender-just and diversity-sensitive way lives more strongly from the spirit of *justice and mercy*. It stands alongside those who were previously marginalized. In doing so, it picks up on the biblical impulse: *"There is no male and female: for you are all one in Christ Jesus"* (cf. Gal 3:28). This view recognizes gender identity and sexual orientation as integral parts of the diversity of creation intended by God. *In the long term, this changes the church profoundly:* liturgies become richer in imagery and better represent the congregation. Church leaders are beginning to see diversity as an asset - for example, by appointing more women and LGBTQIA+ people to leadership roles. There are already prayers asking for precisely this development: for women to have access to all church ministries and to build a church structure based on partnership. What is formulated in intercessions today or tested in small projects could be a natural part of church life tomorrow. A gender-equitable, queer-inclusive spirituality paves the way for a church in which equality is not just a vision, but an everyday reality.

Finally, it is worth taking a look at *spirituality itself*: It gains depth through this competence. If everyone can join in the celebration, the experience of God's presence becomes more intense and credible. In such a church of diversity, new spiritual *awakenings* become possible - perhaps completely new types of community or innovative liturgical forms of expression that draw on the experiences of diverse people.

The ability to shape spirituality in a gender-equitable, queer-sensitive and life-oriented way ultimately promotes a *church of the future*: a church that is supported by Jesus' message of love and carries this love creatively, justly and inclusively into the world. By developing this competence, we are not only changing the church - we are helping more people to feel truly addressed by God's unconditional love. This is an inspiration that reaches far beyond religious education or theological studies - towards a renewed spiritual reality in which *everyone* finds *a place at God's table*.

Exercise 12:
Shaping change, supporting reforms, acting participatively - competence for church, school and democracy today

The exercise deals with the competence to actively shape change, support reforms and act in a participatory manner. The aim is to promote this ability in churches and schools in order to remain credible and sustainable in the face of far-reaching changes. Essential skills include a willingness to change, the ability to engage in dialog, participative action, conflict resolution and moderation skills as well as resilience and determination.

In the church context, this means in particular living synodality - the joint decision-making of all the baptized - as a basic principle of church renewal. In schools, the focus is on promoting a democratic and participatory learning culture. The aim is to develop the "4C skills" (communication, collaboration, critical thinking and creativity) that are necessary to master social, ecological and democratic challenges.

Personal learning paths include practical participation in real change processes, self-reflection, role-playing, simulations and empowerment through experiencing one's own effectiveness. Teaching methods for church and school include project and problem-oriented learning, role reversal, small group work and student participation in everyday teaching. Through these methods, participants learn to make decisions in a participatory manner and to deal constructively with conflicts.

- ***Learning and development objective:*** *The most important personal skill is the ability to engage in dialog, which enables learners to respectfully integrate different perspectives and jointly develop viable decisions. The learning objective is to be able to lead constructive and inclusive dialog processes effectively.*

- **Good practice example:** *"Youth Synod" simulation game, in which pupils take on different roles and learn in a practical way how to make participatory decisions in complex situations in a dialogical and conflict-averse manner.*
- **Church support through:** *The faithful, clergy, priests and bishops can provide support by exemplifying synodal forms of dialog, initiating and accompanying transparent and participatory decision-making processes and promoting open communication in parishes and schools.*
- **Local budget use:** *Community funds can be used specifically for training in moderation, conflict resolution and participatory methods. Specific expenditure includes fees for external experts, materials for workshops and events to promote democratic skills.*
- **Adaptation of the curriculum at school:** *The curriculum in religious education should explicitly include the teaching of participation skills and democratic dialog skills. Modules include exercises in conflict resolution, project work on current church and social issues as well as practice-oriented methods to promote communication, collaboration and responsible decision-making.*

The Second Vatican Council called on the Church to *"search for the signs of the times and interpret them in the light of the Gospel"*. Today, these signs are unmistakable: The Catholic Church is experiencing a deep crisis of trust and credibility. Every year, hundreds of thousands of believers leave; more than half of Germans (56%) even believe that the Church will *"die out if it does not change"*. Believers who remain are demanding tangible reforms instead of accepting stagnation and speechlessness. But change is also growing in the education sector: social and digital upheavals demand a new teaching culture. In order to shape the *"school of the future"*, teachers need interdisciplinary skills - such as personal, digital and, above all, *transformative skills*. In short: in churches *and* schools, it is important to actively shape change processes, support reforms and act together with others in a solution-oriented manner. The ability to do this has become a key competence. The following section explains the teaching objectives and the importance of this competence today, identifies its sub-competences and shows ways in which it can be learned personally and taught in the classroom. Examples of good practice illustrate how participative processes are already being put into practice - and what modern view of the church, education and leadership this promotes.

Importance of competence in church and school

The ability to shape change and act in a participatory manner is particularly important in the current church and school context. It is essential in the church in order to regain lost trust and remain fit for the future. The massive wave of resignations and scandals in recent years have shown that *profound renewal* is needed - otherwise the church is in danger of dying out. Committed believers are therefore calling for more participation and lively discussion instead of mere administration of the status quo. This shows that only a church that acts *synodally* - i.e. involves its members and seeks answers together - can move credibly into the future. Pope Francis himself emphasizes that this synodal path *"is* precisely *what God expects of the Church of the third millennium"*. Synodality, the common journey of all those baptized , has been part of the Church's self-understanding since the early Church.

The ability to shape change is also essential in schools. Education should enable young people to play an active role in shaping society.

Accordingly, democratic and participatory learning is moving into focus. A modern school not only imparts specialist knowledge, but also practises *collaboration, communication, critical thinking and creativity* - the "4C" skills of the 21st century.

Figure25: The skills of the 21st century.

Collaboration, Communicating, Critical thinking and Creativity – the '4Cs' of 21st Century Skills

Collaboration | **Communication**

Critical Thinking | **Creativity**

A modern, clear 2D infographic on the "4K skills of the 21st century": Collaboration, Communication, Critical Thinking and Creativity. The layout is divided into four equally sized sections. Each section features a headline ("Collaboration", "Communication", "Critical Thinking", "Creativity"), a matching icon (handshake, speech bubbles, light bulb with two people, pen and star) and subtle, friendly colors (blue, yellow, red, beige). The style should be flat, friendly and easy to understand - ideal for the education sector. The title at the top reads: "Collaboration, communication, critical thinking and creativity - the '4K' skills".

Teachers today are called upon to modernize their schools "from the inside out" and to respond to social, ecological and democratic challenges with the necessary changes. This willingness to change and ability to innovate are core components of modern professionalism in education. Whether in church or school, the ability to shape change and act in a participatory manner is fundamental in order to do justice to the signs of the times and fulfill one's own mission in a rapidly changing world.

Important sub-competencies: Willingness to change, dialog, conflict resolution, etc.

This overarching competence is made up of several sub-competences that need to be developed. These include, among others:

- **Willingness to change and openness:** the inner attitude of seeing change not as a threat, but as an opportunity. If you want to shape change, you have to be prepared to question old habits and dare to try something new. *A willingness to change, flexibility, agility, vigilance and openness to change processes are basic competencies of a leader* - in church contexts as well as in all other contexts.
- **Participatory action:** The ability to involve others and make decisions together. This includes communicating transparently, delegating tasks and moderating group processes in such a way that everyone involved feels heard and taken seriously. Participatory action means sharing responsibility and anchoring *co-determination* as a value.
- **Church renewal competence:** Especially in the church context, knowledge and skills are needed to support reform processes. This means understanding the structures of the church, but also having the courage to change these structures in the spirit of the Gospel. Synodal communication - a style of dialogue characterized by listening, mutual respect and shared spiritual discernment - is central here. It is about *accompanying change spiritually* and reflecting on it theologically so that reforms are not an end in themselves, but serve the proclamation of faith.
- **Ability to engage in dialog and synodal communication:** The ability to engage in constructive dialog, especially on controversial topics. Anyone who wants to shape change must be able to integrate different perspectives. This includes empathetic listening, formulating one's own points of view without doggedness and searching for common solutions. In

the church, this means bringing laity and clergy, young and old, conservative and progressive voices to the table. In schools, it means bringing students and teachers into a genuine exchange on an equal footing.

- **Conflict resolution and moderation skills**: Change and reforms are often accompanied by tensions. This is why skills in dealing with conflicts are important - from discussing factual differences fairly to mediating deadlocked positions. The ability to moderate groups (such as a local council meeting or a class conference) is also part of managing change processes in a structured and goal-oriented manner. A good moderator remains objective, mediates between positions and ensures that discussions are results-oriented.
- **Determination and perseverance:** Ultimately, shaping change requires *willpower*, patience and tolerance of frustration. Reforms are often met with resistance. An inner resilience, coupled with confidence in the cause, helps not to give up too quickly, but to implement changes step by step. This also requires courage - the courage to support unpopular decisions or to stick to new ideas despite initial skepticism.

These sub-competencies are interlinked. A willingness to change without the ability to engage in dialog would be just as ineffective as participation without conflict resolution skills. The goal is a holistic skills profile that enables people to shape change in a competent, cooperative and value-oriented manner - whether in the renewal of the church or in pedagogical change processes at schools.

How do you learn to shape change? - Personal paths

Skills such as these are primarily acquired through practice. True to the motto: *"Participation can only be learned through participation - not through preparation for participation"*.

Therefore, the best way to develop this ability is to *participate* in change processes *yourself.* For , students who are *actively involved in their university community, youth association or church initiatives learn how to set up projects, motivate fellow campaigners and overcome resistance*. Similarly, students who take on responsibility in the student council or participate in a class council experience democratic negotiation processes first-hand and can reflect on this experience.

Figure26 : Empowerment: The power of self-efficacy.

A young woman stands in the evening light against a golden sky and raises her fist in the air, laughing powerfully. She is wearing a red T-shirt and her curly hair is being moved by the wind. The scene radiates joie de vivre, strength and self-confidence - a symbol of empowerment, self-efficacy and hope. The title of the picture could be: 'The power of self-efficacy'.

Role plays and simulations are also valuable learning methods. In theological training, for example, scenarios could be played out: moderating a heated parish council meeting, resolving a conflict between groups or holding a mini-synod in the seminary in which students take on different roles (bishop, nun, youth representative, etc.). Such exercises make it possible to build up skills, make mistakes and learn from them in a protected environment.

Self-reflection is also essential. Change agents should regularly evaluate their experiences: *What went well, where were there difficulties?* Writing in a diary, spiritual reflection or collegial coaching sessions help them to think through their own actions and develop further. The same applies to management positions: you *never stop learning*. If you want to initiate change, you should always critically question your own practice and remain open to feedback - this is how professional competence grows continuously.

Last but not least, *empowerment* plays a major role: experiencing your own effectiveness. Nothing is more motivating than feeling: *I can make a difference!* Young people in particular are *"prepared to make a big investment when they realize that they can make a difference"*.

It is therefore important to look for opportunities where you have creative freedom - be it managing a project, organizing an event or working on a reform paper. Supportive mentors and networks can provide encouragement here. Those who are accompanied by experienced role models receive valuable feedback and encouragement to take on responsibility. In this way, confidence in your own ability to help shape change grows step by step.

Teaching and promoting competence in religious education and theological training

So how can this competence be taught in educational processes? In religious education and theological training, there are a variety of didactic methods for practicing *participatory action* and *creative competence*. A paradigm shift in the teaching-learning culture is fundamental: *away from frontal teaching and towards dialogical and participatory formats*. What applies to a church council - *"away from read-out speeches and frontal proclamations, towards a dialogical process at eye level"* - also applies to teaching. Learners should not just be recipients of material, but active co-creators of the learning process.

Specifically, teachers can use the following approaches:

- **Project and problem-oriented learning:** For example, a class in the subject of religion chooses a current topic (e.g. *"Can the church change?"*) and develops its own research questions. The students work in groups to develop points of view, perhaps even concrete reform proposals, and present them in a kind of "synodal assembly" in the classroom. Teachers moderate rather than direct, and the class learns how complex but enriching decision-making in the community can be.

- **Role reversal and simulation games:** Similarly to the personal learning phase, simulations can also take place in lessons. For example, you could create a fictitious scenario "Youth synod on topic X" in which learners slip into the role of various synod members and debate a contentious issue. Or a role play about a school conflict that needs to be resolved Such methods promote empathy and a change of perspective and train the ability to take part in discussions.
- **Small groups and discussion groups:** Regular small group work, mumble rounds or "listening phases" in class give everyone a voice. It is important that everyone really gets a chance to speak. Based on synodal processes, you could introduce *listening groups*, for example, in which everyone listens before responding - an exercise in synodal communication culture. Feedback rounds in which students give anonymous feedback on lessons also promote a participatory climate.
- **Pupil participation in everyday teaching:** Participation can also be anchored structurally. A *class council* in religion, for , in which class concerns (including those relating to religious education) are discussed on a monthly basis, can make democratic participation routine. In general, pupils should be allowed to have a say - for example, in the selection of certain lesson content, project topics or class rules for discussions. In this way, they experience school as a shared creative space.

Synodal learning formats are also becoming increasingly important in theological education (university, seminary). Here, for , interdisciplinary workshops are an option, in which prospective theologians work together with students of other subjects (such as social sciences or education) to develop solution strategies for pastoral problems. Open space conferences or future workshops on church topics can also be integrated into the training. It is important to enable future religious education teachers and pastoral workers to lead in a participatory manner. This means that they learn to take on a *dialogue-service-oriented leadership role* in group processes: moderating, encouraging, bringing out the charisms of all. In this way, they already experience during their training what it is like when everyone is "on the journey together" - on a small scale as preparation for the big picture.

Exercise: Listening groups at school: Women in the papal office

An effective and at the same time low-threshold exercise on the topic of "women in the papal office" could be to come together in the form of so-called "listening groups". First, small groups of around five to seven people are formed. Each person is given around three to five minutes to openly share their own personal views, hopes, concerns, theological reflections or biographical experiences regarding the possibility and importance of women in the papal office, without interruption and without immediate questions.

Meanwhile, all other participants listen attentively and empathetically without directly responding to, commenting on or even evaluating what they have heard. Only after all group members have been able to express their thoughts in this first round does a second round follow, in which everyone briefly summarizes what particularly moved or appealed to them while listening. The aim here is to consciously formulate what is understandable about the different positions in an appreciative manner, even if you do not fully agree with their content.

The aim of this exercise is to practice a synodal communication culture of appreciative listening and mindful exchange in the school. By consciously listening first and only then reacting in a reflective manner, space is created for understanding and mutual recognition of different perspectives. This exercise also promotes important skills such as empathy, a change of perspective and respectful interaction with one another - key elements of a synodal church. Finally, the core results from the small groups could be collected and presented and discussed together in plenary to enable deeper reflection and shared learning within the entire group.

Examples of good practice: Experience participation and synodality

Both in schools and in the church, there are already numerous examples that show how participatory processes can succeed. Such practical examples make the abstract competence tangible and offer inspiration:

- **Class council at school:** The class council is an established format in which pupils in a class discuss their living and learning together on their own responsibility. Every week, everyone sits together in a circle and "deliberates, discusses and decides ... on the design and organization of learning and living together in class and school, on current problems and conflicts".

Figure27: Class council at school.

A class council in a school class: young people are sitting in a circle of chairs, several of them have raised their hands. The atmosphere is focused and respectful. 'CLASS COUNCIL' is written in large letters on the blackboard in the background with the keywords 'topics', 'solutions' and 'voting'. The scene shows democratic participation, a culture of discussion and co-determination in everyday school life. The picture is suitable for illustrating student participation, democracy education, class community and social learning.

One pupil chairs the meeting, there are fixed roles (chair, minutes, timekeeper, etc.), and at the end there are joint resolutions. The class council promotes democratic cooperation and participation even in children. In this way, they practise at an early age how to put forward their own concerns, reach compromises and take responsibility. Similar formats are student parliaments or student councils, which anchor participation at school level.

- **Parish council and parish teams:** In the Catholic Church, parish councils provide an important platform for co-determination. This body, consisting of elected volunteers and full-time employees of the parish, has *"the task of participating in an advisory or decision-making capacity in all matters concerning the parish"*.

The parish council was introduced to make the *co-responsibility of all believers* visible - in other words, the principle that the church is not just a matter for priests, but that all baptized people should participate. In many parishes, project-related teams are also formed (for charity, youth, liturgy, etc.) in which lay people plan activities independently. Such a *church of participation* can also be seen in model projects such as the *"parish teams"* of some dioceses, where local groups of volunteers coordinate parish work, especially where no priest is constantly present because the recruiting has to be implemented elsewhere.

- **Youth participation in the Synodal Path:** An outstanding example of participatory church development in recent times is the *Synodal Path* of the Catholic Church in Germany (2019-2023). For the first time, clergy and lay representatives with equal rights came together to discuss reforms on an equal footing. The involvement of the younger generation was remarkable: places in the synodal assembly were also available for young people and young adults under the age of 30, allocated by the Federation of German Catholic Youth (BDKJ). Committed young people were able to apply for a place; many of the selected *young synod members* were active in youth associations and brought the perspective of young people into the deliberations. This participation had a signal effect: it showed that 17 or 25-year-olds can also take part in decisive church discussions and assume responsibility. Although the participation of young people was only part of the Synodal Path, it made it clear that the ability to change is not a question of age - on the contrary, it is often the young who courageously contribute new ideas.

- **Synodal processes on the ground:** In addition to the great synodal path, there are many local synodal initiatives. In some dioceses (e.g. in the diocese of Trier 2013-2016), diocesan synods were held in which the faithful were involved at grassroots level - e.. through parish meetings, working groups and surveys. The global synodal process 2021-2024 uses digital means to gather voices from all over the world church. Synodal principles can also be found at school level: e.g. *school community days* where parents, teachers and pupils discuss school development together. Or projects such as *"Pupils design church services"*, where young people independently plan and conduct a church service or devotional. All of these are opportunities to practice participatory action - whether in a church or school context.

The above examples illustrate this: Where people are genuinely involved, motivation, a sense of community and often creative solutions emerge. Be it a class council that strengthens cohesion and deals with conflicts constructively, or a church parliament that brings a breath of fresh air into encrusted structures - participation pays off. It makes institutions more lively and resilient.

New perspectives: What participatory competence changes in the long term

If the ability to shape change and support reforms is widely developed and practiced, this promotes a much more modern view of the church, education and leadership - with long-term changes.

A culture of *shared responsibility* is emerging *in the church* through synodal processes. The classic hierarchy is beginning to change into a cooperation at eye level. Pope Francis has declared synodality to be a guiding principle, even saying that *"church and synod"* are synonyms. In the long term, this means that the church is understood more as a *community* and less as an authority; decisions are no longer made in isolation "from above", but in dialog, with the participation of those who are affected. Leadership in the church will become more diaconal (serving) and team-oriented, because new talents and charisms of all believers will be allowed to come to the fore.

In this way, the gap between church leadership and the grassroots can be reduced. A participatory church feels the needs of the time more directly - it receives direct feedback through the participation of many and can find pastoral answers that really resonate. This promotes transparency and credibility and counteracts the alienation that many believers have previously perceived. In the long term, a church that lives synodality is also better equipped to remain relevant in a complex world: it learns to constantly renew itself (ecclesia semper reformanda) and thus remains alive.

In the Catholic Church, synodality therefore refers to a form of common journey and decision-making. It means that all members of the Church - laity, priests, bishops - listen together to what the Spirit of God is saying to the Church today. Synodality thrives on dialog, on struggling together to find good ways forward and on the active participation of as many people as possible. It is not just about democratic procedures, but about a spiritually shaped cooperation based on mutual respect, the sharing of responsibility and the common search for truth. Synodality understands the church as a community that is not controlled from above, but grows together through listening, participation and spiritual discernment.

In education, strengthening participation skills brings about a shift towards *schools as vibrant places of learning and living*. When teachers and students alike learn to shape change, schools become a training ground for democracy. Pupils who experience participation at an early age are also more likely to take on responsibility in society and the church later on. The role of the teacher is changing from imparting knowledge to facilitating learning and enabling participation. Leadership in the school system is becoming more collaborative: school leaders are increasingly working in teams and involving staff, pupils and parents to shape school development processes. This promotes a school culture in which *change is not a threat*, but is valued and a natural part of further development.

Participation competence thus refers to the ability and willingness to actively, reflectively and responsibly participate in social, school, political or church processes and to help shape them. It is a key competence in political education, democracy education and in church and school contexts in which co-determination, community and the assumption of responsibility are to be promoted.

The aim of participatory competence is not just to inform or instruct people, but to enable them to help shape their environment themselves. This first requires knowledge of participation opportunities: What committees, spaces or procedures are there in which I can get involved - for example in the class council, in the student council, in the youth council or in church groups? But knowledge alone is not enough. Participation skills also mean being able to express your own interests and opinions clearly and constructively, taking other points of view seriously and being prepared to find compromises.

Another important component is the assumption of responsibility. Those who participate not only contribute to the discussion, but also actively take on tasks and help shape processes. This is linked to the ability to cooperate, to work together in groups and to shape joint decision-making. Empathy also plays a central role: participation succeeds where people understand the life situations of others and are able to put themselves in other people's shoes. This is the only way to make decisions that not only serve one's own interests, but also the common good.

At school, participation skills are evident, for example, when pupils get involved in class councils or project groups, deal with conflicts constructively, involve their classmates and develop solutions together. In church contexts, participatory competence becomes visible when young people or parishioners help to organize church services, campaigns or consultation processes and contribute with their spiritual and social attitude.

Participation competence is therefore more than mere involvement - it is an expression of an inner attitude: the conviction that I am heard, that my voice counts and that I can take responsibility for living together . It promotes democratic processes, strengthens community - and makes an important contribution to the development of responsible personalities.

In the long term, this creates responsible citizens who take away from their time at school that having a say and helping to shape things is desirable and effective. Schools that embrace participation are also more innovative - they can adapt to new challenges more quickly because everyone involved supports changes. Ultimately, this contributes to quality development and the satisfaction of all school partners.

A more modern understanding is gaining *ground in leadership culture* as a whole. Whether in church leadership or school management - authoritarian leadership styles are becoming less plausible. Instead, good leadership means *empowering* others and achieving goals together. Leaders are facilitators of change, not sole decision-makers. They create spaces in which innovation can emerge from the grassroots and support teams in implementing change.

This principle also corresponds to trends in business and society, where agile methods and flat hierarchies are preferred. For churches and schools, this means greater flexibility and adaptability. Institutions that are managed in a participatory manner can adapt more quickly to new requirements because many people are involved in the thinking and decision-making process. *The ability to change* itself becomes a characteristic of resilience. In other words, a church and a school that have learned to constantly reform themselves are better equipped to remain relevant in a changing world.

In summary, it can be said that the ability to shape change, support reforms and act in a participatory manner is not just a learning objective on paper, but a *program for the future*. It enables people to lead change for the better in the spirit of the Gospel and charity - on both a small and large scale. A church that lives synodality and a school that teaches *and* practices democracy will be places where hope grows. Because where many hands and minds work together, change is not experienced as a loss, but as a shared *gain*. Promoting this attitude is a task for all of us - in the training of young theologians, in religious education and in everyday life in parishes and schools. This is how abstract appeals for reform become a lived reality: *Ecclesia semper reformanda* - the ever renewing church - and an education that truly empowers people for life in a changing world.

Appendix

Study guide: Faith and identity in transition - questions and answers

Questions and answers on faith, identity and change in church and society:

1 What is the curator's thesis on artificial intelligence (AI) and its impact on the relationship between humans, knowledge and access to the world?

The curator argues that AI represents a profound turning point, as it fundamentally changes the relationship between humans, knowledge and access to the world - technically, culturally, epistemologically and socially. She sees AI as providing new access to knowledge and promoting the individualization of thought, which can also be reflected in spiritual beliefs.

2 Compare the development of skills in faith with learning to dance, as described in the text.

Learning in faith is compared to dancing, as it is not just about memorizing dogmas, but about acquiring, practicing and developing personal skills and competencies. Similar to dancing, it is about finding your own steps, being sensitive to others and creatively daring to try out new movements.

3 Briefly explain what is meant by "systemic thinking on gender issues" and give an example.

Systemic thinking in gender issues means not looking at gender in isolation, but understanding it in the context of larger social structures. One example is the realization that role models in the church are linked to social power relations and historical traditions.

4 What does "gender-sensitive understanding of power" mean and how can it manifest itself in the behavior of a prospective pastor?

A gender-sensitive understanding of power refers to a keen sense of how power and gender are related and the ability to recognize and critically question gender-specific power dynamics. A prospective pastor with this competence would, for example, ensure that lay people of both genders are appropriately involved in decisions.

5 Describe a mindfulness exercise that can help to become more aware of gender-specific dynamics in everyday life.

One mindfulness exercise is to record in your daily diary when and where you notice differences in the way you deal with gender. Every evening, write down observations on gender issues and how you have reacted in such moments to train your own senses.

6 To what extent can reflecting on one's own biography and influences contribute to building skills in the area of gender equality?

Self-reflection on one's own life story in terms of gender and power enables "aha" experiences and sensitizes people to their own imprints. Questions about advantages or disadvantages due to gender and how to deal with one's own prejudices raise awareness.

7 Explain the term "minority stress" in the context of the text and give two examples of "minority stress factors" in Elias.

"Minority stress" refers to the psychological strain caused by structural exclusion, social pressure and deviant identity. According to Elias, "expected rejection" (fear of ridicule when coming out) and "internalization of negative messages" (internalization of homophobic slogans) are examples of minority stress factors.

8 What theological perspective is mentioned in the text regarding the interpretation of Jesus as being in solidarity with queer experience? Give two reasons for this.

Theologically, it is argued that Jesus can be interpreted as being in solidarity with queer experience because he subverted normative notions of gender and purity (e.g. his relationship with women) and lived tender friendships with men. He also healed marginalized bodies and identities rather than normalizing them.

9 What does "mature faith" mean in the sense of the chapter and which key skills are important for this?

A "mature faith" enables believers to make ethical judgments in a self-determined way and to critically reflect on religious authorities. Central competencies for this are critical thinking, independent judgment, structured acquisition of knowledge, formation of conscience and the ability to engage in dialogue.

10 Describe a practical method for developing the "spiritual power of imagination" with regard to images of God.

A practical method for developing the power of spiritual imagination is guided imagination, in which you imagine a special place and discover a precious book with pictures of God there. You then design the picture that particularly appeals to you in order to gain intuitive access to different concepts of God.

11 To what extent is faith similar to dancing and what skills are important in order to find "safe steps" in faith and in dealing with social issues?

Faith is compared to dancing: a movement that opens the heart, a rhythm that carries you away, a relationship that is characterized by balance, mindfulness and acceptance. Learning to believe is like learning to dance - it's about finding your own steps, being sensitive to others and creatively daring to try out new movements. Important skills for this are systemic thinking on gender issues, a gender-sensitive understanding of power and the ability to break down rigid categories and seek alternative ways of acting.

12 How can individuals develop gender-sensitive skills and what does a gender-sensitive understanding of power mean in church and theological practice?

Developing gender-sensitive skills requires personal learning paths such as reflecting on one's own biography and influences, adopting other perspectives, mindfulness and perception exercises as well as feedback and self-evaluation. A gender-sensitive understanding of power means being aware of power imbalances between the genders, critically questioning them and reflecting on one's own position of power in order to avoid unconsciously exercising authority in a patriarchal manner. In practical terms, this means being sensitive to inequalities and actively working to break down role models and power patterns.

13 To what extent can the figure of Jesus serve as a role model and source of hope for people with so-called "minority stress"?

Although the term "minority stress" did not exist in Jesus' time, Jesus lived in a tense relationship with mainstream society that exhibited many of its characteristics. He was born under questionable circumstances, surrounded himself with marginalized people, broke taboos and questioned authority. Theologically, Jesus can be interpreted as being in solidarity with queer experience as he subverted normative gender ideas, lived tender friendships with men and healed marginalized bodies. Jesus can be a figure of identification for people with minority stress, as he knew exclusion and lived radical inclusion.

14 What does "mature faith" mean and what skills are needed to make ethical judgments in a self-determined way and to critically question religious authorities?

A mature faith enables believers to make ethical judgments in a self-determined way and to critically reflect on religious authorities. Necessary skills are critical thinking, independent judgment, structured acquisition of knowledge, formation of conscience and the ability to engage in dialogue. This includes questioning assertions , examining arguments, developing one's own criteria for moral decisions and defending these responsibly.

15 How can the development of a responsible, pleasurable and socially reflective sexuality be promoted and what role does self-reflection play in this?

The promotion of such a sexuality includes comprehensive sexual education, relationship skills, empathy, justice, power awareness and sexual maturity. Self-reflection is a core competency in which one's own sexuality, identity and biography are openly and honestly examined. This helps to recognize and transform internalized negative messages about sexuality in order to develop a consolidated sexual identity and to deal freely and responsibly with sexuality.

16 Which skills are central to the development of self-acceptance and ethical behavior, and how can these be promoted in everyday life?

Key skills are self-reflection and self-acceptance, dealing with guilt and conscience, empathy and charity as well as social-ethical judgment and commitment. In everyday life, these can be promoted through mindfulness exercises, consciously dealing with feelings of guilt, dealing with ethical issues and self-care. It is important to become aware of one's own limits and to accept oneself in order to be able to treat others with empathy.

17 Why is an open and creative approach to images of God important and what practical ways are there to develop one's own "spiritual imagination"?

An open and creative approach to images of God is important in order to let go of rigid ideas and embrace the diversity of divine reality. Practical ways to develop the power of spiritual imagination include reflecting on one's own images of God, spiritual imagination exercises, reading and learning from a variety of sources, prayer with symbols and names and dialog with others about their ideas of God. The aim is to develop a lively and playful approach to the content of faith and to create an inner "toolbox" of images and symbols.

Essay questions

a) To what extent do the concepts of systemic thinking on gender issues and gender-sensitive understanding of power change traditional theological education and the practice of religious education teachers and clergy? Discuss using examples from the text.

b) Relate the experiences of "minority stress", as explained using the example of Elijah, to the descriptions of Jesus in the text. To what extent can the figure of Jesus be a source of identification and comfort for people who experience minority stress?

c) The text emphasizes the development of a "mature faith". Explain why this competence is important in today's society and within religious institutions and what challenges can be associated with its promotion.

d) The chapter on responsible, pleasurable and socially reflected sexuality advocates "sexual ethical maturity". Discuss how this maturity can be achieved and lived in the area of tension between individual freedom, social norms and religious teachings.

e) To what extent can the conscious reflection and creative reinterpretation of images of God, as described in the relevant chapter, lead to a more inclusive and vibrant faith? Examine the opportunities and possible difficulties of this approach for individuals and for the community.

f) In which maxims does the church fail in relation to queer people? Explain the maxims.

List of figures

The images are generated entirely by AI:

The image of the curator in the masthead was processed using AI filters and algorithms.

Further reading (selection)

Bätzing, Georg / Orth, Stefan: *Rome is not an opponent - Why the Church needs reforms*, 2021.

Bolten, Margit: *Learning empathy - practicing compassion*, 2015.

Bonhoeffer, Dietrich: *Succession*, 1937.

Bordat, Josef: *The conscience. A Catholic point of view*, 2017.

Bordt, Michael: *The art of enduring oneself*, 2011.

Buber, Martin: *I and You*, 1923.

Bubmann, Peter: Queer empathy as a pastoral competence, in: Queer im Pfarrhaus, 2024.

Bucher, Anton A.: *How children imagine God*, 2001.

Diözese Graz-Seckau: Seelsorge mit homosexuellen Menschen, n.d..

Dorst, Brigitte: *Resilience. The resilience of the soul*, 2018

EKHN: Protestant wedding ceremony for all couples, 2024.

Feinschwarz: Can God also be thought queer?, 2020.

Frankl, Viktor E.: *... nevertheless saying yes to life. A psychologist experiences the concentration camp*, 1946.

Francis, Pope: *Laudato Si'. On care for the common home*, 2015.

Ganz, Katharina: *Women in the church - equal rights and self-determination*, 2021.

Grün, Anselm: *Reconcile yourself with your life. Paths to self-acceptance*, 2019.

Gutiérrez, Gustavo: *Theology of Liberation*, 1973.

Halík, Tomáš: *Patience with God. Encounters with the gullible and unbelievers*, 2010.

Huber, Wolfgang: *Conscience*, 2013.

Kessler, Hans: *God and suffering. Answers from a theologian*, 2007.

Kopp, Stefan (ed.): *Church in transition. Ecclesial identity and reform*, 2020.

Küng, Hans: *Does God exist? Answer to the question of God in modern times*, 1978.

Kuschel, Karl-Josef: *Dispute over Abraham. What divides and unites Jews, Christians and Muslims*, 2001.

Leimgruber, Stephan: *Christian sexual pedagogy. An emancipatory reorientation*, 2011.

Lewis, C. S.: *On Pain*, 1961.

McGrath, Alister: *Farewell to illusion: Why faith and reason belong together*, 2015.

Nierop, Jantine: *Gender and the church. Practical theology and gender research*, 2022.

Nouwen, Henri J. M.: *You are the beloved human being. Living spiritually today*, 2018.

Nussbaum, Martha: *Political emotions. Why love is important for justice*, 2014.

Rogers, Carl R.: *Development of the personality. A path to self-development*, 1981.

Roloff, Carola / Drechsler, Katja / van Hoogstraten, Marius (eds.): *Interreligious Dialogue, Gender and Dialogical Theology*, 2019.

Rosenberg, Marshall B.: *Nonviolent Communication: A Language of Life*, 2016.

Rötting, Martin / Sinn, Simone / Inan, Aykan (eds.): *Praxisbuch interreligiöser Dialog. Initiating and accompanying encounters*, 2016.

Schaede, Stephan / Moos, Katharina (eds.): *Das Gewissen (Religion und Aufklärung, vol. 25)*, 2011.

Schellenbaum, Peter: *Images of God. Religion, psychoanalysis, depth psychology*, 1989.

Schockenhoff, Eberhard: *The art of loving. For a new sexual ethic*, 2020.

Scholl, Norbert: *Faith in doubt. Modern man and God*, 2019.

Schreiber, Gerhard: *Im Dunkel der Sexualität - Sexualität und Gewalt aus sexualethischer Perspektive*, 2022.

Schüssler Fiorenza, Elisabeth: *In her memory. Women shape the church's memory*, 1988.

Sölle, Dorothee: *Mysticism and Resistance: Du stilles Geschrei*, 1997.

Sprakties, Gerhard: *Spirituality as a resilience factor in life crises*, 2023

Stettberger, Herbert: *Empathy in religious education*. MThZ 63 (2012:48-59).

Striet, Magnus: *The weariness of faith. Christianity in transition*, 2011.

Zulehner, Paul M.: *Transforming the church. A reform agenda for the future*, 2019.